The Rule of Law in the United Nations Security Council Decision-making Process

The UN Security Council is entrusted under the UN Charter with primary responsibility for the maintenance and restoration of international peace; it is the only body with the power to authorise military intervention legally and impose international sanctions where it decides. However, its decision-making process has hitherto been obscure and allegations of political bias have been made against the Security Council in its responses to potential international threats. Despite the rule of law featuring on the Security Council's agenda for over a decade and a UN General Assembly declaration in 2012 establishing that the rule of law should apply internally to the UN, the Security Council has yet to formulate or incorporate a rule of law framework that would govern its decision-making process.

This book explains the necessity of a rule of law framework for the Security Council before analysing existing literature and UN documents on the domestic and international rule of law in search of concepts suitable for transposition to the arena of the Security Council. It emerges with eight core components, which form a bespoke rule of law framework for the Security Council. Against this framework, the Security Council's decision-making process, since the end of the Cold War, is meticulously evaluated, illustrating explicitly where and how the rule of law has been undermined or neglected in its behaviour. Ultimately, this book concludes that the Security Council and other bodies are unwilling or unable to adequately regulate the decision-making process against a suitable rule of law framework, and argues that there exists a need for the external regulation of Council practice and judicial review of its decisions.

Dr Sherif A Elgebeily is Director of the Centre for the Study of International Peace and Security, Co-chair of the International Law and Policy in Africa Network, and was the 2016 Bingham Centre International Visiting Rule of Law Research Fellow. He has worked for the UN Department of Political Affairs (Iraq Team), the European Commission and has lectured internationally on topics including the rule of law, human rights, and international humanitarian law.

Routledge Research in International Law

Available:

Sovereignty Conflicts and International Law and Politics
A Distributive Justice Issue
Jorge E. Núñez

Queering International Law
Possibilities, Alliances, Complicities, Risks
Dianne Otto

Forthcoming titles in this series include:

Technology and the Law on the Use of Force
New Security Challenges in the Twenty First Century
Jackson Maogoto

International Law and the Rights of those Displaced by Armed Conflict
Elena Katselli Proukaki

International Criminal Law and Sexual Violence against Women
The Interpretation of Gender in the Contemporary International Criminal Trial
Daniela Nadj

Fighting and Victimhood in International Criminal Law
Joanna Nicholson

Human Security Discourse and International Law
A Principled Approach
Shireen Daft

Regionalism in International Law
Ján Klučka

The Rule of Law in the United Nations Security Council Decision-making Process

Turning the Focus Inwards

Sherif A Elgebeily

Routledge
Taylor & Francis Group
LONDON AND NEW YORK

First published 2017 by Routledge

2 Park Square, Milton Park, Abingdon, Oxfordshire OX14 4RN
52 Vanderbilt Avenue, New York, NY 10017

Routledge is an imprint of the Taylor & Francis Group, an informa business

First issued in paperback 2018

British Library Cataloguing in Publication Data
A catalogue record for this book is available from the British Library

Library of Congress Cataloging in Publication Data
Names: Elgebeily, Sherif, author.
Title: The rule of law in the United Nations Security Council decision-making process: turning the focus inwards / Sherif Elgebeily.
Description: New York: Routledge, 2017. | Series: Routledge research in international law | Includes bibliographical references and index.
Identifiers: LCCN 2016046643 | ISBN 9781138220249 (hbk) | ISBN 9781315413457 (ebk)
Subjects: LCSH: United Nations. Security Council—Powers and duties. | Rule of law.
Classification: LCC KZ5038 .E44 2017 | DDC 341.23/23—dc 3
LC record available at https://lccn.loc.gov/2016046643

ISBN: 978-1-138-22024-9 (hbk)
ISBN: 978-0-367-19340-9 (pbk)

Typeset in Galliard
by Keystroke, Neville Lodge, Tettenhall, Wolverhampton

To the one who arrived last first;
And the one to whom belongs my future;
And the ones to whom I owe my beginning;
And the shadow who shall follow me forever.

Contents

Acknowledgements

This book is the culmination of many years research and work. It would not have been possible without the immense and unconditional support of my wife and parents.

I would also like to thank my doctoral supervisory team at the University of Westminster, under whom the majority of this work was researched: Professor Marco Roscini, Professor Hélène Lambert and Dr Ruth MacKenzie. My thanks go also to Dr Paresh Kathrani for his ongoing friendship, kindness and support both on and off this book.

My dearest thanks go to Othmane Benlafkih and Brian Chui for their assistance in researching and collating material into this final draft.

Finally, my thanks to Olivia Manley for her kind assistance and support at Routledge in answering queries, liaising with editors and various (what I can only imagine are) tedious tasks.

Definitions and abbreviations

Assembly/UNGA	United Nations General Assembly
Chapter VII	United Nations Charter, Chapter VII
Charter	United Nations Charter (1945)
Council/UNSC	United Nations Security Council
CTC	United Nations Counter Terrorism Committee
Daesh	Al-Dawla Al-Islamiya fi al-Iraq wa al-Sham (Islamic State in Iraq and the Levant), also referred to as Islamic State or ISIS
DPRK	Democratic People's Republic of Korea
DRC	Democratic Republic of Congo
EU	European Union
GDP	Gross Domestic Product
IAEA	International Atomic Energy Agency
ICC	International Criminal Court
ICJ	International Court of Justice
ICTR	International Criminal Tribunal for Rwanda
ICTY	International Criminal Tribunal for Yugoslavia
MONUSCO	UN Stabilization Mission in the Democratic Republic of the Congo
NGO	Non Governmental Organisation
OHCHR	Office of the High Commissioner for Human Rights
P5	Permanent Five
Res	Resolution
Russia	The Russian Federation
UK	United Kingdom of Great Britain and Northern Ireland
UN	United Nations
UNJHRO	United Nations Joint Human Rights Office (DRC)
UNMIBH	United Nations Mission in Bosnia Herzegovina
UNMIL	United Nations Mission in Liberia
US	United States of America
USSR	Union of Soviet Socialist Republics

Introduction

The rule of law has become synonymous with principles of democracy, equality, freedom, good governance and other elements of a civilised society, which are generally agreed to be beneficial to mankind. Similarly, the United Nations may conjure up images for many of a utopian ideal that values strength in diversity and leads the way in impartiality of procedure and composition. After all, the General Assembly offers in its structure, amongst other benefits, a means of placing less developed nations on a par with industrialised states: Nauru and China on the same stage despite their massive size difference; the DRC alongside the United States despite their divergent respective GDPs; and states openly hostile towards one another such as Iran and Israel viewed equally in the Assembly chamber and granted equal rights. Indeed, even the seating arrangement of states, ordered alphabetically and in proximity to the front rotated based on a ballot, is swimming in even-handedness and fairness. However, whereas UN member states in the General Assembly are equally represented, meaning each has a single vote irrespective of size, population, economic size or other distinguishing feature, the Security Council is an inherently different system altogether.

Although not in contradiction to international principles of state sovereignty owing to the fact that all members of the UN have voluntarily chosen to be bound by the UN Charter, which itself regulates the Security Council mechanism, the Council can appear this way at first glance. The Council is formed of 15 members,[1] only 10 of which are alternated every two years on a staggered basis: five each year. The remaining five permanent members are equipped with the power unilaterally to prevent a resolution from even coming into existence through the power of veto.[2] Furthermore, the Council has been mandated by the UN Charter to maintain the international peace and security by any means necessary, including, but not limited to, the use of sanctions and the use of force. Recent decades have seen the definition of international *peace and security* expand, although not without concern by member states, non-governmental organisations and scholars.[3]

Thus, with one-third of seats within the organ occupied by permanent members wielding the veto and the Security Council's apparently unfettered powers to subject UN member states to legally binding obligations without their consent,[4] the Council is far from proportionally representative or equal in its composition. Calls for reform have fallen on deaf ears for decades, with the exception of token changes such as the 1963 expansion of the number of non-permanent seats on the Council from 6 to 10, bringing the total from 11 to 15 members.[5]

It would seem, then, that despite purporting to be an organ that claims to represent the entirety of the United Nations member states, the Council must be accepted as a flawed system, at least from the perspective of the proportional representation, standards of equality and other democratic principles that the General Assembly displays. Perhaps more concerning than the flawed system itself is the notion that Council action is not subject to any adjudication, review, standards of accountability or other elements of what those involved in the fields of law, politics and international relations might term *the rule of law*.

However, this situation seemed to be on the cusp of change earlier this decade when, on 24 September 2012, the UN General Assembly adopted a landmark declaration that 'the rule of law applies to all states equally, and to international organisations, *including the United Nations and its principal organs*, and that *respect for and promotion of the rule of law and justice should guide all of their activities* and accord predictability and legitimacy to their actions'.[6] After years of debate on UN reform and discussion on how the rule of law can be internationalised, the question transitioned from *whether* the rule of law should be applied to the United Nations and its organs to *how* this can be done.

The UN Charter allows the Security Council to set its own agenda in maintaining international peace and security, without defining the term or giving it a specific mandate with respect to armed conflict or any other definition. While the expansive nature of a 'threat to the peace'[7] can be argued to have evolved since 1945 – when the Council was established – from the perspective of an inquisitive and legal researcher, the lack of oversight or monitoring of its decisions is a metaphorical thorn in the side. The competence of the Council to self-regulate as well as regulating others, such as appointments to the International Court of Justice[8] and the post of Secretary-General of the UN,[9] allows it a great deal of freedom without the type of review one may traditionally associate with comparable domestic organisations.[10] Similarly, as arguably the closest organisation to a 'world government', with the power to impose economic sanctions, military intervention and, most recently, criminal sentences,[11] the Council does not benefit from the impartiality and separation of powers that a domestic government that abides by the principles of a rule of law might.

To add to this situation, the focus of the United Nations, as well as other international organisations and governments, has shifted increasingly towards the establishment of the rule of law. It is found in the doctrines, resolutions, statements and official records of the United Nations at all levels and has been cited as one of the core foundations for peace and security. Indeed, since 2004, the rule of law has increasingly featured on the agenda of the Security Council itself and held numerous thematic debates on the subject;[12] yet it was only recently that the United Nations began looking internally when discussing the rule of law and even more recently that any action was taken in moving the United Nations towards compliance with a rule of law. In the aftermath of the General Assembly's 2012 declaration on the rule of law, I examine how the rule of law can be applied to the Security Council, what it would be comprised of, how it can inform decisions taken under Chapter VII of the UN Charter dealing with threats to the international peace and the extent to which it has shaped Council policy in recent years and decades.

This book does not primarily seek explicitly to trace an evolution in practice, although evolving practices will indicate a willingness of the Security Council to change its approach to responding to threats to the international peace as well as the UN's – and by extension the Council's – ability to self-reflect on the most appropriate methods of upholding its responsibilities under the UN Charter. Rather, this book primarily focuses on the establishment of a bespoke rule of law for the Council and the comparison of Council behaviour with this rule of law. Therefore, owing to the concept of peace and security and its development throughout the decades since the establishment of the United Nations, I have chosen primarily to limit the scope of this book to resolutions dating from 1990 – after the fall of communism and the collapse of the USSR – which over the course of my research I have found to be more illustrative of modern Council practice.[13]

First, the end of the Cold War appears to be a point that scholars agree constituted a great shift in Security Council politics and heralded the beginning of an increased activity on its part in the maintenance of international peace and security.[14] The impact of the Cold War on the work of the Council is starkly contrasted with a post-Soviet Security Council, exemplified most clearly by the juxtaposition of the paralysis suffered prior to 1990 to the cascade of Council-mandated and related activity on the front of peacekeeping activities,[15] adopted Council resolutions,[16] proliferation of subsidiary bodies[17] and significant decline in the number of vetoes used by P5 member states;[18] this increased cooperation of the Council members after 1990 is sure to have impacted on the stance and behaviour of its decision-making process.

Secondly, to discuss the threat to international peace from the early 20th century, in the aftermath of the Second World War, at the height of the Cold War or prior to the expansion of the definition of a *threat* by the Security Council would be irrelevant; ultimately, the emergence of new threats to international peace[19] and a greater focus on the impact of intra-state conflict on regional stability rather than the now antiquated inter-state conflicts[20] highlights that the international arena the peace of which the Council is tasked to maintain or restore has change drastically.

Thirdly, this work must endeavour to remain relevant and contemporary – the decision-making process of the Security Council may well have changed over the course of 70 years and to identify a pattern in the mid-20th century that no longer exists would produce no answers as to the extent to which the Council maintains the rule of law today. As a result, the focus of this research must be relatively recent and (just over) a quarter of a decade appears a naturally suitable period of time for examination, while also allowing sufficient scope for detailed and varied illustrations of Council behaviour.

Finally, it would be remiss to attempt to impose a standard of the rule of law, mention of which as a concept itself only appeared on the Security Council agenda at the advent of the new millennium, with the standards of the Charter drafters at San Francisco in 1945; as a concept only recently acknowledged as applying internally to the UN system, there would be little use in measuring the decision-making process of the Council against a standard that did not exist a quarter of a century ago. Such analysis would attempt an *ex post facto* critique of the Council that violates the principle of *nullem crimen sine lege*.

Nonetheless, there remains a vast quantity of Security Council material for comparison and numerous conflicts and threats that are ripe for discussion. Even within the period 1990 onwards the Council has passed over 1600 resolutions,[21] which seems a wealthy pool of resources from which to derive patterns of behaviour and, most importantly, timely, relevant and pertinent examples.

Notes

1 UN Charter (1945) art 23(1).
2 ibid art 17(3).
3 See eg Jacob Cogan, 'Noncompliance and the International Rule of Law' (2006) 31 *Yale Journal of International Law* 189; Simon Chesterman, 'The UN Security Council and the rule of law: the role of the Security Council in strengthening a rules-based international system: final report and recommendations from the Austrian Initiative, 2004–2008' (Institute for International Law and Justice 2008) 33; Jared Schott, 'Chapter VII as exception: Security Council action and the regulative ideal of emergency' (2008) 6(1) *Northwestern Journal of International Human Rights* 24; Björn Elberling, 'The *ultra vires* character of legislative action by the Security Council' (2005) 2 *IOLR* 337.
4 See eg UNSC Res 2304 (12 August 2016) UN Doc S/RES/2304; UNSC Res 1970 (26 February 2011) UN Doc S/RES/1970; UNSC Res 1593 (31 March 2005) UN Doc S/RES/1593; and UNSC Res 955 (8 November 1994) UN Doc S/RES/955.
5 UNGA Res 1991A (1963) UN Doc A/RES/17/1991A.
6 Declaration of the High-level Meeting of the General Assembly on the Rule of Law at the National and International Levels, UNGA Res 67/1 (2012) UN Doc A/RES/67/1 para 2 (emphasis added).
7 UN Charter (n 1) art 39.
8 Statute of the International Court of Justice (1945) art 4(1).
9 UN Charter (n 1) art 97.
10 Domestic governments are traditionally subject to checks and balances to ensure that the rule of law is maintained effectively.
11 The subsidiary organs of the ICTY and ICTR, in addition to the ICC to which the Council may refer situations under Rome statute art 16, are enabled with the power to hand down criminal sentences to convicted parties. This is attributable to the Security Council and thus, indirectly, the Security Council has granted itself the power to hand down criminal sentences. For imputability of actions of a subsidiary to an organ back to the parent organ, see generally, Antonios Tzanakopoulos, *Disobeying the Security Council: Countermeasures against Wrongful Sanctions* (Oxford University Press 2011) and Danesh Sarooshi, *The United Nations and the Development of Collective Security: The Delegation by the UN Security Council of its Chapter VII Powers* (Oxford University Press 1999).

12 See eg UNSC Presidential Statement 15 (2003) UN Doc S/PRST/2003/15; UNSC Presidential Statement 2 (2004) UN Doc S/PRST/2004/2; UNSC Presidential Statement 32 (2004) UN Doc S/PRST/2004/32; UNSC Presidential Statement 30 (2005) UN Doc S/PRST/2005/30; UNSC Presidential Statement 28 (2006) UN Doc S/PRST/2006/28.

13 Some analysis of resolutions prior to this will be necessary to derive Council interpretation of its mandate and powers at the time of and shortly after its establishment. For example, the Council's approach to its reform, its transparency, its interaction with other UN organs and the use of the veto are not issues that must be necessarily temporally limited.

14 See eg Susan Lamb, 'Legal limits to UN Security Council powers' in Guy Goodwin-Gill and Stefan Talmon (eds), *The Reality of International Law: Essays in Honour of Ian Brownlie* (Oxford University Press 1999) 361; Antonios Tzanakopoulos, 'Transparency in the Security Council' in Andrea Bianchi and Anne Peters (eds), *Transparency in International Law* (Cambridge University Press 2012) 368; Björn Elberling, 'The *ultra vires* character of legislative action by the Security Council' (2005) 2(2) *International Organizations Law Review* 337; John Dunbabin, 'The Security Council in the wings: exploring the Security Council's non-involvement in war' in Vaughan Lowe and others (eds), *The United Nations Security Council and War: The Evolution of Thought and Practice Since 1945* (Oxford University Press 2010) 495.

15 Between 1990 and 1994, the UN's annual peacekeeping budget rose from US$500 million to over US$3 billion; during the same period, the number of peacekeepers deployed rose from 10,000 to 70,000 troops. See Security Council Report, 'UN peacekeeping: deployments and budgets, 1946–2013' (2014).

16 In the years 1985–89, 87 resolutions were passed – an average of 17 every year; in the period 1990–1994, a total of 323 resolutions were passed – around 64 every year.

17 There are only a handful of existing subsidiary organs that date back prior to 1990: three standing committees (the Committee of Experts (1946); the Committee on Admission of New Member States (1946); and the Committee on Meetings away from UN Headquarters (1972)) and one Charter-mandated subsidiary body (the Military Staff Committee (1946)). Since 1990 the Council has created three ad hoc committees (the UN Compensation Committee (1991), the Counter-Terrorism Committee (2001) and the Weapons of Mass Destruction Committee (2004)), three ad hoc International Tribunals (the ICTY (1993), the ICTR (1994) and the International Residual Mechanism (2010)), six working groups (on Peacekeeping operations (2001), on Resolution 1566 (2004), on Children and Armed Conflict (2005), on Conflict Prevention and Resolution in Africa (2002), on Documentation and other Procedural Questions (1993), on International Tribunals (2000)) and 13 sanctions committees (on Somalia and Eritrea (2002, 2009), Al-Qaeda (1999, 2011), the Taliban (2011), Iraq (2003), Liberia (2003), Democratic Republic of Congo (2003), Côte d'Ivoire (2004), Sudan (2005), Lebanon (2005), Democratic People's Republic of Korea (2006), Iran (2006), Libya (2011) and Guinea-Bissau (2012)).

18 In 1989 the same number of veto votes were cast as throughout the entire decade of the 1990s (9 in total); the 1970s saw 51 vetoes and the 1980s saw 72, while the 1990s saw only 9 and the 2000s saw 16.

19 See eg non-proliferation, international terrorism, climate change, gender inequality and others.

20 Typified by the discussions and responses of the Council on and to the former Yugoslavia, Rwanda, Libya, Syria, Kosovo, Iraq, Haiti and numerous other internal state conflicts.

21 Figures calculated through the author's own analysis of UN documents. There were 646 resolutions passed between the years 1946 and 1989; since then there have been over 1600 resolutions passed.

Part I

Defining the rule of law for the Security Council: how, why and what?

1 Yoking the giant *Pantagruel*: why the Security Council needs a rule of law

> [V]oicy sorty Pantagruel, tout velu comme un ours, dont dict une d'elles en esprit prophétique: 'Il est né à tout le poils, il fera des merveilleuses, et, s'il vit, il aura de l'eage'.[1]

Introduction

Why should the Security Council be subject to a rule of law? Why should the Security Council – a political body – even be held subject to the rule of law? To what extent should it be held accountable for its actions? This chapter examines these research questions and focuses on four core reasons why the establishment of such a framework for the Council's work is essential. The notion that the Council 'cannot be subject to the rule of law in any meaningful way'[2] is antiquated; such a theory predates the 2012 declaration bringing the Council under the scrutiny of rule of law elements. This declaration by the General Assembly has made it clear that the rule of law can and must form part of the working practices of the Security Council; the existence and need for implementation of an international rule of law for the Security Council is no longer debatable nor, indeed, is it necessary intricately to examine the reasons and arguments for and against such a rule of law. Nonetheless, it would be prudent to identify four clear arguments favouring a rule of law for the Security Council to determine objectively the importance of this book's scope and content.

Why is the rule of law necessary for the Security Council?

> We remain convinced that the best way for the Security Council to promote international law and the rule of law is to lead by example. We challenge the view—and, to some extent, the conventional wisdom—that regards the Council as a purely political body. Its authority is based on the world's supreme international treaty, the United Nations Charter. The Council is legally bound by the applicable rules of the Charter and of international law. Those rules leave the Council much room to take decisions based on political, legal and other considerations—but that room is not without limits. It is both

a legal necessity and a wise policy choice for the Council to respect and promote international law and the rule of law.[3]

The limited composition of the Security Council

Although the Council consists of only 15 members,[4] originally 11, it is tasked with acting on behalf of them all[5] – these members represent 193 states, each with its own respective government, political agenda and interests. Without doubt, frequently the interests of states are aligned and cooperation is assured; however, the Security Council was created as maintainer of international peace and security. Given that the UN Charter provides that '[t]he Republic of China, France, the Union of Soviet Socialist Republics, the United Kingdom of Great Britain and Northern Ireland, and the United States of America shall be permanent members of the Security Council'[6] (P5), one can infer that their interests and the interests of those aligned to them will be perpetually represented on the Council. But selected interests and topics of discussion and debate will not suffice for a body that purports to truly represent all states; the question then arises-how does the Security Council ensure that it is truly representative as it was created to be? Given the low ratio of Council members to UN member states, a rule of law would ensure that its procedures and decisions are more representative of the general will of the UN member states, as it was arguably envisioned in the Charter.[7]

The decision-making process and use of the veto

The manner, too, in which decisions are reached should also be noted: '[d]ecisions of the Security Council on [non-procedural] matters shall be made by an affirmative vote of nine members including the concurring votes of the permanent members'.[8] This is the clause upon which the power of veto,[9] held by the P5 members, is built; in essence, all non-procedural matters are conditioned on the non-opposition[10] of all P5 members. Thus, no Chapter VII resolution emerges from the Security Council without at least P5 acquiescence, and it is not difficult to imagine, given this power, how self-serving political agendas can rapidly colour the decision-making process in order to protect the P5 members and their allies from the far-reaching jurisdiction of the Council. This was an issue raised by both the Ecuadorian and Venezuelan delegates at San Francisco in 1945, who were concerned that the Charter 'contains such a broad delegation of the powers of the [United Nations] to the Security Council that it appears practically inacceptable . . .'.[11] Stretching beyond the previous point on the representative nature of the Council, and taking into consideration the inherent bias attributed to the veto power given to the P5, the question here, then, is how does the Security Council ensure that its decisions are free of improperly biased agenda?[12]

The extended competence of the Council

The scope of Security Council jurisdiction has expanded far beyond that initially envisioned at the time of its creation-issues that have been deemed to pose a threat to the international peace and security such as the AIDS epidemic in Africa[13], climate change[14] and women in conflict[15] have slowly crept into the remit of the Security Council's Chapter VII powers during the last 60 years. While these are all valid issues in their own rights, the question must be whether they were originally envisioned in the minds of drafters when granting the Council such all-pervasive control. As Palau's Permanent Representative to the UN noted, 'the Council may employ "such action . . . as may be necessary to maintain or restore" [international peace and security]. Such constitutional carte blanche, as well as the Council's increasing invocation of Chapter VII to justify quasi-legislative and quasi-judicial actions, gives cause for concern to detractors wary of an unrepresentative Council whose powers continue to broaden in scope faster than do corresponding guarantors of accountability and legitimacy'.[16] Indeed, as the representative from Brazil argued at the establishment of the ICTY:

> [i]t is precisely because the Council exercises a delegated responsibility in a field as politically sensitive as the maintenance of international peace and security that the task of interpreting its competences calls for extreme caution, in particular when invoking language of Chapter VII of the Charter . . . [T]he definition of such powers must be construed strictly on the basis of the text of the relevant Charter provisions. To go beyond that would be legally inconsistent and politically unwise.

Joyner comments on the expansion of both the scope and quality of the expansion of Security Council powers, stating that the Council now believes that it

> is empowered not only to act as an *executive body*, but rather also to act as a *legislative body* crafting proactive and permanent legal edicts covering important areas of international relations including terrorism (UNSC Resolution 1373) and weapons of mass destruction proliferation (UNSC Resolution 1540) and even further to act as a *judicial body* determining the legal rights and obligations of UN members (UNSC Resolutions 1874 and 1929).[17]

This is in direct correlation to the fears of Ecuador at San Francisco, who wished to 'forbid the Council – as the Inter-American Juridical Committee has wisely suggested – to establish or modify principles or rules of law'[18] and which submitted an amendment to this effect,[19] unsuccessful though it may have been.

The legally binding nature of Council resolutions

Membership to the United Nations obliges all states to 'agree to accept and carry out the decisions of the Security Council in accordance with the [UN] Charter'.[20] At times, these decisions are even to be imposed on non-Members, since the UN is also charged with ensuring that 'states which are not members of the United Nations act in accordance with these Principles so far as may be necessary for the maintenance of international peace and security'.[21] This effectively brings non-member states under the jurisdiction and control of the Security Council and its decisions. The debate over what constitutes a legally-binding decision of the Security Council as opposed to an advisory opinion or non-binding resolution is one that has been entered into by other authors[22] and which I will not enter into at length, but which, owing to the integral necessity for a *legally binding* resolution to exist in order for there to be a *rule of law*, a brief encounter with arguments for and against the binding nature of Council resolutions is required.

Briefly, the parameters of a legally binding resolution have been argued to be not necessarily analogous with any resolution adopted under Chapter VII of the UN Charter; that is to say, there are some resolutions the obeisance to which is paramount, whereas other resolutions might tolerate less compliant behaviour. There appear to be clear examples of situations where Council action is not legally binding; for example, under article 26 of the UN Charter, the Council has the authority to formulate plans 'for the establishment of a system for the regulation of armaments'[23] with the goal of 'the establishment and maintenance of international peace and security with the least diversion for armaments of the world's human and economic resources'.[24] However, both Joyner and Kelsen observed that: '[m]embers may . . . choose either to accept or reject these plans'[25] and that such plans 'are binding upon the members only if accepted by them . . . Article 26 does not provide expressly for the "adoption" of the plan by the members . . .'.[26] Nonetheless, while both Chapters VI and VII relate to the Council's responsibilities with respect to international peace and security, some scholars argue that it is only Chapter VII that allows the Council to pass legally binding resolutions.[27] In its *Namibia*,[28] the ICJ suggested that Article 25 of the UN Charter[29] was an obligation that should be carried through on *all* Security Council when it stated that,

> Article 25 is not confined to decisions in regard to enforcement action but applies to 'the decisions of the Security Council' adopted in accordance with the Charter. Moreover, that Article is placed, not in Chapter VII, but immediately after Article 24 in that part of the Charter which deals with the functions and powers of the Security Council. If Article 25 had reference solely to decisions of the Security Council concerning enforcement action under Articles 41 and 42 of the Charter, that is to say, if it were only such decisions which had binding effect, then Article 25 would be superfluous, since this effect is secured by Articles 48 and 49 of the Charter.[30]

The debate rages on the exact definition of a legally-binding resolution and where obligations of compliance cease for states. However, one point upon which almost all parties appear to agree is that there exists a point at which resolutions *do* become legally-binding upon states. The question of exactly where these boundaries lie is not central to this book; it is sufficient to note that the Council, in certain circumstances, benefits from the discretion to impose legal obligations upon states member to the UN.

Thus, there is nothing and, seemingly, no state beyond the reach of the Security Council.[31] The Council is tasked with representing all states, yet the great power bestowed upon it by the founding delegates in San Francisco is undoubtedly at risk of abuse by some in the decision-making process. More hazardously, perhaps, these politicised decisions are binding on member states. Brownlie noted in 1998 that '[t]he active agenda of the Security Council and its relative solidarity creates a paradox. Its increased political power is a source of hope but the modalities of the exercise of power present problems of principle and of legal control'.[32] In the years since he made this observation, the international political arena has not become any less complex or dark: terrorist attacks have struck the United States, UK, Spain, Nigeria and elsewhere; wars have since broken out in Afghanistan, Iraq; internal conflict has fatally fragmented countries such as Syria, Sudan, Myanmar, Sri Lanka and others. As Tamanaha remarked in 2002, '[o]ne must wonder whether the same has not been said at all times, but around the world today there appears to be more than the usual doses of war, oppression, and insecurity'.[33] Indeed, the Security Council was born of war[34] and found itself confronted with its first ideological conflict '[o]n 19 January 1946, before the first Security Council had ever met, [when] the Iranian ambassador addressed to it a letter complaining about the failure of Soviet troops to evacuate Azerbaijan . . .'.[35] It is therefore of the utmost importance for the Security Council to work as effectively and impartially as possible, in order to maintain international peace and security as it has been tasked with.

Notes

1 '[O]ut comes Pantagruel, as hairy as a bear, whereupon one of them said prophetically: "He has been born with all of his hair, he will do wonderful things, and, if he lives, he will grow old"' (author's translation).

2 Christine Gray, 'The Security Council and the rule of law: an overview' (2009) 103 *American Society of International Law* 245, 246.

3 Liechtenstein, UNSC Verbatim Record (29 June 2010), UN Doc S/PV.6347 (Resumption 1), 6.

4 UN Charter (1945) art 23(1).

5 ibid art 24(1): The UN Charter states that '[i]n order to ensure prompt and effective action by the United Nations, its Members confer on the Security Council primary responsibility for the maintenance of international peace and security, and agree that in carrying out its duties under this responsibility the Security Council acts on their behalf'.

6 UN Charter (n 4) art 23.

7 Although the Charter does not explicitly state that the Council should be *representative* of member states, art 24(1) does state that 'the Security Council acts

on [UN Members'] behalf'. The allusion to 'equitable geographical distribution' in art 23(1) and the fact that the non-permanent members of the Council are rotated on a staggered basis every two years for a four year term also heavily suggest that all member states can and should be part of the decision-making process, both directly as serving Council members and indirectly through their geographical blocs.

8 UN Charter (n 4) art 27(3).

9 The word *veto* is Latin and translates as 'I forbid'. Its usage within the context of the Security Council denotes a decision unilaterally to cease the passing of a resolution or to overrule a decision being made by other members, which is the substantive effect of art 27(3) of the UN Charter.

10 That is to say, P5 members must not vote against; either affirmative votes or abstentions are acceptable.

11 United Nations Conference on International Organization (UNCIO) vol 4 (1945), 253.

12 As political decisions, resolutions of the Security Council will inherently be politically biased, for example, in situations where the Council decides to take action against a state by means of sanctions, which will be fundamentally biased against the state in question. However, the issue is how to ensure this political bias used appropriately to ensure that veto-holders do not abuse the powers they have been granted under the Charter.

13 UNSC Res 1983 (7 June 2011) UN Doc S/RES/1983.

14 UNSC Verbatim Record (20 July 2011) UN Doc S/PV.6587, 2.

15 UNSC Res 1325 (31 October 2000) UN Doc S/RES/1325.

16 Jared Schott, 'Chapter VII as exception: Security Council action and the regulative ideal of emergency' (2008) 6(1) *Northwestern Journal of Human Rights* 24.

17 Daniel Joyner, 'The Security Council as a legal hegemon' (2012) 43 *Georgetown Journal of International Law* 225, 226 (original emphasis).

18 United Nations Conference on International Organization (UNCIO), Vol 3 (1945), 408.

19 Ecuador's proposed amendment read: 'In the fulfilment of the duties inherent in its responsibility to maintain international peace and security, the Security Council shall not establish or modify principles or rules of law but shall respect and enforce and apply the principles or rules of existing law', United Nations Conference on International Organization (UNCIO), Vol 3 (1945), 438.

20 UN Charter (n 4) art 25; see also arts 2(5) and 49.

21 ibid art 2(6).

22 Orakhelashvili argues that the 'Security Council's interaction with international law can take place in two dimensions . . . represented by the number of Council resolutions in which the Council confirms its support for the validity and enforcement of the relevant international norms and instruments . . . [or] resolutions by which the Council either purports to impact, qualify or modify the existing legal position under international law . . .'. See Alexander Orakhelashvili, 'The acts of the Security Council: meaning and standards of review' (2007) 11 *Max Planck Yearbook of United Nations Law* 143. Wood's standard definition of the legally binding nature of resolutions comprises three segments: '[W] hen the resolution in question (or an earlier closely related one) states that the Council has determined that such-and-such is, or continues to be, a threat to the peace; that it is acting under "Chapter VII" or under a specific provision in Chapter VII, such as Article 41; and that it "*decides*" that something shall be done'. See Michael C Wood, 'The UN Security Council and international law' (Hersch Lauterpacht Memorial Lectures 2006, Cambridge, 7 November 2006), para 39 (original emphasis). Hurd argues that resolutions 'are generally seen as important documents in international politics, but this certainly does not mean

they are automatically followed. Despite the legal obligations they might create, Council resolutions clearly do not necessarily elicit full and complete compliance by nation-states. States still seem to "pick and choose" from Council decisions those elements they respect while pretending other elements do not exist'. See Ian Hurd, *After Anarchy: Legitimacy and Power in the United Nations Security Council* (Princeton University Press 2008) 4. In support of this assertion, Hurd refers to Joseph Grieco, 'Anarchy and the limits of cooperation: a realist critique of the newest liberal institutionalism' in David A Baldwin (ed), *Neorealism and Neoliberalisation: The Contemporary Debate* (Columbia University Press 1993) and John J Mearsheimer, 'The false promise of international institutions' (1994/5) 19(3) *International Security* 5.

23 UN Charter (n 4) art 26.

24 ibid.

25 See Joyner (n 17) 225, 233.

26 Hans Kelsen, *Collective Security under International Law* (Lawbook Exchange 2011) 214.

27 For the non-binding nature of Chapter VI resolutions see eg Philippe Sands and Pierre Klein (eds), *Bowett's Law of International Institutions* (Sweet & Maxwell 2011) 46; David Schweigman, *The Authority of the Security Council Under Chapter VII of the UN Charter* (Kluwer Law International 2001) 33; Ken Matthews, *The Gulf Conflict and International Relations* (Routledge 1993) 130; André De Hoogh, *Obligations Erga Omnes and International Crimes* (Nijhoff 2012) 371.

28 *Legal Consequences for States of the Continued Presence of South Africa in Namibia (South West Africa) notwithstanding Security Council Resolution 276 (1970)* (Advisory Opinion) [1971] ICJ Rep 16.

29 UN Charter (n 4) art 25: 'Members of the United Nations agree to accept and carry out the decisions of the Security Council in accordance with the present Charter'.

30 *Legal Consequences for States of the Continued Presence of South Africa in Namibia (South West Africa) notwithstanding Security Council Resolution 276 (1970)* (n 28) para 113. The ICJ continues to qualify this statement, however, by noting that '[t]he language of a resolution of the Security Council should be carefully analysed before a conclusion can be made as to its binding effect' para 114. Wood builds on this suggestion, finding that, although there are no definite standards, a resolution should have three elements to be legally binding: '*First*, a determination by the Council, under Article 39 of the Charter, of the existence of a threat to the peace, breach of the peace, or act of aggression. *Secondly*, evidence that the Council is indeed acting under Chapter VII. And *thirdly*, that the Council has taken a decision within the meaning of Article 25'. See Wood (n 22) para 38 (original emphasis).

31 The advent of international criminal law in the late 20th century was not foreseen in its entirety when the Council was created, despite ad hoc trials such as the Nuremburg and Tokyo trials. I will examine the relationship between the Security Council and the International Criminal Court (ICC) in a later chapter, as this relationship appears to be an additional route for Security Council jurisdiction to be extended to cover the new field of international criminal law.

32 Ian Brownlie, *The Rule of Law in International Affairs: International Law at the Fiftieth Anniversary of the United Nations* (Nijhoff 1998) vii.

33 Brian Z Tamanaha, 'The rule of law for everyone?' (2002) 55 *Current Legal Problems* 97.

34 The Security Council, and indeed the United Nations as a whole, was created in the wake of the Second World War and the permanent five members of the Council reflect the victors and major powers at the time.

35 Evan Luard, *A History of the United Nations: Vol I* (St Martin's Press 1982) 106.

2 The shifting sands of the rule of law

Introduction

What should the rule of law be at the Security Council level? What is the rule of law in the domestic and international spheres? How and why does a rule of law for the Security Council differ from the rule of law in other contexts? Now that the need for a rule of law for the Council has been established, it is important to address what the rule of law entails at the domestic level and how our understanding of this can inform a definition of the rule of law on the international plane, including an engagement with the argument that the international rule of law can be directly transposed from the domestic rule of law, which some academics have attempted to suggest. Building upon these existing rule of law principles, this chapter will establish a rule of law specific to the Security Council drawing on primary sources of the UN itself, such as declarations, resolutions and statements. This will result in a comprehensive definition of the rule of law as it pertains to the Security Council in order to set the stage for Part II of this book, in which Council action is examined against the framework of the rule of law.

What do we mean by 'the rule of law'?

Despite the almost sacred importance and the quasi-religious connotations of the rule of law, the concept has been 'widely embraced at the domestic and international levels without much precision as to what the term means'.[1] In many minds[2] and political systems,[3] the national incarnation of the rule of law has become synonymous with good governance, maintenance of human rights and an equitable, robust judicial system – it is 'a signal virtue of civilized societies'.[4] However, surprisingly, it is certain that there is no singular, simplified definition of a domestic rule of law; indeed, it has been described as 'an exceedingly elusive notion'.[5] It is truly a labyrinthine and tortuous term that would not be difficult imagining collapsing under its own weight. In fact, it has been posited that 'the phrase "the Rule of Law" has become meaningless thanks to ideological abuse and general overuse'.[6] There are at least five pertinent points that all contribute to the tortuously meandering convolutions of the term 'the rule of law'.

First, the definition itself of the term in the legal domain is obscure and opinion is divided on its components: curiously for a legal term, no-one has agreed on an exact definition.[7] Secondly, the exact meaning of the concept differs not only between academics and scholars, but also along geographical lines: despite the rule of law featuring heavily for centuries in literature and legal texts, after the end of the Cold War – when the concept itself spread most notably – in Latin America the rule of law meant a focus on judicial reform, in the Eastern European states legal change alone was thought sufficient and the US viewed the phrase 'rule of law' to mean assistance efforts to support legal judicial and law enforcement reform efforts undertaken by foreign governments.[8]

Thirdly, beyond geographical borders, the term 'rule of law' has transgressed legal borders, pervading discussions in the economic arena, where it 'is held to be not only good in itself, because it embodies and encourages a just society, but also as a cause of other good things, notably growth'.[9] Fourthly, as this chapter will show, the rule of law has also evolved to become not only a concept related to *what* rules should be included, but also now *how* these rules are created, enforced and maintained.[10] Finally, the rule of law has transitioned from being a strictly domestic concept to one that is now discussed and incorporated in international law; as such, there are two types of the rule of law that need to be discussed: the domestic rule of law and the international rule of law.

The origins of the rule of law

While Dicey was perhaps the first to popularise the phrase 'rule of law',[11] the ethereal content of his tripartite proposal[12] dates back to Greek philosopher Plato's *Politicus*,[13] in which the notion is advocated that law should be a means through which to rule, but not an impediment to the ruler himself,[14] and later *Laws*.[15] Subsequently, his student Aristotle expounded this notion[16] recognising, as Plato before him, the corruptibility and fluidity of man's nature.[17] In the centuries even before the Middle Ages, during the eras of the Ancient Romans[18] and the Ancient Chinese,[19] the rule of law underscored revolutionary political theories of governance and popular equality; indeed, under the Islamic Caliphates the subordinance of rulers to the supremacy of law was heavily entrenched from the outset in accordance to Sharia Law.[20]

The fledgling insistence on what we recognise today as being a rule of law gradually formed in the West more solidly through such works as Samuel Rutherford's *Lex, Rex*. John Locke's *Second Treatise of Government* and Montesquieu's *Esprit des Lois* each coined a branch of the *trias politica* theory of separation of powers that lies at the core of modern Western governments. Such works entrenched themselves in direct opposition to the theories of Thomas Hobbes[21] and other advocates of absolutist monarchies[22] and, although it can be argued that the 1215 Magna Carta was the start of the imposition of limitations on the powers of a monarch, it was not until the Bill of Rights Act 1689, that British 'kings could no longer suspend or dispense with the laws, were obliged to acknowledge the privileges of Parliament and to seek legislative approval to raise revenue',[23] essentially entrenching the subjugation of the monarchy to the representatives of the people. Since this time, legal professionals,[24] international declarations,[25] UN resolutions[26] and academic scholars[27] have consolidated the existence of the domestic rule of law, leading to its enshrining at the foundation of modern democratic societies around the globe.

The International Bar Association (IBA) has deemed the rule of law to be 'the foundation of a civilised society',[28] incorporating, non-exhaustively, '[a]n independent, impartial judiciary; the presumption of innocence; the right to a fair and public trial without undue delay; a rational and proportionate approach to punishment; a strong and independent legal profession; strict protection of confidential communications between lawyer and client [and] equality of all before the law'.[29] To add even further complication, as the Council of Europe found, 'the discussion is also muddied by the fact that the meaning of the term "rule of law" may not be the same in different languages;[30] the term is subject to various definitional and normative disputations in the respective countries'.[31] The United States Supreme Court has offered yet another slightly different definition,[32] shifting the passive role of law as being an avenue that should be made available if and when needed to an active role where the law is obliged to *devise*, *maintain* and *empower*.[33]

As a result of these myriad influences no exhaustive list of components of a rule of law has emerged. The reason for these discrepancies in interpretation appears to be that the rule of law represents different ideas to each analyst or theorist; indeed, as Chesterman notes, '[s]uch a high degree of consensus on the virtues of the rule of law is possible only because of dissensus as to its meaning'.[34] Referring to judges' varying interpretations of law, Dworkin suggests that 'the artist can create nothing without interpreting as he creates, [and the critic] creates as he interprets'.[35] If one takes this analogy further, it seems logical that the rule of law might seem slightly, if not vastly, different according to ones positioning and environment. Each individual's experiences, outlooks and moral school of thought subtly but significantly colour their personal definition not only of the rule of law itself as a concept, but also all others' definitions – a constant echo of interpretative reverberations.

The concern that emerges, then, is that with differing contextual practices and laws, standards between nations can differ depending on the specific circumstances of that environment. For example, where a government dictates that certain moral codes allow for employment discrimination in favour of previously disadvantaged groups, the social backgrounds or racial profile of potential employees become disproportionately important in relation to qualifications, allowing, or even encouraging, employers to choose those who will fulfil certain criteria on paper and leaving a significant number of the population struggling to compete in the job market. Moreover, the rule of law is adapted to serve specific national needs that would be irrelevant or even counter-intuitive in other states. In post-Apartheid South Africa, the introduction of Black Economic Empowerment (BEE) legislation[36] may be deemed appropriate for social cohesion and political, economic or other national advancement, but would clearly be erroneous and abhorrently discriminatory if imposed in another nation. Thus, the rule of law is this case is clearly only judged as being equal and transparently rational relative to the domain to which it relates.

The domestic rule of law

There are, however, certain elements that appear to be inherently shared between all of these varied descriptions and the purpose of this chapter is to analyse whether such elements of a domestic system can be transposed or adapted to fit the international legal model. In order to do so, one must first analyse the domestic model: the definition of a 'political ruler' and the various components of 'a rule of law' as opposed, for example, to 'rule *by* law'. This latter notion is not technically opposed to absolute monarchic system since a political ruler who imposes laws arbitrarily and for the sake of personal gain, for example, would still be ruling *by* law; what the rule *of* law encapsulates at its very inception is the subjugation of all individuals, irrespective of stature, creed or other defining characteristic, to laws promulgated by the representatives that are appointed to do so by democratic means. Paradoxically, the 'rule of law' is in itself a misnomer – law cannot rule: 'being a human creation, [it] must be subject to human will'.[37]

Therefore, to assess the rule of law requires analysis of both the 'political ruler' and the intended beneficiaries, as well as the standards to which actions will be held accountable. In such a system, actions taken by any actor, ranging from the individual citizen to the government itself, are accountable – normative law. One should recall, however, that incorporation of elements of the rule of law does not amount to comprehensive definition. The transient nature of the rule of law is reflected in the difficulty of identifying an exhaustive list of its components and the hitherto lack of precise definition; it seems that there is much literature[38] and debate[39] about its origins, what it might consist of and what it might seek to avoid, yet no standard or all-encompassing pithy delineation.

Two overarching attributes of the rule of law seem evident: the first is that a set of laws is established; the second is that this set of laws is equally enforced. The two exist in unison and are inter-reliant: a set of laws that is arbitrarily or sporadically enforced is ineffective in achieving the goals of uniformity and would reduce the rule of law to a game of probabilities, where committing an illegal act is balanced against the likelihood of repercussions for its commission, or a corrupt and nepotistic system whereby those in select positions such as those of government and power are above the laws and able to escape the negative consequences of illegal acts with impunity; similarly, in order to follow a set of laws effectively and consistently, the framework of laws by which a structure is governed must be put in place based upon stable pillars that are communicated to those it governs, with a clearly evident chain of events that enumerates both what acts or actions are outlawed and the punishment for the commission of said acts or actions.

The rule of law as a concept must, nevertheless, have certain elements upon which most, if not all, parties can agree. The phrase 'rule of law', or a variation thereof, is explicitly mentioned as being at the core of domestic constitutions the world over;[40] the elements, nonetheless, remain elusive. The late practitioner and rule of law authority Thomas Bingham attempted to unravel the mystery of a definition of its elements in one volume, entitled quite aptly *The Rule of Law*.[41]

The principles identified by Bingham in *The Rule of Law* were no doubt derived from intensive study of different constitutions; they are enshrined widely across nations as being at the core of the rule of law at the domestic level. Equality can be seen in Belgium's constitutional protection that: '[n]o class distinctions exist in the State . . . Belgians are equal before the law'[42] or Australia's affirmation that: 'all laws made by the Parliament of the Commonwealth under the Constitution, shall be binding on the courts, judges, and people of every State and of every part of the Commonwealth'.[43] Judicial review through the separation of powers is woven into the fabric of many constitutions, such as those of the United States,[44] South Africa,[45] Brazil,[46] Belgium[47] and France.[48] The right to a fair trial is also enshrined in the constitutions of South Africa[49] and Canada,[50] as are the accessibility of the law, also understood as clarity or legal certainty,[51] and non-arbitrariness, which incorporates the prohibition of *ex post facto* law and *habeas corpus* rights.[52]

Legal aid is also available in some nations[53] but does not appear to have reached the level of being a constitutional right.[54] Therefore, although there are undoubtedly a relatively large number of elements upon which many states and scholars are able to agree, the exact definition of a rule of law remains debatable; this in turn makes the definition of an international rule of law all the more difficult. Despite the fact that there are inherent differences between the two systems of domestic and international law, there do exist arguments both for and against the motion to use the domestic rule of law as the foundation for an international rule of law.

Searching for a definition of the international rule of law for the Security Council

There appear to be two paths available when making the leap between domestic and international rule of law systems – the more straightforward approach is to isolate each component of the domestic rule of law and simply attempt to apply these to international law; however, as this section will explore, there are elements of the domestic rule of law that are unsuitable for transposition in this manner, since the structure of domestic law, as previously mentioned, frequently differs greatly from that of the international sphere. Therefore, this approach is simply the starting point. The second, more complex, bespoke method of deducing an international rule of law is to build upon this first approach, examining each of these components and attempting to add to or detract from them in order to create the most legitimately applicable rule of law system possible; this would be far more suitable to the idiosyncrasies of the international legal system and pays heed to the dissimilarities between it and the domestic legal model.

Direct transposition of domestic norms to the international plane

If there is equivocality in agreeing definitions of the domestic rule of law, then this is doubly true for the international sphere.[55] Brownlie states that 'it would be absurd if it were not possible to evaluate the workings of the international system in terms of the Rule of Law'[56] but stops short of filling in the blanks.[57] Bingham's assertion that 'the rule of law in the international order is, to a considerable extent at least, the domestic rule of law writ large'[58] is not unanimously shared within the academic community.[59] There is, it appears, some debate over the distinction to be made between the rule of law at the domestic level and the international rule of law.

The argument against direct transposition is strengthened by the fact that traditional concepts of international law such as state sovereignty must be accommodated in a discourse on the rule of law at the international level. Moreover, the fields of diplomacy and international politics are reliant on undocumented negotiations, which although one might find at the domestic level appear to be more prevalent in international relations and politics. As Eijsbouts notes: '[e]ven in the European Union, with its relatively high degree of transparency in the legislative process, there is no record of the final exchanges leading up to the enactment of legal instruments . . .'.[60] There are, of course, the *travaux préparatoires* of the meetings that result in these documents; nonetheless, one cannot say the same of all UN Security Council resolutions, for example, which may begin with a closed-door meeting of selected Council members, allowing for political bargaining or negotiations the details of which will never see the light of day and may merely be distilled to a yes or no vote in the Council chambers with no subsequent explanation.[61]

Another fundamental distinction that must be made between the rule of law at the domestic level and any comparable rule of law at the Security Council level is that, whereas at the domestic level an integral part of the rule of law is that no individual should be beyond the reach of the law, no organisation above scrutiny and no *body* exempt from judicial oversight, the Security Council appears to be all three. Although the UN Charter stands as both the founding text and regulatory document for the Security Council, there is no independent judiciary that reviews its actions or decisions. In a domestic rule of law setting, clearly enumerated laws are promulgated by the legislature to be uniformly enforced upon all citizens, irrespective of power or status. These laws are heavily scrutinised by an independent judiciary to ensure they are not unconstitutional or similarly invalid and in the event that a citizen wishes to challenge the validity of a law, adequate channels of impartial judicial recourse are made available. Such a separation of powers ensures that there exists an environment for the rule of law to be established and continue to thrive.

Transposing this to the Security Council framework, the UN Charter contains a hazy definition of Security Council powers, which has led to a plethora of understandings and interpretations; nevertheless, in the hypothetical situation that it were to be more specific and expansively definitive, there exists no body established to ensure that the Council adheres to its mandate – a counterpart to the judiciary on the domestic level. Thus, in the event that the Security Council is capable of acting ultra vires, there exists no mechanism to state this fact; 'the Security Council may request the International Court of Justice to give an *advisory opinion* on any legal question'[62] but as a principal organ of the United Nations on a par with the General Assembly, the Security Council, the Economic and Social Council, the Trusteeship Council and the Secretariat,[63] and with the Statute annexed to and forming part of the UN Charter, the ICJ does not have any jurisdiction over the Security Council, particularly given that the Court's jurisdiction is over any 'legal question'[64] and '[t]he Council is a political body *par excellence*'.[65] As an organ of the UN parallel to the Security Council, a sibling relationship between the ICJ and Security Council appears insufficient to satisfy standards of judicial review.

For these reasons, the cautious approach advocated by Chesterman is the more pragmatic and adoptable of proposals for the framework of a rule of law for the Council. In his report for the Austrian Initiative, Chesterman expands on this notion and identifies more acutely the discrepancy between the domestic rule of law and the international rule of law, finding that:

> [a]t the national level, [the rule of law] requires a government of laws, the supremacy of the law, and equality before the law. Strengthening a rules-based international system by applying these principles at the international level would increase predictability of behaviour, prevent arbitrariness, and ensure basic fairness. For the Council, greater use of existing law and greater emphasis on its own grounding in the law will ensure greater respect for its decisions.[66]

The structure of the international plane, in addition to the legal obligations on states as opposed to citizens, are poles apart from the domestic counterpart, and the mechanisms and structures in place are accordingly disparate. The assertion that not all norms may translate well to the international sphere calls for a measured approach to which norms can work and which are obsolete or unsuitable for the international level.

A more cautious examination

UNGA Resolution 67/1 tackled these issues and enumerates several aspects of what an international rule of law should strive for; in addition to 'predictability and legitimacy',[67] the declaration calls for the international rule of law to comprise 'fair, stable and predictable legal frameworks',[68] 'economic, financial or trade measures'[69] that are consistent with international law, 'the independence of the judicial system, together with its impartiality and integrity'[70] and 'equal access to justice for all'.[71] Furthermore, it identifies that the 'rule of law and development are strongly interrelated and mutually reinforcing'.[72]

It is clear from this description that the rule of law at the international level differs quite significantly from the rule of law at the domestic level; in addition to direct references in Resolution 67/1 to the work of four of the principal organs of the United Nations – the Security Council,[73] the Economic and Social Council,[74] the International Court of Justice (ICJ)[75] and the General Assembly[76] – mention of supra-national organisations such as the International Criminal Court[77] and 'the International Tribunal for the Law of the Sea as well as other international courts and tribunals'[78] show not only that the scope of this declaration, and the concept of the international rule of law of which it speaks, is far broader and more far-reaching than that of the domestic rule of law, but also that the United Nations itself is one of, if not the main, members of the audience to which the declaration speaks.

The declaration also stresses 'the importance of strengthened international cooperation, based on the principles of shared responsibility and in accordance with international law',[79] stressing its international direction. Although it enumerates many beneficial results that the international rule of law can and should create[80] and potential threats and hindrances to the rule of law,[81] there is no exhaustive list of where the parameters of an international rule of law might lie. Reinforcing the need for an expansive approach, in order to delve deeper into the question of what an international rule of law comprises, it is necessary to read this declaration in conjunction with other documents that have emerged from the General Assembly or United Nations in general.

In 2008, Bühler noted that: 'it is only since a few years that the United Nations has started to develop comprehensive common concepts, coordinate, and give coherent policy direction to the manifold activities of the UN system in the field of rule of law . . . [before which] activities of the United Nations followed a piecemeal approach, were limited in scope . . . and lacked coordination and a coherent policy'.[82] Indeed, despite the fact that the Assembly has considered rule of law as an agenda item since 1992[83] and numerous thematic debates spear-headed by the Security Council,[84] until recently the internalised rule of law for the United Nations, and in particular the Security Council, appeared to be neither a feasible reality nor a goal towards which the evidence suggested the Council could be seen to be working. Although the Council had in the past adopted resolutions reiterating the importance of the international rule of law, it had always done so within the framework of connected issues such as women, peace and security,[85] children in armed conflict,[86] the protection of civilians in armed conflict[87] and counter-terrorism.[88]

Insofar as a bespoke working definition of the rule of law for the Council as a tool for comparison to its decision-making process, these tend to have hitherto focused on policy proposals. An Australian initiative in partnership with the Australian National University[89] was the most recent to have done this, with a focus on transparency, consistency, accountability and engagement. Prior to this, the Austrian Rule of Law Initiative[90] attempted to address this gap but falls short of creating a comprehensive or requisite standard. Notwithstanding the 17 bespoke recommendations for the Security Council outlined,[91] each pertaining to an aspect of Council behaviour within the framework of the rule of law, the report does not enumerate a list of components of the rule of law, resorting instead to a piecemeal approach of Council actions that revolve centrally around issues of transparency,[92] accountability[93] and review.[94]

There are quite clearly elements of the rule of law in domestic legal orders that can be adopted at the international level; transparency, equality before the law and the avoidance of arbitrariness are all examples of rule of law elements that are equally important at the international level as at the domestic. However, there are components that need to be added to the domestic elements to reflect the international nature of law governing and between states – international human rights law and the abidance by international human rights treaties is a prime example of this, as well as elements that are not applicable to the Security Council, such as the public promulgation of laws. Finding that these reflect the core components highlighted, this book therefore aims to hone these elements of the international rule of law into a workable model to fit the mould of the Security Council.

A definition for the UN Security Council

For the purposes of delineating the specificities of an international rule of law, perhaps the most important document is the definition given in 2004 by the then-serving Secretary-General of the United Nations, Kofi Annan. The work of the Secretary-General Ban Ki-Moon is referred to explicitly in UNGA Resolution 67/1,[95] specifically with reference to the 2012 Report of the Secretary-General 'Delivering justice: programme of action to strengthen the rule of law at the national and international levels';[96] however, this report also does not create a list of international rule of law components. Rather, it refers[97] back to Annan's 2004 report to the Security Council and uses the same definition of the rule of law which Annan announced four years prior.

This definition, which relates to 'a concept at the very heart of the Organization's mission . . .',[98] can be read to apply not only to states themselves, but also to international organisations and the United Nations itself. It stated that the rule of law was a principle of governance in which all persons, institutions and entities, public and private, including the state itself, are accountable to laws that are publicly promulgated, equally enforced and independently adjudicated, and which are consistent with international human rights norms and standards. It requires, as well, measures to ensure adherence to the principles of supremacy of law, equality before the law, accountability to the law, fairness in the application of the law, separation of powers, participation in decision-making, legal certainty, avoidance of arbitrariness and procedural and legal transparency.[99]

Accounting for some duplication, there appear to be 11 components of an international rule of law suitable for application to the Security Council, as derived from Annan's report:[100] public promulgation of laws; consistency with international human rights norms and standards; supremacy of the law; equality before the law; accountability to the law; fairness in the application of the law; the separation of powers; the equitable participation in decision-making processes; legal certainty; the avoidance of arbitrariness; and procedural and legal transparency. Finding that these reflect the core components highlighted by both domestic and international rule of law scholars, these are the components that this book accepts as the definition of the rule of law for the Council.

Moreover, I would not be alone in adopting them as such; with respect to the applicability of these principles to the Security Council, the UN High Commissioner for Human Rights and others[101] have deemed Annan's definition to constitute a rule of law that can be taken for all United Nations organs.[102] This seems particularly the case given the 2012 General Assembly declaration that seems to put to rest any arguments over whether the rule of law should be applied internally to the United Nations.

Naturally, this did not immediately end all debate about the components of the rule of law, nor stem the debate about the concept. Like a proverbial game of snakes and ladders, a later working paper from the Secretariat sent the debate back to square one in its quite explicit statement that: 'there is no universal agreement as to what the term rule of law actually means . . . The rule of law is a system of interrelated principles that extend widely into social, economic, cultural and other structures in present-day societies'.[103] However, perhaps spurred on by the necessity of establishing a working definition of the term *rule of law* given the attention it has been given in recent years imposed on both the Secretariat and General Assembly the obligation to adopt one and Annan's has seemingly been the reference to which resolutions have pointed since.

The fact that the definition was furnished by the then-serving Secretary-General of the United Nations imports additional relevancy to the definition for the purposes of this book, for who could be better placed than he to know the mandate of the United Nations, its regulations, direction and the intricate workings of the organisation, allowing his report pin-point accuracy and topical pertinence to this book? In addition, given the questions this book raises around the impartiality and independence of the Security Council, a definition from the Secretary-General is more reliably independent than one from the Council itself and will ensure that any standards of the rule of law compared to Council actions will not be tautologous, biased or self-serving.

Following Annan's report to the Council, member states unanimously recognized the need for 'universal adherence to and implementation of the rule of law at both the national and international levels' and reaffirmed their commitment to 'an international order based on the rule of law and international law'[104] at the United Nations World Summit in September 2005. This echoed far earlier calls in documents such as the Declaration on Principles of International Law Concerning Friendly Relations,[105] which in 1970 referred to the 'promotion of the rule of law among nations'[106] and inextricably linked the rule of law to a 'contribut[ion] to the strengthening of world peace'.[107] This declaration, which was adopted without a vote, also proclaimed that 'States shall comply in good faith with their obligations under the generally recognized principles and rules of international law with respect to the maintenance of international peace and security, and shall endeavour to make the United Nations security system based on the Charter more effective'.[108]

In 2012, the Assembly indeed found that 'the Charter . . . , international law and justice, and . . . an international order based on the rule of law . . . are indispensable foundations for a more peaceful, prosperous and just world'.[109] The seeds of the international rule of law can be viewed as having been sown several decades ago, in the drafting states' decisions to 'promote through joint and separate action universal respect for and observance of human rights and fundamental freedoms . . . the duty to refrain from any forcible action which deprives peoples referred to above in the elaboration of the present principle of their right to self-determination and freedom and independence . . . [or] the duty to comply fully and in good faith with its international obligations'.[110] Similarly, in the 2000 Millennium Declaration,[111] member states resolved to 'strengthen respect for the rule of law in international as in national affairs'.[112] Although the rule of law was mentioned in passing in this document, it is significant that it was done within the section dealing with 'Peace, security and disarmament'[113] as this couches the rule of law in the pursuit of peace and security.

It is, perhaps, also worthy of note at this point that there is no specific role laid out for the Security Council in Annan's definition; all organs of the United Nations are treated in the same way. That each organ of the United Nations would interpret the provisions of the Charter and the means of implementation of its provisions which concerned its activities was a decision taken at the very outset of the creation of the United Nations;[114] it therefore follows that each organ should decide how best to implement the international rule of law, particularly in light of the *equality* and *competence* principles[115] that prohibit organs from either instructing one another or depending upon another organ in the conduct of their mandates and missions. Indeed, just as organs can and should be independent in deciding the manner or path chosen in reaching their respective goals, so too in the implementation of the rule of law internally it would be remiss for the Secretary-General, or the Assembly, to impose structures and specificities upon the Council's behaviour. Annan's definition of the rule of law understandably, then, does not distinguish between the organs of the United Nations; however, there can be no doubt that Annan's definition of the rule of law is sufficient, having been included, and thereby endorsed, by Secretary-General Ban Ki-Moon in the Secretary-General's 2008 *Delivering Justice* report and again by the General Assembly in UNGA Resolution 67/1.

The legitimacy of the UN definition

Although not unilaterally legally binding,[116] certain resolutions of the General Assembly[117] can still be argued to amount to the custom of states for the purposes of international customary law.[118] Indeed, it has been posited in relation to resolutions of the UN on the use of outer space that there is a concept of 'instant customary law', where 'unanimously adopted General Assembly resolutions (or draft texts of other bodies) reflect a *communis opinio juris* which in itself will suffice for the formation 'overnight' of customary law'.[119] The Statute of the International Court of Justice (ICJ) does not elaborate on the components of customary law, stating simply that customary norms must be supported by 'evidence of a general practice accepted as law'.[120] Although the ICJ agreed in principle with the possibility of General Assembly resolutions bearing some weight under some circumstances, any interpretations of customary law still require the twofold standard of 'the material element of State practice and psychological element of acceptance of norms thus practiced as legally binding',[121] which has previously been supported by the ICJ.[122]

In the ICJ's *Nicaragua* case, both the near-universal acceptance of the UN Charter and the wide approval of relevant General Assembly resolutions resulted in finding that the non-intervention rule had reached a customary legal status.[123] Indeed, individual General Assembly resolutions have also been recognised as representing *opinio juris*: in the *Nicaragua* case, 'the adoption by states of [resolution 2625(XXV) on Principles of International Law Concerning Friendly Relations] afford[ed] an indication of their *opinio juris* as to customary international law on the question'.[124] UNGA Resolution 67/1 shows a similar *opinio juris* to UNGA Resolution 2625(XXV); both were adopted by consensus[125] and enumerated rules and standards that had been accepted by a large number of states, most importantly without record of opposition.[126]

Supportive of state practice are the sheer number of represented states[127] and organisations[128] at the high-level meeting, in addition to the existing actions taken and efforts made by states to implement the core themes of UNGA Resolution 67/1 at the domestic level.[129] UNGA Resolution 67/1 can be seen, then, not only as an affirmation of state willingness but as an exercise in stock-taking; states attending the high-level meeting put forward examples, some over a decade-old, of how they have been implementing the rule of law at both the international and domestic levels. UNGA Resolution 67/1 is, in a sense, reiterating the existing practices and willingness in the form of an official written document and setting out a plan for further expansion of state practice in the form of pledges – it is a codification of principles that does amount to the existence of a customary norm. The rule of law, then can only be seen as an obligatory norm for a modern democratic society.[130]

While comments of states focus mainly on the rule of law at the national level and how to implement international obligations domestically, a few states have commented on the relationship between the UN system and the need for a rule of law to apply to it internally. On the whole, however, member states did so within the context of criticism of the Security Council itself to be failing to implement the rule of law internally, be that through 'the undemocratic and unrepresentative nature of the Security Council',[131] the need to 'completely reform and change the rules and regulations governing the Security Council, in terms of both its powers and its structures'[132] or simply the belief 'that [the Council] is far from making a positive contribution to the rule of law'.[133]

In fact, the rule of law for the Security Council, or even the United Nations system as a whole, is explicitly mentioned but a handful of times throughout the comments – the UN Secretary-General argued that 'rule of law activities . . . deserve a central place in the structure of [UN] work';[134] the President of the ICJ articulated his view that 'the concept of the rule of law is, and should be at the very heart of the Organization's mission';[135] and the European Commission's President recognised 'the importance of linking the rule of law agenda to the work of the United Nations on peace and security, human rights and development, which are simultaneously preconditions for and enablers of democracy and the rule of law'.[136]

In light of these statements, UNGA Resolution 67/1 therefore grants authority and gravitas to the concept of an international rule of law for the Security Council – leaders from over 80 states were present at the meeting.[137] As the deliberative organ of the UN tasked to 'initiate studies and make recommendations for the purpose of . . . promoting international co-operation in the political field and encouraging the progressive development of international law and its codification',[138] the Assembly's official recognition of the applicability of the rule of law internally to the United Nations and its organ signifies a landmark event in the organisation's history and a concrete base upon which to establish a rule of law framework. However, it cannot be said to yet constitute international customary law in relation to the applicability of the rule of law to the Security Council, or even the United Nations in general.

The Council itself has also previously emphasised its commitment 'to ensure that all United Nations efforts to restore peace and security themselves respect and promote the rule of law'[139] and maintained that 'the rule of law is an important concept in the work of the Security Council',[140] citing the thematic debates, presidential statements and Council resolutions on the topic of the rule of law. Somewhat promisingly, the President of the Council offered measurable targets for change in Council procedure in the form of Council commitment 'to fair and clear procedures for placing individuals and entities on sanctions lists and for removing them, as well as for granting humanitarian exemptions',[141] although this could cynically also be argued to have been either a moot point in light of or a direct result of the quasi-judicial review undertaken by the European Court of Justice in the *Kadi* decision.[142] The fact remains, though, that the Council acknowledges the need for the rule of law in its own decision-making process and attempts to place on record its willingness, intent and quantifiable steps to do so.

Notes

1 Simon Chesterman, 'The UN Security Council and the rule of law: the role of the Security Council in strengthening a rules-based international system: final report and recommendations from the Austrian Initiative, 2004–2008' Executive Summary (Institute for International Law and Justice 2008) ii. See also Venice Commission, 'The rule of law: concept, guiding principle and framework' (2010) Council of Europe Doc CDL-UDT(2010)022 at 3; and generally, Declaration of the High-level Meeting of the General Assembly on the Rule of Law at the National and International Levels, UNGA Res 67/1 (2012) UN Doc A/RES/67/1.

2 See eg Brian Z Tamanaha, 'The rule of law for everyone?' (2002) 55 *Current Legal Problems* 97, 107; E P Thompson, *Whigs and Hunters: The Origin of the Black Act* (Penguin 1975) 266; International Commission of Jurists, *The Rule of Law in a Free Society: A Report on the International Congress on Jurists, New Delhi, India January 5–10, 1959* (International Commission of Jurists 1959) vii.

3 In addition to UN declarations on the rule of law, which are formed of sovereign States and therefore political systems, individual states such as Russia and China have come forward to highlight the importance of the rule of law. See eg Alexander Lebed, 'Rule of law for Russia' *The Moscow Times* (1 June 1996); Erik Eckholm, 'China signs UN pact on rights and rule of law' *New York Times* (21 November 2000).

4 Neil MacCormick, *Rhetoric and the Rule of Law: A Theory of Legal Reasoning* (Oxford University Press 2009) 12.

5 Brian Tamanaha, *On the Rule of Law: History, Politics, Theory* (Cambridge University Press 2004) 9.

6 Judith N Shklar, 'Political theory and the rule of law' in Allan C Hutchinson and Patrick Monahan (eds), *The Rule of Law: Ideal or Ideology?* (Transnational 1987) 1.

7 See eg Thomas Bingham, *The Rule of Law* (Penguin 2011) 8; Fredrich Hayek, *The Road to Serfdom* (Routledge 1994) 54; Philip Allott, 'Law and the re-making of Humanity' in Prosser Gifford and Norman Dorsen (eds), *Democracy and the Rule of Law* (CQ Publications 2001) 19; Ian Brownlie, *The Rule of Law in International Affairs: International Law at the Fiftieth Anniversary of the United Nations* (Nijhoff 1998) 213–14; Brian Z Tamanaha, 'The rule of law for everyone?' (n 2) 102; Cheryl Saunders and Katherine Le Roy, 'Perspectives on the rule of law' in Cheryl Saunders and Katherine Le Roy, *The Rule of Law* (Federation Press 2003) 5; Jean Ely and Richard Ely (eds), *Lionel Murphy: The Rule of Law* (Akron Press 1986).

8 Rachel Kleinfeld, 'Competing definitions of the rule of law' in Thomas Carothers (ed), *Promoting the Rule of Law: In Search of Knowledge* (Carnegie Endowment for International Peace 2006) 33.

9 'Economics and the rule of law: order in the jungle' *The Economist* (13 March 2008).

10 Rachel Kleinfeld, 'Competing definitions of the rule of law' in Thomas Carothers (ed), *Promoting the Rule of Law: In Search of Knowledge* (Carnegie Endowment for International Peace 2006) 33–44.

11 Albert V Dicey, *An Introduction to the Study of the Law of the Constitution* (8th edn, Liberty Classics 1982) 107.

12 No one can be punished or made to suffer except for a breach of law proved in an ordinary court; no one is above the law and everyone is equal before the law regardless of social, economic, or political status. The rule of law includes the results of judicial decisions determining the rights of private persons.

13 Julia Annas and Robin Waterfield (eds), *Plato: The Statesman* (Cambridge University Press 1995).

14 Plato, *The Dialogues of Plato translated into English with Analyses and Introductions by B. Jowett, M.A. in Five Volumes* (3rd edn, Oxford University Press 1892) 504.

15 Plato, *Laws* (trans. Benjamin Jowett, Cosimo 2008) 221. In his earlier *Republic*, Plato supported the rule of 'Philosopher Kings', ruled by knowledge but above the law.

16 Aristotle, *Politics* (William Ellis trans, Echo Library 2006) 79.

17 ibid.

18 Marcus Tullius Cicero, *The Orations of Marcus Tullius Cicero* (Charles D Yonge trans, London 1856) Ch 53 s 146.

19 See eg Randall P Peerenboom, *Law and Morality in Ancient China: The Silk Manuscripts of Huang-Lao* (SUNY Press 1993) 171.
20 See eg Bernard Lewis, *The Political Language of Islam* (Chicago University Press 1991) 91; Christopher G Weeramantry, *Justice Without Frontiers: Furthering Human Rights: Vol 1* (Kluwer Law International 1997) 132.
21 See eg Thomas Hobbes, *Leviathan* (Oxford World's Classics 2008).
22 For an examination of absolute monarchist and enlightened absolute monarchist themes see eg Niccolò Machiavelli, *The Prince* (Penguin 1988); Voltaire, *Candide* (Penguin 1998).
23 Caroline A Edie, 'Revolution and the rule of law: the end of the dispensing power, 1689' (1977) 10 *Eighteenth Century Studies* 434.
24 See International Commission of Jurists conferences, which brought together judges, lawyers and professors from 53 countries in the Act of Athens (1955); Declaration of Delhi (1959); Law of Lagos (1961); Resolution of Rio (1962); Declaration of Bangkok (1965); Declaration of Colombo (1966).
25 See eg Universal Declaration of Human Rights (adopted 10 December 1948) UNGA Res 217 A(III) (UDHR) preamble; Convention for the Protection of Human Rights and Fundamental Freedoms (European Convention on Human Rights, as amended) (ECHR) preamble.
26 See eg UNGA Res 61/39 (18 December 2006) UN Doc A/RES/61/39; UNGA Res 62/70 (8 January 2008) UN Doc A/RES/62/70; UNGA Res 63/128 (15 January 2009) UN Doc A/RES/63/128; UNGA Res 64/116 (15 January 2010) A/RES/64/116; UNGA Res 65/32 (10 January 2011) UN Doc A/RES/65/32.
27 See Ronald Dworkin, *Law's Empire* (Hart 1998); see also Bingham, *The Rule of Law* (n 7); Freidrich A Hayek, *The Constitution of Liberty* (Routledge 1976).
28 International Bar Association, 'Rule of law resolution' (September 2005).
29 ibid.
30 See eg '*Etat de droit*' (France), '*Rechtsstaat*' (Germany), '*Stato di diritto*' (Italy), '*verkhovensto prava*' (Russia) or '*estado de derecho*' (Spain).
31 Venice Commission, 'The rule of law: concept, guiding principle and framework' (n 1) (original emphasis).
32 Justice Anthony Kennedy, 'Remarks to the American Bar Association' (ABA Annual Meeting, Honolulu, 5 August 2006).
33 Once again, this is diametrically opposed to the prevalent Hobbesian theory of government in the 17th century. See eg Thomas Hobbes, *Leviathan* (n 21).
34 Simon Chesterman, 'An international rule of law?' (2008) 56(2) *American Journal of Comparative Law* 331, 332.
35 Ronald Dworkin, 'Law as interpretation' in Dennis Patterson (ed), *Philosophy of Law and Legal Theory: An Anthology* (Wiley-Blackwell 2003) 382.
36 The Broad-based Black Economic Empowerment Act 53 of 2003. See eg *Report of the Black Empowerment Commission* (Skotaville Press 2001) 2.
37 Philip Allott, 'Law and the re-making of humanity' in Prosser Gifford and Norman Dorsen (eds), *Democracy and the Rule of Law* (CQ Publications 2001) 62.
38 See eg Bruce Broomhall, *International Justice and the International Criminal Court – Between Sovereignty and the Rule of Law* (Oxford University Press 2003); Gerhard Werle, '"We asked for justice and got the rule of law": German courts and the totalitarian past' (1995) 11 *South African Journal of Human Rights* 70; David Tolbert and Andrew Solomon, 'United Nations reform and supporting the rule of law in post-conflict societies' (2006) 19 *Harvard Human Rights Journal* 45; Davis R Robinson, 'The role of politics in the election and the work of judges of the International Court of Justice' (2003) 97 *Proceedings of the American Society of International Law* 277; Eric A Posner and John C Yoo, 'Judicial independence in international tribunals' (2005) 93 *California Law*

Review 899; Gerald Fitzmaurice, 'The law and procedure of the International Court of Justice, 1951–54: treaty interpretation and other treaty points' (1957) 33 *British Yearbook of International Law* 203; Susan Kneebone, 'The rule of law and the role of law: refugees and asylum seekers' in Susan Kneebone (ed), *Refugees, Asylum Seekers and the Rule of Law* (Cambridge University Press 2009); John Laughlin, *Travesty: The Trial of Slobodan Milosevic and the Corruption of International Justice* (Pluto Press 2006); Simon Chesterman, *Just War or Just Peace?: Humanitarian Intervention and International Law* (Oxford University Press 2002), 128; Ruth MacKenzie and others, *Selecting International Judges: Principle, Process, and Politics* (Oxford University Press 2010); Jennifer A Widner, *Building the Rule of Law* (Norton 2001).

39 Simon Chesterman, 'The UN Security Council and the rule of law' (n 1); International Bar Association, 'Rule of Law resolution' (September 2005).

40 Constitution of the Republic of South Africa 1996 para 1(c); Constitution Act, c 11 (UK), Schedule B, 1982 preamble; Constitution de la République française, 1958, art 1; La Constitución Española, 1978 preamble.

41 See Bingham, *The Rule of Law* (n 7).

42 The Constitution of Belgium 2012 art 10. For similar rights see also Constitution of the Republic of South Africa 1996 art 9; Constitution of Brazil 1998 art 5; Constitution of India 2011 art 14; Constitution Act c 11 (UK), Schedule B, 1982 art 15(1).

43 An Act to constitute the Commonwealth of Australia [1900] 63–64 Victoria, ch 12 para 5. See also Constitution of the Republic of South Africa 1996 art 9.

44 Articles I, II, III of the US Constitution delineate the exact roles of the legislative, executive and judiciary branches of the US government. United States Constitution (1787).

45 Constitution of the Republic of South Africa 1996 art 40.

46 Constitution of Brazil, 1998 art 18.

47 Constitution of Belgium 2012 art 36.

48 Constitution de la République française 1958 art 34.

49 Constitution of the Republic of South Africa 1996 art 34.

50 Constitution Act c 11 (UK), Schedule B 1982 art 11.

51 ibid; Constitution of India 2011 art 20.

52 Indian constitution, ibid art 22; Constitution of the United States 1787 Amendment VI; Constitution Act c 11 (UK), Schedule B 1982 arts 9–10; Constitution of the Republic of South Africa 1996 art 35; Constitution of Belgium 2012 art 12.

53 In the EU, Member States must provide legal aid in accordance with the Charter of Fundamental Rights of the European Union 2000 art 47, although the UK in 2010 removed funding from legal aid pertaining to cases of family law, clinical negligence, education, employment, immigration, benefits, debt and housing cases under Schedule 2 of the Access to Justice Act 1999; India guarantees legal aid under art 39A of its constitution. In New Zealand this is covered by the Legal Services Regulation 2011.

54 In Canada, legal aid was identified in *Canadian Bar Assn v British Columbia*, 2008 BCCA 92, to not be a constitutionally protected right. The USA provides state-funded legal aid in criminal cases to those unable to afford legal services themselves, but does not do so in civil cases; in Australia there are eight legal aid commissions established in partnership with the government under the National Partnership Agreement on Legal Assistance Services 2010.

55 Declaration of the High-level Meeting of the General Assembly on the Rule of Law at the National and International Levels, UNGA Res 67/1 (2012) UN Doc A/RES/67/1 para 2.

56 Ian Brownlie, *The Rule of Law in International Affairs: International Law at the Fiftieth Anniversary of the United Nations* (Nijhoff 1998) 213.

57 See also William Bishop, 'The international rule of law' (1961) 59 *Michigan L Review* 553.
58 See Bingham, *The Rule of Law* (n 7) 111.
59 See eg Thomas Eijsbouts, 'Introduction' in Thomas A Vandamme and Jan-Herman Reestman (eds), *Ambiguity in the Rule of Law: The interface between National and International Legal Systems* (Europa Law 2001) 6; Simon Chesterman, 'The UN Security Council and the rule of law' (n 1) para 12; Cheryl Saunders and Katherine Le Roy, 'Perspectives on the rule of law' in Cheryl Saunders and Katherine Le Roy, *The Rule of Law* (Federation Press 2003) 14; Franz L Neumann, *The Rule of Law: Political Theory and the Legal System in Modern Society* (Berg 1985) 4.
60 See Eijsbouts (n 59).
61 See eg W M Reisman, 'The constitutional crisis in the United Nations' (1993) 87 *American Journal of International Law* 83, 85.
62 UN Charter (1945) art 96(1) (emphasis added).
63 ibid art 7(1).
64 ibid art 96(1). For a legal analysis of the political question doctrine see the US Supreme Court's discussions, definition and reasoning in *Marbury v Madison*, 5 U.S. 137 (1803) and *Baker v Carr*, 369 U.S. 186, 217 (1962). See also *Accordance with International Law of the Unilateral Declaration of Independence in Respect of Kosovo* (Advisory Opinion) [2010] ICJ Rep 403.
65 Morten Bergsmo, 'Occasional remarks on certain state concerns about the jurisdictional reach of the International Criminal Court, and their possible implications for the relationship between the Court and the Security Council' (2000) 69 *Nordic Journal of International Law* 87, 111.
66 Simon Chesterman, 'The UN Security Council and the rule of law' (n 1) i.
67 Declaration of the High-level Meeting of the General Assembly on the Rule of Law at the National and International Levels, UNGA Res 67/1 (2012) UN Doc A/RES/67/1 para 2.
68 ibid para 8.
69 ibid para 9.
70 ibid para 13.
71 ibid para 14.
72 ibid para 7.
73 ibid paras 28–29.
74 ibid para 30.
75 ibid para 31.
76 ibid para 41.
77 ibid para 23.
78 ibid para 32.
79 ibid para 24.
80 ibid paras 17–18.
81 ibid paras 24–26.
82 Konrad G Bühler, 'The Austrian rule of law initiative 2004–2008' (2008) 12 *Max Planck Yearbook of United Nations Law* 409, 410.
83 See UNGA Res 61/39 (18 December 2006) UN Doc A/RES/61/39; UNGA Res 62/70 (8 January 2008) UN Doc A/RES/62/70; UNGA Res 63/128 (15 January 2009) UN Doc A/RES/63/128; UNGA Res 64/116 (15 January 2010) A/RES/64/116; UNGA Res 65/32 (10 January 2011) UN Doc A/RES/65/32.
84 See UNSC Presidential Statement 15 (2003) UN Doc S/PRST/2003/15; UNSC Presidential Statement 2 (2004) UN Doc S/PRST/2004/2; Declaration of the High-level Meeting of the General Assembly on the Rule of Law at the National and International Levels, UNGA Res 67/1 (2012) UN Doc A/RES/67/1;

UNSC Presidential Statement 30 (2005) UN Doc S/PRST/2005/30; UNSC Presidential Statement 28 (2006) UN Doc S/PRST/2006/28; UNSC Presidential Statement 28 (2006) UN Doc S/PRST/2006/28; UNSC Presidential Statement 11 (2010) UN Doc S/PRST/2010/11.

85 UNSC Res 1325 (31 October 2000) UN Doc S/RES/1325; UNSC Res 1820 (19 June 2008) UN Doc S/RES/1820; UNSC Res 1888 (30 September 2009) UN Doc S/RES/1888.

86 UNSC Res 1612 (26 July 2005) UN Doc S/RES/1612; UNSC Res 1882 (4 August 2009) UN Doc S/RES/1882.

87 UNSC Res 1674 (28 April 2006) UN Doc S/RES/1674; UNSC Res 1894 (11 November 2009) UN Doc S/RES/1894.

88 UNSC Res 1373 (28 September 2001) UN Doc S/RES/1373; UNSC Res 1456 (20 January 2003) UN Doc S/RES/1456; UNSC Res 1566 (8 October 2004) UN Doc S/RES/1566; UNSC Res 1904 (17 December 2009) UN Doc S/RES/1904.

89 Jeremy Farrall, Hilary Charlesworth and Alan Ryan, 'Strengthening the rule of law through the United Nations Security Council: policy proposals' https://securitycouncilanalysisnetwork.files.wordpress.com/2016/03/arc-linkage_rol-policy-proposals.pdf (last accessed 11 November 2016).

90 See Chesterman, 'The UN Security Council and the rule of law' (n 1).

91 ibid i–iii.

92 ibid para 42.

93 ibid para 30.

94 ibid para 29.

95 Declaration of the High-level Meeting of the General Assembly on the Rule of Law at the National and International Levels, UNGA Res 67/1 (2012) UN Doc A/RES/67/1 para 39.

96 Report of the Secretary-General, 'Delivering justice: programme of action to strengthen the rule of law at the national and international levels: Report of the Secretary-General' (2012) UN Doc A/66/749.

97 ibid para 2.

98 ibid para 6.

99 Report of the Secretary-General, 'The rule of law and transitional justice in conflict and post-conflict societies' (2004) UN Doc S/2004/616 para 6.

100 Fitschen comments that Annan identifies no less than fifteen elements that are decisive for his understanding of the rule of law; see Thomas Fitschen, 'Inventing the rule of law for the United Nations' (2008) 12 *Max Planck Yearbook of United Nations Law* 347, 351.

101 Report of the High Commissioner for Human Rights, 'Human rights and transitional justice' (2006) UN Doc A/HRC/4/87 para 3; Scott Carlson, 'Legal and judicial rule of law work in multi-dimensional peacekeeping operations: lessons learned study' (2006) 22 https://www.un.org/ruleoflaw/files/Legal%20and%20judicial%20RoL%20work%20in%20multi%20dimensional%20pKping%20operations%20_Lessons%20Learned%20Study.pdf (last accessed 11 November 2016).

102 Fitschen might take a pessimistic view of the report, stating that the Secretary-General 'strictly avoids even to suggest that what he has termed a "concept" for internal use by the United Nations was meant to define the rule of law in a way that could apply also outside the Secretariat [i.e. other organs of the United Nations]'. See Fitschen (n 100) 347, 355.

103 'Promoting the Rule of Law and Strengthening the Criminal Justice System: Working Paper prepared by the Secretariat' Tenth United Nations Congress on the Prevention of Crime and the Treatment of Offenders (Vienna 10–17 April 2000) (14 December 1999) UN Doc A/CONF.187/3 para 5.

104 UNGA Res 60/1 (24 October 2005) UN Doc A/RES/60/1 para 134.
105 UNGA Res 2625 (XXV) (24 October 1970) UN Doc A/RES/25/2625, 121.
106 ibid preamble.
107 ibid.
108 ibid s 1.
109 ibid para 1.
110 ibid.
111 UNGA Res 55/2 (18 September 2000) UN Doc A/RES/55/2.
112 ibid para 9.
113 ibid II.
114 United Nations Conference on International Organization (UNCIO) Vol 13 (1945), 709–710; United Nations Conference on International Organization (UNCIO) Vol 13 (1945), 831.
115 Mohammed Bedjaoui, *The New World Order and The Security Council: Testing the Legality of Its Acts* (Nijhoff 1994) 12–13.
116 UN Charter arts 10, 11(1), 13(1), 14. In contrast, the binding nature of certain resolutions emerging from the Security Council are referred to in eg UN Charter (1945) arts 2(6), 25, 48(1).
117 See eg Declaration of the High-level Meeting of the General Assembly on the Rule of Law at the National and International Levels, UNGA Res 67/1 (2012) UN Doc A/RES/67/1.
118 For the ICJ definition of a customary norm see *Continental Shelf case (Libyan Arab Jamahiriya v Malta)* (Judgment) [1985] ICJ Rep 13 para 27. For a discussion of the impact of General Assembly resolutions on peremptory norms see eg Alexander Orakhelashvili, *Peremptory Norms in International Law* (Oxford University Press 2006) 117–119. See also Mark E Villiger, *Customary International Law and Treaties: A Manual on the Theory and Practices of the Interrelation of Sources* (Nijhoff 1997) 52.
119 Bin Cheng, 'UN resolutions on outer space: "instant" international customary law?' (1965) 5 *Indian Journal of International Law* 23. For a discussion of custom as both habit and convention see also James Bernard Murphy, 'Habit and convention at the foundation of custom' in Amanda Perreau-Sassine and James B Murphy, *The Nature of Customary Law: Legal, Historical and Philosophical Perspectives* (Cambridge University Press 2007) 53–78.
120 Statute of the International Court of Justice (1945) art 38.
121 Alexander Orakhelashvili, *Peremptory Norms in International Law* (Oxford University Press 2006) 113.
122 *Legality of the Threat or Use of Nuclear Weapons* (Advisory Opinion) [1996] ICJ Rep 226 para 70.
123 *Military and Paramilitary Activities in and against Nicaragua (Nicaragua v United States)* (Merits, Judgment) [1986] ICJ Rep 14 para 188.
124 ibid para 191; see also ibid para 188.
125 UNGA Verbatim records (24 October 1970) UN Doc A/PV.1883 para 7 for the adoption of resolution 2625(XXV). In contrast, although in *Legality of the Threat or Use of Nuclear Weapons* (Advisory Opinion) [1996] ICJ Rep 226 para 70 the ICJ found no 'conventional rule of general scope, nor a customary rule specifically proscribing the threat or use of nuclear weapons *per se*', this was due to 'tensions between the nascent *opinio juris* on the one hand, and the still strong adherence to the practice of deterrence on the other' (ibid para 73) – essentially, the fact that 'resolutions under consideration in the present case [had] been adopted with substantial numbers of negative votes and abstentions' (ibid para 71) undermined any assertions of *opinio juris.*
126 UNGA Verbatim records (24 September 2012) UN Doc A/67/PV. It has been recognised that 'the statements in the preparatory and plenary phases, the absence

of "reservations" by States, and the voting records (namely unanimous patterns) may constitute first instances of State practice, which contribute towards a new customary rule by stating its substance and effects, and by revealing the *opinio juris* of member States'. See Mark E Villiger, *Customary International Law and Treaties: A Manual on the Theory and Practices of the Interrelation of Sources* (Nijhoff 1997). See also *Western Sahara* (Advisory Opinion) [1975] ICJ Rep 12 para 32; *Barcelona Traction, Light and Power Company, Limited* (Judgment) [1970] ICJ Rep 3 para 320; *South West Africa, Second Phase* (Judgment) (Judge Tanaka Dissenting Opinion) [1966] ICJ Rep 6 para 291.

127 29 heads of state, with a further 35 nations represented by other high-level officials.

128 Addressing the meeting were the High Commissioner for Human Rights, the UNDP Administrator, UNODC Executive Director, President of the Security Council as well as representatives of the UN Commission on International Trade Law, International Development Law Organisation, International Crisis Group and the International Institute of Higher Studies in Criminal Science.

129 Maldives, UNGA Verbatim records (24 September 2012) UN Doc A/67/PV.3, 18; Mongolia, UNGA Verbatim records (24 September 2012) UN Doc A/67/PV.3, 21; Gabon, UNGA Verbatim records (24 September 2012) UN Doc A/67/PV.3, 21; Kenya, UNGA Verbatim records (24 September 2012) UN Doc A/67/PV.3, 26; Bangladesh, UNGA Verbatim records (24 September 2012) UN Doc A/67/PV.3, 33.

130 See eg the comments of the EU, ibid 32; Austria, ibid 13; Bulgaria, ibid 17; Albania, ibid 23.

131 President Jacob Zuma of South Africa, ibid 29.

132 President Mahmoud Ahmadinejad of Iran, ibid 14.

133 Venezuela, ibid 40. See also, Cuba, ibid 41; and Bolivia, ibid 42–43.

134 Ban Ki-Moon, ibid 3.

135 Peter Tomka, ibid.

136 Jose Manuel Barroso, ibid 32.

137 UN Press release, 'World leaders adopt declaration reaffirming rule of law as foundation for building equitable state relations, just societies' (24 September 2012).

138 UN Charter (1945) art 13(1).

139 UNSC Presidential Statement 11 (2010) UN Doc S/PRST/2010/11. See also President of the Security Council, UNGA Verbatim records (24 September 2012) UN Doc A/67/PV.3, 5.

140 ibid.

141 ibid 6.

142 Joined Cases C-402/05P and C-415/05P, *Yassin Abdullah Kadi and Al Barakaat International Foundation. v Council of the European Union and Commission* [2008] ECR I-06351.

3 The components of a bespoke Security Council rule of law

Introduction

Chapters 1 and 2 of this book identified its scope and focused on the background to the establishment of a rule of law framework for the Council – the what, the why and the how of a Council-specific rule of law. This chapter delves into further detail on the parameters of each component, highlighting what the specificities of the eight components of the framework that can be used both to measure previous and reshape future decision-making in the Council.

Certain components of the rule of law are addressed together, owing to the fact that they may not perhaps examine various independent elements of the vast field of international law, but rather different facets of Security Council action. These groups, which will be examined in greater detail below, are as follows: clarity of action (incorporating procedural transparency and public promulgation); legal certainty; equality before the law; the predictability paradox (incorporating the avoidance of arbitrariness, supremacy of the law and fairness in the application of the law); consistency with international human rights and humanitarian norms; the separation of powers; the equitable participation in the decision-making process; and accountability before the law. It is also essential to note that there is a degree of overlap between some of the components; this emerges as a result of different facets to Council actions, or similar means to decipher whether and to what extent the Council is abiding by the rule of law.

Clarity of action

Although these two components are separate concepts under the rule of law at the domestic level, their similarity in practice when discussing a Council rule of law lend them to an amalgamation. They are, essentially, two facets of the same theme of clarity in Security Council action and I have elected to address them first for the simple reason that they are the information channels through which all other elements are measured; together they form the administrative component of the rule of law. The primary sources that emerge from the Security Council are only as beneficial as they are detailed and widely available. Irrespective of how adherent the Council may be in its work to the rule of law, without procedural transparency and the public dissemination of material, it would be impossible to discern the facts or circumstances around its decisions.

Procedural and substantive transparency is therefore vital to the work of the Council, meaning that the way in which a decision of the Council was taken and the reasons for this outcome must be comprehensible. The language should be accessible and understandable, the goals should be clear and the decisions taken should be unambiguous; this last aspect on decisions is doubly important for states when duties are imposed upon them. Resolutions displaying a high level of procedural transparency would include full verbatim minutes and a full outline of voting, allowing those states to access the information to see clearly whether decisions have been taken in accordance with the correct procedure and what factors, if any, played a role in the final decisions.

Verbatim records allow the reader to gain full details on the political stance of each voting state and gives the most accurate picture of the sequence of events leading from the introduction of a proposed resolution and the conclusion of the meeting. Verbatim records are also vital for pursuing a specific situation or debate through various resolution proposals, some of which may have failed to be adopted. Verbatim records should therefore also be available for meetings where resolutions were not adopted, as well as for meetings where they were.

Running parallel to this is public promulgation, which in the case of the Security Council requires the full dissemination of each resolution and the debates around its adoption. Although debates and discussions are frequent between states on either bi-lateral or multi-lateral diplomatic levels, the finalised text should contain elements such as when the resolution shall come into force, the temporal limits of the resolution and should be publicly and readily available prior to its adoption. Resolutions that are effectively publicly promulgated 'should be legible and accessible in the formal sense of having been . . . brought forth in public debate, having made their appearance in and become part of the public realm and having attracted the public's involvement and attention'.[1] In the case of the Security Council, the immediate concern is for that of member states of the UN, although these resolutions and peripheral material such as voting records should also be accessible to the general public directly.

Clarity of action is integral to the work of the Security Council for several reasons, most notably as a means of establishing the actual meaning of a resolution, for 'there cannot be a Rule of Law without rules of law . . . Values like legal certainty and legal security can be realized only to the extent that a state is governed according to pre-announced rules that are clear and intelligible themselves'.[2] Clarity of action is therefore central to the process of resolutions themselves; it would render futile even the most pioneering resolution on reinstating peace or eliminating a threat if the member states that are bound to abide by it did not agree on the meaning of the content, or were not in swift receipt of it. To fail to comprehend the path taken by the Council as well as the reasons behind a resolution's passing or the use of a veto would reduce all but the serving Council members at the time obsolete and would subvert the Charter's stipulation that the Council 'acts on their behalf'.[3]

Of the 195 UN state members, only 15 are allocated seats in the Council chamber and therefore, for the vast majority of states wide-ranging, swift dissemination of high calibre, transparent and complete information is one of the key means of maintaining credibility of Council decisions among UN member states.

However, a transparent legal text does not ensure that it will be enforced consistently, nor that it is constitutionally sound, nor indeed that the law itself is impartial. In a domestic example of a government that abides by the rule of law, citizens are assured of the knowledge that should a government pass an unconstitutional law or engage in pernicious behaviour, citizens have the option to refer to a legal system or, more simply, vote in a new government at the following elections; there is no such assurance with the Council; the P5 members sit in perpetuity at the table. As the organ responsible for electing the Secretary-General, it is also important that this is conducted transparently and fairly.

Legal certainty

This element of the rule of law asks whether Chapter VII resolutions, which contain legally binding elements are accessible, clear and predictable. This component explores whether states can reasonably be expected to comprehend the regulations and stipulations of the resolutions, or whether there are elements of the resolutions that are vague, convoluted or open to interpretation.

Legal certainty would require that the results of non-compliance by states to a resolution be predictable in order to allow UN member states to regulate their conduct in accordance with the legally binding obligations of a resolution.[4] A lack of legal certainty risks not only eliciting confusion about the correct avenues of compliance but also paves the way for the legitimate refusal of a member state to comply, with the defence that the legal text did not stipulate sufficiently the provisions and parameters of its scope. In the absence of a judicial review mechanism or constitutional court to clarify meaning, it is even more imperative that the Council be clear in its documents. Sanctions, for example, are ideal candidates for legal certainty. It is not difficult to imagine a situation where vague or ambiguous terminology might result in certain states inadvertently, or perhaps knowingly, acting in contravention of a resolution where sanctions have been imposed, or where the Council has passed the imposition of a no-fly zone, arms embargo or repercussions.

Legal certainty also assists in predicting future violations of resolutions. In an equation where the Council acts to maintain the international peace, legal certainty of resolutions should enable states reasonably to predict other actions that might result in similar resolutions. For example, resolutions based on human rights violations or the failure of a state to adhere to an international principle should contain structured and detailed examples of the exact threats to the international peace, in order to allow states to predict under what circumstances their behaviour might fall foul of the Council. Similarly, where similar violations have been committed by states, one would expect to find that the Council has responded in the same manner, to the same extent and with the same degree of proportionality.

This component will therefore look for a clear legal basis in all Chapter VII resolutions. In the first instance, resolutions that are taken under Chapter VII should explicitly state that the Council is acting under these Charter powers and should enumerate whether this is under article 41, article 42 or any other relevant provisions. All resolutions relating to maintenance of peace and security must explicitly state this in the text and must delineate the boundaries of both Council action and the action of entities, states or organs that it tasks with any related action, for example, in cases of military intervention; the legal justification for this action must also be apparent and clearly explained. The existence of this in a resolution would be a clear indication that the Council views legal certainty as being imperative to its role; conversely, failure to stipulate this could suggest a desire for ambiguity.

The second legal basis that I will seek is the identification of the exact threat to the peace that the Council is aiming to eliminate by taking such Chapter VII action. Moreover, it is essential that the Council stipulate specifically what the nexus between the threat and its proposed action is; that is to say, the Council has an obligation to explain how the actions outlined in the Council resolution will assist in the restoration of international peace and security.

Contrastingly, the absence of legal bases might primarily suggest that the Council does not value the importance of legal certainty and, by virtue of this element, the rule of law; secondly, it could suggest that the Council cherishes its prerogative to ambiguity, in which case this component will establish where the Council provides a legal basis and where it neglects to do so, attempting also to discover why; finally, the lack of legal certainty could suggest an abuse of power on the part of the Council that is thinly veiled behind its uncertainty of legality, which is indicated by its failure to justify its actions clearly within the boundaries of law.

Equality before the law

On a domestic level, equality before the law ensures that all individuals are subject to the same laws and the same rights, avoiding a hierarchical structure. At the Council level, where legally-binding resolutions are being discussed, the question has two core elements. The first is ensuring the equitable application of the resolution to all states and avoiding targeting resolutions that would inherently impede or adversely affect either individual or a selection of states; put simply, resolutions should not arbitrarily target a particular faith, nationality, ethnicity or other characteristic – this is most easily compared to non-discrimination laws at the domestic level and is, perhaps, the simpler of the two to maintain in an increasingly globalised, open world where cosmopolitan lifestyles, open borders and multi-nationalism is increasingly becoming the norm for a larger proportion of the global population, in contrast to the more closed world in which the UN was created.

The second element is that all states should be subject to the same standards, whether these are human rights norms, financial sanctions or any other stipulations of a resolution. Essentially, there should not be one rule for the powerful, and another for the weak. The Charter explicitly states that 'the Security Council acts on [UN Member States'] behalf'[5] and Bingham writes that: 'although the citizens of a democracy empower their representative institutions to make laws which, duly made, bind all to whom they apply . . . nothing ordinarily authorizes the executive to act otherwise than in strict accordance with those laws'.[6] Within the Council context it is vital, then, that the states passing the resolution are seen to adhere to its contents, meaning and purposes. Resolutions that display a high level of adherence to equality before the law will contain provisions that are applied to all members of the Security Council as well as the intended subjects of a resolution.

Resolutions will also adhere to the component of equality before the law when there is a similar reaction by the Council to similar threats or situations; it seems self-evident that where an armed conflict has broken out the Council must act to quash the threat to the peace. Although the sources of the conflict are often different and require different approaches, the Council has a responsibility to end bloodshed, violence and conflict as soon as possible. As a result, Council members are obliged to provide reasoned arguments for their actions or inaction – where clear evidence of the necessity for Council intervention is apparent through the statements, declarations and resolutions of other UN organs, agencies and representatives and the Council fails to act, the risk of inequality before the law is high.

This component will also argue that resolutions should impose the same standards upon all states, as opposed to different standards for different states. Equality before the law requires that resolutions contain provisions that are equally applied to all members. At its core, this component is fundamentally speculative, although certain evidence of bias can be found in statements made on the domestic level – for example, the declaration of a P5 member's unwavering support for another state.[7] Nonetheless, the most that this component can hope to prove is that certain decisions of the Council *appear* to contravene the principle of equality before the law.

The predictability paradox

The predictability paradox is the amalgamation of non-arbitrary action, the supremacy of the law in decision-making processes and fairness in the application of the law. It is highly successful when states are able to forecast the Council's decisions based upon existing clearly elucidated decisions (as highlighted in the component on clarity of action), the legal basis for comparable situations (as in legal certainty), the knowledge that the Council's actions will not be arbitrary and that legally sound decisions will be fairly applied. The difficulty lies, however, in analysing where the Council has reacted either similarly or differently to a similar threat and has done so unfairly or arbitrarily.

The Council, as a political body that was established to adapt to shifting definitions of a threat, must necessarily change its approach accordingly when faced with each threat; therefore, it is insufficient to claim that where it has reacted differently to an analogous threat, it has failed in the principle of fairness or avoidance of arbitrariness. Conversely, where there has been a marked shift in approach or where states are not held accountable to the same principles or standards, without compelling and thorough explanation of the reasons for the Council shift in approach, it will be clear that there has been arbitrary behaviour and a lack of fairness and equality in the application of its powers.

The Council is, by definition, a political body and to impose upon it the stiff restrictions of an unwavering set of standards would both defeat the purpose of its existence by crippling its diplomatic and political capabilities and run contrary to the intentions of the drafters at San Francisco to allow it a wide berth in which to operate. Indeed, as Bingham notes:

> . . . even judges should enjoy a measure of discretion when passing sentence on convicted criminals, since if they are obliged to impose a prescribed penalty for a given offence they are unable to take account of the difference between on offence and another and between one offender and another . . . The rule of law does not require that official or judicial decision-makers should be deprived of all discretion, but it does require that no discretion should be unconstrained so as to be potentially arbitrary. *No discretions may be legally unfettered.*[8]

Concern arises when 'the behaviour of states, on which the rule of law ultimately depends, often is arbitrary and self-interested, in a way that is the antithesis of rule of law norms'.[9] The Council is charged with the primary maintenance of international peace and is tasked with 'discharging these duties . . . in accordance with the Purposes and Principles of the United Nations',[10] which include 'international co-operation in solving international problems . . . [and] harmonizing the actions of nations in the attainment of these common ends'.[11]

This component therefore argues that Council members, when acting on official Council business, should pay primary attention to the maintenance of the peace above their own national interests; that is to say, the maintenance of international peace should be valued at all costs, even perhaps controversially at the expense of domestic welfare. While it may seem to be politically naive to suggest this hierarchy, and it would not be surprising to find that such a system did not exist, the scope of this book confines its approach to the letter of the UN Charter, which states that the Council shall exercise its duties within the parameters of the purposes and principles of the UN[12] – far from advocating unilateral decisions and self-serving actions, article 1(1) of the Charter refers to 'collective measures'.

To use a domestic analogy, representatives of the subjects of the law – members of parliament – are the source of outrage when it is revealed that laws and decisions are taken to benefit their own personal, affiliated or company interests and in some cases are fatal to their political careers; fairness and supremacy of law for the Council should elicit the same standards of integrity, particularly given the high stakes of international peace and the repercussions that Council decisions have not only on individuals but on entire populations.

The first element of non-arbitrary behaviour of the Council is a clear legal basis for its action or decision – this is an example of the overlap between Security Council rule of law components. In the case of resolutions, they should contain the component of legal certainty and in the case of decisions that do not result in the passing of a resolution, sound judgement must be displayed with a reasoned argument for the decision that is clearly outlined in the statements or speeches made. Secondly, a clear pattern of action should be evident; for example, when dealing with the same situation, previous decisions and resolutions should be taken into consideration to ensure that a clear trajectory is charted, rather than an ad hoc response that differs in proportionality, direction and substance. Thirdly, resolutions should take account of comparable situations, where Council action should not differ vastly. In essence, this means that where similar situations have a clear causal link it should be evident why the same action was taken or why a different course was pursued.

Consistency with international human rights norms and standards

Recent decades have heralded a wave of concern from international bodies with respect to the human rights implications of actions and decisions; indeed, they have even been at the core of decisions to create international criminal tribunals and at the root of relatively new phenomena such as the erosion of state sovereignty[13] and the new hierarchy that places human rights above state immunities. The potential impact of project outcomes on the human rights situation are carefully assessed by the UN, certainly more expansively than initially envisioned in the UN Charter.[14]

Human rights elements can be found as considerations in resolutions that primarily deal with other issues; for example, UNSC Resolution 1373 on the freezing of terrorist assets might not initially be seen to concern human rights, but it was based on 'the rights of the defence, in particular the right to be heard, and the right to effective judicial review of those rights'[15] as well as the 'unjustified restriction of his right to property'[16] that the European Court of Justice overturned the Council of the EU's implementation of the resolution. It would appear, then, that the Council at times does not fully contemplate the human rights effect of its resolutions and this sub-section intends to discover the extent of this phenomenon.

Human rights can be relevant to the Security Council in two ways: as a competence and as a limitation. Whereas the competence element acts as a catalyst for Council action, this component also explores whether Council action is bound by some limitations imposed on it by human rights law. However, the debate reaches further than this to one of the Council's adherence to *jus cogens* and international customary norms relating to human rights. This component asks whether the Council is bound by these norms or the Council can act outside of international human rights law, asking whether the Council has acted consistently with *jus cogens* and customary norms and if so, how it balances these with the maintenance of international peace and security. Resolutions and decisions that include smart sanctions and the establishment of review committees might suggest that the Council considers it bound by them, whereas the absence of their mention in resolutions could suggest that the Council sees its role as maintainer of peace and security to incorporate an exemption.

Potential violations can be seen not only as the effects of a resolution to be considered during deliberations on the drafting and passing of a resolution, but also as the reason for the creation of a resolution itself. Although human rights often lie at the root of a decision to act, there is the argument that human rights violations are not always effectively handled in a timely fashion, or even that certain states block the passing of resolutions that centre around human rights issues for reasons that run contrary to the philanthropic goals upon which the UN is built. The question is, then, whether every decision of the Security Council to act, or not to act, accommodates its responsibility to ensure the protection of human rights or whether there is a selective approach to the response to human rights depending on other factors. If the latter is true, these factors will be addressed.

The separation of powers and acting ultra vires

Linked to the accountability issue, at first glance this particular element of the rule of law might not stand out as applicable to the Security Council, given the independent core organs that the UN system is formed of and the horizontal nature of the international sphere in comparison to the domestic system. However, it is in fact a pertinent topic for discussion when addressing the Council; this component takes the view that it is vitally important that the Security Council ensure that it does not act ultra vires in the course of its action and discusses the limits to Chapter VII resolutions and the expansion of its powers to include legislative authority in pursuing apparent breaches of or threats to the peace.

In the wake of international terrorist attacks in the early 21st century, the Council took the unprecedented step of imposing legally binding, general and non-temporally limited obligations upon states through Chapter VII resolutions;[17] this precedent was recently bolstered by another general resolution combatting terrorism in 2014.[18] In 2005, by imposing binding obligations on all states to adopt legislation to prevent the proliferation of nuclear, chemical and biological weapons,[19] the Council's powers were again called into question, as it was alleged to have installed itself as a form of global governor in contravention to principles of state sovereignty. The separation of powers component intends to identify any situations where the Council appears to have overstepped the boundaries defined for it in the UN Charter, either by trespassing on the territory of another UN organ or extending its reach to impose legally binding obligations upon states that were not in accordance with its powers in the Charter, both of which should be examined within the constraints of the parameters set out for the Council in the UN Charter.

The equitable participation in decision-making processes

This component mirrors that of to the above point on equality before the law; whereas equality before the law relates to the subjects of a law – in the context of the Council, these are member states that are bound to abide by the stipulations of a given Chapter VII resolution – and is therefore *externally-facing*, the equitable participation in decision-making is introspective. It relates to the background of such resolutions and the history of a given resolution from tabling to passing, or failure, incorporating consultations with member states and the inclusion or at least consideration of the diverse opinions that are often expressed in the Security Council chamber during resolution discussions.

Perhaps the most obvious of issues that spring to mind when discussing the equitable participation of states in the decision-making process of the Security Council is the existence of the veto power available to the P5 members. This book does not tackle the thorny subject of altering the *status quo* of P5 veto power, but rather attempts to define how an equitable participation in the decision-making process can exist alongside it. The existence of a select group of members that have the power unilaterally to block the passing of a resolution may appear to be a lopsided system that undermines the very fabric of equitable participation, but it is a structure that has not changed since the conception of the Council and, despite repeated reform efforts, looks to remain cemented thus for the foreseeable future.

The equitable participation in the decision-making process demands that representatives of the UN member states be consulted on all decisions of the Council. In order to discern whether this component has been satisfied, I will first examine the Charter for the principles relating to voting and composition of the Council, as well as the Rules of Procedure of the Council. Does the Charter contain specific provisions that oblige the Council to offer equitable participation? If so, it would suggest that, with the exception of the veto, an equitable process for Council decision-making was envisioned for the Council under the Charter. However, if not it would suggest that an inherent bias was created from the outset, although this does not negate the need for it entirely as a component of the rule of law for the Council.

I will then address the procedure of the Council in its decision-making and try to establish whether a practice of closed-door meeting and agreement between states, in the same vein as took place prior to the establishment of the UN at Yalta and Dumbarton Oaks, still exists or whether decisions, debates and full and frank disclosure have been incorporated in the Council's decision-making process. Even in instances where the veto has been used, it is vital that the P5 member making use of this privilege be forthcoming in its explanation of the reasons why it feels the course of action it disagrees with cannot benefit the restoration and maintenance of the international peace. In order to discern these points, it is not the text of the resolutions that will be most important but rather the comments of states – the verbatim records – that will grant proof of compliance. For example, evidentially-based accusations by member states of collusion or agreement of some states prior to official Council meetings would run contrary to this component of the rule of law.

Accountability before the law

Accountability is akin to a thread that runs through all elements of Council decision. If clarity of action and transparency are the starting points of the rule of law for the Council, accountability is the end; it is the means of measuring and reviewing how effectively the Council has adhered to the principles of the rule of law and gives a forum for amendments to Council practice. Accountability of the Council is not something that is likely to be found entrenched in the resolutions of the Council, since the notion of its accountability is clearly not a matter that the Council considers a requirement.

Identifying that '[a]n important element of the rule of law is the ability to have one's grievances heard before an impartial judge',[20] accountability requires a mechanism in place to which states may turn should they suspect that the Council has taken an illegitimate or *ultra vires* decision; accountability also requires the existence of an independent monitor of the Council's compliance with the rule of law. Article 24(3) of the UN Charter stipulates that the Council is to 'submit annual and, when necessary, special reports to the General Assembly for its consideration'. However, these reports are insufficient for the purposes of accountability, since they do not fulfil the requirements of judicial review and fit more within the context of procedural transparency and public promulgation.

The structure of the Council and its position as an organ of the United Nations dictates that any accountability mechanisms be horizontal; discussions on the benefits and disadvantages, as well as the feasibility and practicality of review by a fellow UN organ such as the ICJ have been conducted by delegate states at the formational meetings of the United Nations itself in addition to more recently by scholars. This component will build on these proposals by discussing the powers of UN organs to monitor and review the decision-making process of the Council itself.

Chapter conclusions

These components of the rule of law have been tailored to fit the Council and reflect the behaviour expected of it in order to abide by rule of law principles. I have grouped certain components together owing to similarities in both substance and methodology, as well for ease of examination since certain elements are inherently linked or overlap. In concluding Part I, I have partly answered one of my two major research questions, namely, what the rule of law is at the Security Council level. I have also succeeded in answering the three sub-questions that

I aimed to address at the start of this chapter: what the rule of law is in the domestic and international spheres; how a rule of law for the Council differs from this; and why the Council should be subject to the rule of law at all. Part II will continue to expand on the points that I have highlighted here and analyse in more depth how the Council has or has not complied with the provisions of each element; its chapters will now examine the components that I have identified here in further detail.

Notes

1 Thomas Eijsbouts, 'Introduction' in Thomas A Vandamme and Jan-Herman Reestman (eds), *Ambiguity in the Rule of Law: The Interface between National and International Legal Systems* (Europa Law 2001).
2 Neil MacCormick, *Rhetoric and the Rule of Law: A Theory of Legal Reasoning* (Oxford University Press 2009) 12.
3 UN Charter (1945) art 24(1).
4 See eg *Sunday Times v United Kingdom* (1979) 2 EHRR 245, 271 para 49.
5 UN Charter (n 3) art 24(1).
6 Thomas Bingham, *The Rule of Law* (Penguin 2011) 60.
7 It can also be found in the internal criticism found in verbatim records of meetings, such as the vitriolic assault on China and Russia by several members, including the P5 members of France, UK and USA, over the use of the veto in UNSC Draft Res S/2012/77 (2012); see China, UNSC Verbatim Record (21 February 2012) UN Doc S/PV/6717 at 5–6; Russia, UNSC Verbatim Record (21 February 2012) UN Doc S/PV/6717 at 5–6.
8 Thomas Bingham, *The Rule of Law* (n 6) 53–54 (emphasis added).
9 Cheryl Saunders and Katherine Le Roy, 'Perspectives on the rule of law' in Cheryl Saunders and Katherine Le Roy, *The Rule of Law* (Federation Press 2003) 15; see also Ian Brownlie, *The Rule of Law in International Affairs: International Law at the Fiftieth Anniversary of the United Nations* (Nijhoff 1998); and Martin Loughlin, *Sword and Scales* (Hart Publishing 2000).
10 UN Charter (n 3) art 24.
11 ibid art 1(3)–(4).
12 ibid art 24(2).
13 For example, the responsibility to protect (R2P).
14 Human rights are only mentioned as being directly within the remit of the General Assembly (UN Charter (n 3) art 13(b)); ECOSOC (UN Charter (n 3) art 62(2), 68); and the Trusteeship Council (UN Charter (1945) art 76(c)).
15 Joined Cases C-402/05 P and C-415/05 P, *Yassin Abdullah Kadi and Al Barakaat International Foundation v Council of the European Union and Commission* [2008] ECR I-06351 para 334.
16 ibid para 370.
17 UNSC Res 1373 (28 September 2001) UN Doc S/RES/1373.
18 UNSC Res 2178 (24 September 2014) UN Doc S/RES/2178.
19 UNSC Res 1540 (28 April 2004) UN Doc S/RES/1540.
20 Jennifer A Widner, *Building the Rule of Law* (Norton 2001).

Part II

Exploring the components of the rule of law

4 Clarity of action

Introduction

This element of the rule of law examines the extent to which the Council's decision-making process is clear, transparent and publicly available to other Council member states, non-Council member states and the general public. The dissemination of information around the path taken to reach any given decision by the Council is integral to public awareness of Council action and reflects a transparent procedural process. The absence of clear information is the hallmark of secretive decision-making and opens the door to arbitrary action; it is vital that all states are able to understand the options considered by the Council and the reasoning behind the decision that emerged from their meeting and discussions. Similarly, if such information exists but is not released to the public, this might suggest a hierarchy in the United Nations (UN), wherein some states are permitted to be privy to discussions and knowledge and others are not.

The same principle applies to the citizens of each member state, to whom the governments and authorities on a domestic level, represented at the UN by delegates and ambassadors, are ultimately answerable. Therefore, one could advance the theory that any lack of public promulgation of detailed documents and information at the Council level impacts upon the rule of law at a domestic level in each member state and that this element of the rule of law for the Council has a global domestic knock-on effect.[1]

Clarity of action in relation to the remainder of the components of the rule of law can be viewed as what the Vienna Convention on the Laws of Treaties is to international law – a secondary source of interpretation. Transparency of itself provides little independent use, but is valuable when examined in tandem with another component of the rule of law. In this sense, too, it is integral to accountability,[2] as 'it enables critique and control by the public of the actor one is seeking to hold accountable'.[3] Accordingly, it is also the gateway to interpretation; without transparency, it is unlikely that any component of the rule of law can be examined fully, as the information accessible would be unreliable, incomplete or erroneous. The presence in Council discussions of non-member states and non-state actors is part of the issue of procedural transparency and closely linked also to the rule of law at the domestic level.[4] The inability, should it exist, of a relevant non-state actor or member state to participate in proceedings would surely be a substantial failing of the component of both clarity of action and equitable participation.

I have identified two major elements to this component of the rule of law: the first is textual analysis and the dissemination of information. This requires examining what rules are in place for the dissemination of official Council documents and whether the Council complies with these obligations. The second is the access to information and the degree to which actions of the Council are conducted in secret unnecessarily or arbitrarily; key examples of these are Council meetings and election of the Secretary-General.

Council obligations for procedural transparency

Under the UN Charter, the Council is obligated to present to the Assembly 'annual and special reports . . . includ[ing] an account of the measures that the Security Council has decided upon or taken to maintain international peace and security'.[5] Moreover, as part of the Secretary-General's responsibility to 'make an annual report to the General Assembly on the work of the Organization',[6] an inference exists that communication between the Council and Secretariat will be forthright, transparent and timely in order to facilitate the preparation of the report. The Security Council's Rules of Procedure are also clear on the requirement that verbatim records, 'records of meetings . . . [a]ll resolutions and other documents shall be published in the languages of the Security Council'[7] are to be made simultaneously available in all five official, working languages of the UN: English, French, Arabic, Spanish and Standard Chinese.[8]

The Council's Rules of Procedure also take into consideration the necessity of rapid and accurate documentation of meeting minutes, imposing a standard that 'the verbatim record of each meeting of the Security Council shall be made available to the representatives on the Security Council and to the representatives of any other states which have participated in the meeting not later than 10 a.m. of the first working day following the meeting'.[9] There is a similar deadline on the dissemination of the public record to states and parties that did not participate in the meeting. Indeed, even for members of the public and academics such as this author, the ease of access to the repertoire, rules of procedure, working methods, annual reports, letter exchanges, official statements, meeting records, voting records, a full history of resolutions and a variety of other recent Council-related documents are easily accessible online in various languages.[10]

However, there are several formats of meetings that can take place at the Council level and this is where compliance by the Council to the component of clarity of action begins to deteriorate. Meetings of the Security Council can be held in public, including open debate,[11] debates,[12] briefings[13] or adoption[14] meetings – or private – including both closed public private meetings[15] and Troop Contributing Country (TCC)[16] meetings. Although official records of public meetings are minuted and made available to the public, official records of private, or closed, meetings are made in single copy and kept by the Secretary-General, with access to this copy only being granted to the select few Council member states that participated in the meetings.

Perhaps more worryingly, meetings of the Members of the Security Council can take place in 'informal consultations of the whole' to which non-Council members are not invited and no official record is made; indeed, the French delegation expressed concern as early as 1994 at the fact that 'nearly all the work of the Council takes place in the form of informal consultations to which States not members of the Council do not have access'.[17] Moreover, speaking on behalf of the 115 Non-Aligned Movement States in 2006, the representative from Cuba addressed the Council with a damning list of examples of Council behaviour undermining transparency, openness and consistency, including:

> . . . unscheduled open debates with selective notification, reluctance in convening open debates on some issues of high significance, frequent restrictions on the participation in some of the debates and discrimination between members and non-members of the Council, particularly with regard to sequencing and time limits of statements during the open debates, failure to submit special reports to the General Assembly, as required under Article 24 of the Charter, the submission of annual reports still lacking sufficient information and analytical content, and lack of minimal parameters for the drawing up of the monthly assessment by the Security Council presidencies.[18]

There is, therefore, a problem that arises with the actual information both made available through attendance at Council meetings and contained within the documentation disseminated.

Private (informal) meetings

Although implicitly permitted by the Council's own Rules of Procedure,[19] private meetings run contrary to a transparent Council; whereas *public* meetings are a matter of *public* record and the verbatim records and other documents are easily accessible by not only UN member states but also the wider public in many guises and media, *private* meetings are almost wholly segregated from the public eye. While it might seem reasonable for the Security Council – which deals with matters of international security and potentially sensitive and classified information – to conceal sensitive information, private meetings are of concern for two primary reasons: first, there appears to be no standardised threshold that needs to be met in order to trigger a private meeting; and, secondly, private meetings have steadily increased in usage by states in place of the public forum. What this means, in reality, is that a Council member may decide, for whatever reason, that it wishes to meet with another Council member to discuss a matter in private, with no obligation to divulge the details of the topics discussed. Nonetheless, they are frequently made use of, can be attended by any number of invited members and carry with them no stipulation for compulsory records analogous to public meetings. Although this is inherent to the nature of politics – and the Council is, after all, a political body – the risk then comes with the repeated use of behind the scenes discussions that leave other member states and the wider international community at a loss as to what has been discussed:

> Like a parliamentary matryoshka (doll), [the Council] now contains ever-smaller 'mini-Councils', each meeting behind closed doors without keeping records, and each taking decisions secretly. Before the plenary Council meets 'in consultation' . . . the P-5 have met in 'consultation' . . . and before they meet, the P-3, composed of the United States, the United Kingdom and France, have met in 'consultation' in one of their missions in New York . . . After the fifteen members of the Council have consulted and reached their decisions, they adjourn to the Council's chamber, where they go through the formal motions of voting and announcing their decision. Decisions that appear to go further than at any time in the history of the United Nations are now ultimately being taken, it seems, by a small group of states separately meeting in secret.[20]

This observation, made in 1993, appears only to have gained momentum as the years have passed, expanding to include other discussion topics besides those initially criticised. Despite increased recourse to Council action in the 1990s, the use of closed meetings has grown rapidly since 1999, prior to which closed meetings were used for specifically mandated reasons such as the reappointment of the Secretary-General in 1996:[21] 1999 saw only four closed meetings[22] leaping drastically to nineteen in 2000.[23] Since 2000, there have been over 400 closed meetings and at one point over 20 per cent of Council meetings were conducted in private.[24] The fact that the use of private meetings has increased so markedly since their introduction flies in the face of the Council's 2010 reaffirmation of 'its commitment to increase recourse to open meetings, particularly at the early stage in its consideration of a matter'.[25] The reliance on closed meetings, to which members of the public have no access, raises grave concerns of transparency and has long led to calls for reform by non-Council member states.[26] The representative of Kazakhstan summed up this sentiment, when he stated that:

> [w]e non-member States of the Security Council have the right to know first-hand what are the possible decisions being discussed within the Council and what are the positions of each Council member on current issues, and should not have to find this out through the prism of the mass media. Complete knowledge of the nature of internal developments in the Council, which are important for the entire international community, are of critical importance for our Governments, which depend upon objective information in adopting decisions. As concerned members of the international community, we believe that we have the right to be informed.[27]

One of the principal concerns with this format, aside from the selective nature of participation in the meetings themselves,[28] is that the Council 'may decide that for a private meeting the record shall be made in a single copy alone . . . [to be] kept by the Secretary-General'.[29] Corrections to this record are permitted only through the Secretary-General, by states that have attended these private meetings and within a time frame of 10 days;[30] access to this sole copy is limited to 'representatives of the Members of the United Nations which have taken part in a private meeting . . . or authorized representatives of other Members of the United Nations'[31] and the release of meeting records are subject to the Council's discretion. Indeed, 'in the case of informal consultations, there have also been instances in which the most directly concerned parties were denied participation in open meetings'.[32]

It can be argued that such private meetings appear not to be entirely segregated from the public eye; at 'the close of each private meeting the Security Council shall issue a communiqué through the Secretary-General'[33] and in the instances where they have taken place, communiqués have indeed been submitted.[34] However, they are heavily redacted or brief to the point of undermining the worth of their issuance in the first place. Indeed, the extent that is known about these meetings is the intended topic of discussion, the parties privy to the meeting and, usually, that there has been 'an exchange of views'.[35] There is no means of determining the nature of the discussion, arguments, counter-arguments or, indeed, any elements of the discussion or exchange; by all measures, these private meetings are selective, exclusive and divisive, as they encourage the formation and consolidation of pro and con camps for resolutions with respect to voting.

Recent practice appears to have moved away from such closed meetings: in 2014, most of the closed-door meetings were conducted with TCCs and in both 2015 and 2016 the only closed-door meetings related to such TCC meetings. Nonetheless, closed meetings pose a problem primarily for non-Council members, owing to the lack of transparency that is inevitably associated with them. For example, 'States that are not members of the Security Council are forced to spend more time searching for information in any way they can. As a result, they learn either too late or not at all about closed consultations'.[36] States must therefore sometimes refer to the information gleaned from interviews given to the press by Council members in attendance in order to derive any semblance of awareness of the subject and content of the meetings.[37] Other UN member states, too, have noted this deficiency in the transparency of the Council proposing that in compliance with its requirements 'the Security Council should consider the wisdom and propriety of granting the wish of member states, particularly non-Council members, to receive full information on issues discussed by the Council'.[38] Speaking on behalf of the Pacific small island developing states, the representative of Tonga noted that: '[m]any of the agreements reached by the Council are negotiated through experts meetings, which are not open to non-members . . . and the summaries of the discussions are not readily available'.[39]

The issue does not appear to centre entirely on the lack of a structure or regulation of the type of meetings, but rather the fact that the existing structure is being abused or misinterpreted. There are agreed measures in place for the holding of meetings, both public and private, as well as rules governing the appropriate circumstances under which each should be held.[40] At the heart of the matter seems to be, as Pakistan noted, that: 'these provisions, which are mostly agreed provisions, are not being faithfully implemented . . . [which] has a direct negative bearing on the Council's efficiency, effectiveness and legitimacy . . . [and calls into question whether] the Council is effective in carrying out its core mandate, namely, the maintenance of international peace and security'.[41]

Such closed or restricted meetings, while perhaps serving a political imperative as an 'indispensable tool to facilitate prompt and timely decisions',[42] clearly run contrary to the rule of law. They are, however, seen by UN staff as 'a valuable time-saving device'[43] and an inhibition to 'diplomats and U.N. officials from using the U.N. organization as a forum to attain personal political goals'.[44] Quantitative research has led to the explanation that: '[a]ccording to one former Security Council President, under these circumstances, the real issues are discussed, whereas in larger meetings, members tend to use "more diplomatic, but less clear language," which is likely to obscure rather than clarify important issues'.[45]

Informal consultations

A further element of concern comes in the form of informal consultations of the whole, to which non-Council state members are not invited, and the even more exclusive informal dialogues that frequently now precede any actual vote of the Security Council, thereby reducing it from a forum of discussion to a forum of formalisation of preconceived and previously agreed decisions:

> In many cases the general membership and even the countries concerned are kept totally uninformed of the negotiations on draft resolutions or statements directly affecting them, let alone being asked their views on the Council's outcome documents. That is also the case with regard to non-permanent members, which frequently face situations of secretive negotiation between a few permanent members on important issues.[46]

Informal meetings can be central to the achievement of diplomatic and political goals, allowing the achievement of 'compromises that delegations initially accept ad referendum and not on the basis of instructions from the Governments. Holding such negotiations in public would obviously slow them and paralyse them'.[47] This was shown to be the case after the collapse of the USSR 'when, after a long period of paralysis owing to the Cold War, the Security Council has had to learn to work as a unit in order to ensure prompt and effective action by the Organization in accordance with Article 24 of the Charter'.[48] However, the same cannot be said to be true today, over two decades later, when the stagnant condition of Council affairs owing to the rigidity of the US and USSR has loosened considerably.[49] In contrast to the factual evidence of increased Council activity since the fall of the Soviet Union,[50] transparent meetings have decreased and informal meetings appear to be increasingly relied upon.

This upwards trend of usage of informal meetings worryingly has only sought to increase during the last decade: prior to 2006, there are only two documented instances of informal meetings being used – once in 1996 for a General discussion of Council issues in connection with the visit of the President of Italy to the UN and a special meeting in 2006 on the relationship between the UN and the USA briefed by the chairman of the United States Senate Committee on Foreign Relations. Conversely, in the years between 2006 and 2011, a total of 25 informal meetings are documented to have taken place – an average of five a year and over 12 times the number in the preceding decade. Informal consultations – undocumented, entirely verbal discussions between states – are even more concerning and prompted the French foreign minister to transmit an *aide memoire* to the Secretary-General on 9 November 1994,[51] in which he lamented the evolution of Council procedure:

> . . . there is a certain uneasiness in relations between the Security Council and Members of the United Nations . . . result[ing] in large part from the fact that *informal consultations have become the Council's characteristic working method*, while public meetings, originally the norm, are increasingly rare and increasingly devoid of content: *everyone knows that when the Council goes into public meeting everything has been decided in advance.* Thus, all of the Council's work takes place behind closed doors, without observers and without a written record. We think this is a dangerous departure. First of all, it runs counter to rule 48 of the Council's provisional rules of procedure . . . Public meetings are therefore the rule, and non-public meetings the exception. *I should note that informal meetings are not even real Council meetings at all; they have no official existence, and are assigned no number. Yet it is in these meetings that all the Council's work is carried out.* The result of this situation is strong frustration and a lack of information. There is frustration among nonmembers of the Council; and members of the Council have inadequate information because there are too few opportunities for debate for them to understand the general feelings of those interested in items on the Council's agenda.[52]

Council efforts to reform

Discussions on working methods

The 3483rd meeting, held on 16 December 1994 – almost 50 years from the establishment of the Security Council – was the first instance that the Security Council ever held an open meeting to discuss its working methods and procedure. Parallel to this is the fact, that since the early 1990s, the Security Council has been faced with a volume of work not previously encountered; it is estimated that: '[n]inety-three percent of all Chapter VII resolutions passed from 1946 to 2002 have been adopted since the end of the Cold War'.[53] However, it would appear that the Council began carrying out most of its work in its closed consultation room, meeting in public only to adopt resolutions already agreed upon, to provide a forum for set speeches regarding the resolutions or to give the Council's President a platform for statements reflecting understandings reached in private consultation. The adoption of UNSC Resolution 1695 (2006) highlights this in the verbatim records, where the Argentinian delegate ended his speech by thanking 'the Ambassador of the United Kingdom for his intervention to achieve agreement'.[54]

Non-Council member states – and the wider international community – are left wondering what the extent of this intervention was and why the representative of the UK was singled out for thanks when the UK delegation was one of eight members – Denmark, France, Greece, Japan, Peru, Slovakia and the US being the other seven – to have sponsored the original draft resolution, S/2006/488. What exactly transpired in the meeting that brought about harmony in the wording of the resolution remains privy only to the members attending the informal consultation.

Documentation

The Council has taken some steps to improve the process by which it addresses issues concerning its documentation; 'the desire to enhance the flow of information and the exchange of views between the Security Council and the General Assembly lay behind the Council's decision of June 1993 to establish an informal working group on documentation and other procedural matters'.[55] This Informal Working Group (IWG) was designed to make recommendations concerning the Council's documentation and other procedural questions and in order to promote 'efficiency and transparency of the Council's work, as well as interaction and dialogue with non-Council members, the members of the Security Council are committed to implementing [these] measures'.[56]

Indeed, the IWG 'has met regularly, and a number of important steps have been taken following recommendations made by it',[57] such as making available draft resolutions to non-members of the Council and the tentative forecast of the Council's monthly work programme, as well as briefing member states on the progress of informal consultations. The *UN Journal* now announces both formal and informal consultations of the Council. However, as the representative of Lichtenstein noted in 2008, the frequency of their meetings has decreased rapidly,[58] and there have been calls for its formalisation following questions as to why it remains an *informal* working group when it deals with such an integral and vital aspect of the Council's work.[59]

Elections of the Secretary-General

The most recent round of elections has seen the most transparent and open election process for the role of the Secretary-General in the UN's history. The Secretary-General, in accordance with Article 97 of the UN Charter, is a two-stage process – 'appoint[ment] by the General Assembly upon the recommendation of the Security Council'.[60] Historically, the Secretary-General has been chosen in secret in a process that falls short of the UN's own principles and basic recruitment standards. With no job description, selection criteria or public scrutiny of candidates, the Secretary-General nomination process has typically been shrouded in secrecy and open to back-room deals for election.

General Assembly Resolution 69/321[61] – passed in 2015 as a result of intense pressure by many governments and the 1 for 7 billion campaign – marked at least a partial new beginning for the process. Stressing gender and geographical balance[62] and calling for informal dialogues,[63] among other initiatives, the resolution paved the way for a more transparent election process for the election of the Secretary-General. In April 2016, three days of public dialogue were held where nine candidates were interviewed; these were streamed live over the internet, as well as being televised. Representatives from civil society were also included in the process, with almost every country represented in the audience and the opportunity for questions to be posed directly to candidates during the dialogue.

There do, however, remain obstacles to transparency even in this process. From the outset of discussions on UNGA Resolution 69/321, opposition from some groups meant that reform of the process did not extend as far as originally intended by other states:

> Important questions remain to be addressed. One is how to ensure a more active role for the General Assembly in nominating the Secretary-General, according to article 97 of the Charter of the UN, so as not to merely rubber-stamp a Security Council decision. Another is the possibility of the Security Council sending more than one name for consideration by the General Assembly. Moreover, although supported by a substantial number of delegations, language including a suggestion to discuss the duration of the appointment and the renewability of the term of office of the Secretary-General could not be included in this resolution for the sake of consensus.[64]

Moreover, despite opening with a transparent process, the elections themselves will be held in secret ballot and have maintained the use of secret 'straw polls' in which support for candidates is gauged anonymously. The outcomes of the straw polls are not designed to be communicated, a fact that has been recognised by the GA President not to 'live up to the expectations of the membership and the new standard of openness and transparency'.[65] Finally, it seems clear that front-runners for the role of the next Secretary-General are invariably male, dealing a blow to gender equality at an organisation at the forefront of recognising the significant nexus between women, peace and security.

Conclusions

In theory, there should be a wide range of methods through which information is disseminated to non-Council member states. However, it would appear that these are not fully made use of, or in some cases neglected entirely. Interactive wrap-up sessions at the end of a Council presidency that were designed 'to take into account an assessment and evaluation of its work during the preceding month'[66] and 'to be somewhat interactive, so that members would ask questions and raise issues'[67] gradually waned,[68] were not subject to any set procedure[69] and were last formally held in March 2005.[70] Similarly, more substantive and analytical reports would improve the transparency of Council procedure. 'Publications and submissions of the Council could be qualitatively improved to allow the wider membership to gain more insight into its work';[71] in particular, the annual reports submitted by the Council in accordance with Article 24(3) of the UN Charter require refinement 'to add analytical value', rather than merely giving descriptions of the work of the Council during a given year.[72]

Many States have lamented the fact that Security Council reform, particularly review of Council working methods, has 'not been accorded due attention'.[73] Such states have emerged with reasonable and feasible amendments that would ameliorate the current situation and improve transparency in the Council's working methods but these have been ignored or cast aside by Council practice. In essence, despite repeated protestations by smaller and medium-sized states for Council reform of its working methods, no substantive changes have come about. The use of informal mechanisms that render the Council landscape opaque seem to show no signs of tapering; votes in the official meetings are undermined by private discussions between all or a selection of Council Members, rendering them a formality that is necessitated by the Charter and the Council's Working Methods; and non-Council member states continue to scramble for information not only relating to meetings to which they were barred from attending, but also the locations or existence of meetings that they were eligible or invited to attend. These practices, omissions or reluctance to include non-Council member states cannot be seen as compatible with any but the most basic degree of clarity of action: there is superficial transparency insofar as information on public meetings can be found after the event; however, there is still a great deal to be done on the part of the Council to ensure that the inclusion of all UN member states is adequately accommodated.

Notes

1 Antonios Tzanakopoulos, 'Transparency in the Security Council' in Andrea Bianchi and Anne Peters (eds), *Transparency in International Law* (Cambridge University Press 2012) 386. See also Vaughan Lowe, 'The politics of law-making: are the method and character of norm creation changing?' in Michael Byers (ed), *The Role of Law in International Politics* (Oxford University Press 2000) 213–16.

2 See eg Anne Peters and Geir Ulfstein, *The Constitutionalization of International Law* (Oxford University Press 2009) 327; Carol Harlow, *Accountability in the European Union* (Oxford University Press 2002) 7.

3 Antonios Tzanakopoulos, 'Transparency in the Security Council' (n 1) 392.

4 In order for the criteria of transparency to be fully satisfied, it is essential that all parties to an issue be given fair and equitable access to the floor to highlight potential issues from, undoubtedly, a closer and more knowledgeable perspective.

5 UN Charter (1945) art 15.
6 ibid art 98.
7 UNSC Provisional Rules of Procedure (1946) UN Doc S/96/Rev.7, rr 45–46.
8 ibid r 41.
9 UNSC Provisional Rules of Procedure (1946) UN Doc S/96/Rev.7, r 49.
10 http://www.un.org/en/sc/documents (last accessed 10 November 2016).
11 Non-Council members may be invited to participate in the discussion upon their request.
12 Non-Council members that are directly concerned or affected or have special interest in the matter under consideration may be invited to participate in the discussion upon their request.
13 Only Council members may deliver statements following briefings.
14 Non-Council members may or may not be invited to participate in the discussion upon their request.
15 Non-Council members may be invited to participate in the discussion upon their request.
16 Parties prescribed in Resolution 1353 (2001) are invited to participate in the discussion, in accordance with the resolution.
17 'Letter dated 9 November 1994 from the Permanent Representative of France to the United Nations addressed to the Secretary-General' (11 November 1994) UN Doc S/1994/1279 (Annex) 2.
18 Cuba, UNSC Verbatim Record (27 August 2008) UN Doc S/PV.5968 at 32–33.
19 UNSC Provisional Rules of Procedure (1946) UN Doc S/96/Rev.7, r 51.
20 W M Reisman, 'The constitutional crisis in the United Nations' (1993) 87 *American Journal of International Law* 83.
21 UNSC Verbatim Record (19 November 1996) UN Doc S/PV.3714, on the reappointment of the Secretary-General, which can be argued to be necessarily held in private and is specifically mandated by Rule 48 of the Council's Rules of Procedure.
22 UNSC Official Communiqué (26 October 1999) UN Doc S/PV.4058; UNSC Official Communiqué (5 November 1999) UN Doc S/PV.4061; UNSC Official Communiqué (8 November 1999) UN Doc S/PV.4062; UNSC Official Communiqué (30 December 1999) UN Doc S/PV.4086.
23 UNSC Official Communiqué (16 February 2000) UN Doc S/PV.4102; UNSC Official Communiqué (6 March 2000) UN Doc S/PV.4108; UNSC Official Communiqué (25 April 2000) UN Doc S/PV.4132; UNSC Official Communiqué (15 June 2000) UN Doc S/PV.4157; UNSC Official Communiqué (16 June 2000) UN Doc S/PV.4158; UNSC Official Communiqué (21 June 2000) UN Doc S/PV.4163; UNSC Official Communiqué (3 August 2000) UN Doc S/PV.4183; UNSC Official Communiqué (14 September 2000) UN Doc S/PV.4196; UNSC Official Communiqué (19 September 2000) UN Doc S/PV.4198; UNSC Official Communiqué (29 September 2000) UN Doc S/PV.4202; UNSC Official Communiqué (12 October 2000) UN Doc S/PV.4206; UNSC Official Communiqué (26 October 2000) UN Doc S/PV.4210; UNSC Official Communiqué (31 October 2000) UN Doc S/PV.4212; UNSC Official Communiqué (10 November 2000) UN Doc S/PV.4217; UNSC Official Communiqué (10 November 2000) UN Doc S/PV.4218; UNSC Official Communiqué (17 November 2000) UN Doc S/PV.4226; UNSC Official Communiqué (20 November 2000) UN Doc S/PV.4228; UNSC Official Communiqué (27 November 2000) UN Doc S/PV.4233; UNSC Official Communiqué (27 November 2000) UN Doc S/PV.4234.
24 In 2002, 55 of the 272 Council meetings were conducted in private, equating to 20.22% of all Council meetings.
25 UNSC 'Note by the President of the Security Council' (26 July 2010) UN Doc S/2010/507 para 28.

26 See eg Djibouti, UNSC Verbatim Record (16 December 2014) UN Doc S/PV.3483, 14; New Zealand, UNSC Verbatim Record (16 December 2014) UN Doc S/PV.3483, 11; Italy, UNSC Verbatim Record (16 December 2014) UN Doc S/PV.3483, 15; Austria, UNSC Verbatim Record (16 December 2014) UN Doc S/PV.3483, 19; Iran, UNSC Verbatim Record (16 December 2014) UN Doc S/PV.3483, 22.
27 UNSC Verbatim Record (27 August 2008) UN Doc S/PV.5968 (Resumption 1) at 4.
28 These meetings are always closed to the public and closed to non-Council Member States unless they are granted express permission to attend.
29 UNSC Provisional Rules of Procedure (1946) UN Doc S/96/Rev.7, r 51.
30 ibid 51.
31 ibid 56. Such authority is granted by the Security Council, although criteria for allowing this access are lacking.
32 Pakistan, UNSC Verbatim Record (27 August 2008) UN Doc S/PV.5968 (Resumption 1) 24.
33 UNSC Provisional Rules of Procedure (1946) UN Doc S/96/Rev.7, r 55.
34 See eg UNSC Official Communiqué (19 December 2010) UN Doc S/PV.6456; UNSC Official Communiqué (10 December 2010) UN Doc S/PV.6443; UNSC Official Communiqué (3 December 2010) UN Doc S/PV.6433; UNSC Official Communiqué (11 November 2010) UN Doc S/PV.6420.
35 See eg UNSC Official Communiqué (30 October 2010) UN Doc S/PV.5558, where: 'Members of the Council, General Cissé and His Excellency Mr Elie Dote, Prime Minister of the Central African Republic, had an exchange of views'; UNSC Official Communiqué (30 April 2013) UN Doc S/PV.6957, where 'The members of the Council heard a briefing by the representative of Jordan . . . [and] had an exchange of views'.
36 Venezuela, UNSC Verbatim Record (27 August 2008) UN Doc S/PV.5968 (Resumption 1) at 4.
37 ibid.
38 Philippines, ibid 9. See also Canada, ibid 10.
39 Tonga, ibid 21.
40 Chapter XI of the Council's Rules of Procedure is dedicated to the publicity of meetings and records.
41 Pakistan, UNSC Verbatim Record (27 August 2008) UN Doc S/PV.5968 (Resumption 1) 24.
42 'Letter dated 4 August 2008 from the Permanent Representative of Belgium to the United Nations addressed to the Secretary-General' (6 August 2008) UN Doc S/2008/528 (Annex), 3.
43 Discussion with Secretariat official (9 March 1984) and discussion with Secretariat official (1 March 1984) in Loie Feuerle, 'Informal consultation: a mechanism in Security Council decision-making' (1985–1986) 8 *New York University Journal of International Law & Policy* 267, 272–73. cf Simon Chesterman, 'The UN Security Council and the rule of law: the role of the Security Council in strengthening a rules-based international system: final report and recommendations from the Austrian Initiative, 2004–2008' (Institute for International Law and Justice 2008).
44 Feuerle (n 43) 271.
45 ibid 272.
46 Iran, UNSC Verbatim Record (27 August 2008) UN Doc S/PV.5968 (Resumption 1) 11–12.
47 France, UNSC Verbatim Record (16 December 2014) UN Doc S/PV.3483, 3.
48 'Letter dated 9 November 1994 from the Permanent Representative of France to the United Nations addressed to the Secretary-General' (11 November 1994) UN Doc S/1994/1279 (Annex) 2.

49 The renewed anti-US sentiments harboured by the Sino-Russian partnership in recent years will be covered briefly in a later sub-chapter; nonetheless, it cannot compare with the precarious Cold War deadlock that lasted for decades and ended in the 1990s.
50 In the years 1985–1989 a total of 86 resolutions were passed by the Council; in the years 1990–1994, the total was 323. In fact, more resolutions were passed in 1993 alone than in 1985–89 combined.
51 'Letter dated 9 November 1994 from the Permanent Representative of France to the United Nations addressed to the Secretary-General' (11 November 1994) UN Doc S/1994/1279.
52 UNSC Verbatim Record (16 December 2014) UN Doc S/PV.3483 (emphasis added). See also the reports of Security Council presidential statements, eg UNSC Presidential Statement (14 October 1994) UN Doc S/PV.3436, 2.
53 ibid 19.
54 Argentina, UNSC Verbatim Record (15 July 2006) UN Doc S/PV.5490, 6–7.
55 UK, UNSC Verbatim Record (16 December 2014) UN Doc S/PV.3483, 3.
56 UNSC 'Note by the President of the Security Council' (26 July 2010) UN Doc S/2010/507, 1.
57 UK, UNSC 'Note by the President of the Security Council' (26 July 2010) UN Doc S/PV.3483, 3.
58 Lichtenstein, UNSC Verbatim Record (27 August 2008) UN Doc S/PV.5968 (Resumption 1) 12.
59 Egypt, UNSC Verbatim Record (27 August 2008) UN Doc S/PV.5968 (Resumption 1) 2.
60 UN Charter art 97.
61 'Revitalization of the work of the General Assembly', Resolution adopted by the General Assembly on 11 September 2015 UN Doc A/RES/69/321 (22 September 2015).
62 ibid para 38.
63 ibid para 42.
64 Brazil, Verbatim Records UN Doc A/69/PV.103, 6.
65 'Letter to All Permanent Representatives and Permanent Observers to the United Nations from the President of the General Assembly' (21 July 2016).
66 UNSC 'Note by the President of the Security Council' (29 June 2001) UN Doc S/PV.4343, 2.
67 ibid 4–5.
68 Five sessions were held in 2002; three in 2003; none in 2004; one in 2005.
69 Some were held in public, such as UNSC Verbatim Record (30 April 2003) UN Doc S/PV.4748 under Mexico and UNSC Verbatim Record (30 March 2005) UN Doc S/PV.5156 under Brazil, whereas others were held in private.
70 Since then, some Council members have held informal briefings such as Brazil in February 2011, South Africa in January 2012. Some have been open, most have been closed. Both private (four) and public (five) sessions were held in 2014; a further four public sessions were held in 2015 and, so far in 2016, there have been three public sessions.
71 Korea, UNSC Verbatim Record (27 August 2008) UN Doc S/PV.5968 (Resumption 1) 19.
72 ibid.
73 Iran, ibid 11. See also Canada, ibid 11; Philippines, ibid 8; Lichtenstein, ibid 14 and Argentina, ibid 16.

5 Legal certainty

Introduction

Legal certainty as a component of the rule of law is inherently linked to both the legality and legitimacy of Security Council action under Chapter VII. It examines the legal argument for Council action, demanding that resolutions should highlight which article of Chapter VII any resolutions are taken under and its parameters, as well as clearly stating the legal justification for taking such action, the nature of the threat which the resolution intends to address and the nexus between the threat and the course of action pursued. That is to say, legal certainty is the explanatory element of a resolution, showing what the Council has identified as a threat, why it has chosen to respond in this way and what the extent of such response should be. While initially eager to adhere to the letter of the law after the hard-fought negotiations and text that emerged from the Dumbarton Oaks, Yalta and San Francisco meetings and conferences, it is documented that the practice of referring legal questions to a committee of legal experts quickly fell by the wayside as the years progressed, essentially heralding the age of Council unilateralism that can be argued to exemplify the current *status quo*.[1]

This practice runs contrary to the provisions of the Charter, which clearly stipulate the exact procedure that the Council must follow if it is to invoke the clauses of Chapter VII.[2] With the argument in mind that the Council and all its actions are governed by its founding text – the UN Charter – it is vital that Council action abide by the stipulations therein. Thus, the Charter is the first port of call when exploring what the Council is permitted to carry out and what, if any, constraints are imposed upon it. As such, the Charter is quite clear in the opening article of Chapter VII on what the Council must provide prior to any further Chapter VII action.[3]

Articles 41 and 42 of the Charter, authorising non-military and military action respectively, are subordinate to Article 39, which provides the threshold of identification of a threat *prior* to any action being instigated under the Council's Chapter VII powers. There is, then, a staged progression that safeguards from arbitrary or frivolous use of Articles 41 and 42, albeit a caveat that is wildly ambiguous in itself; in order for Chapter VII to be invoked, the threat, breach or act *must* be expressly stated in the resolution. A determination under Article 39, however, does not immediately presuppose action under Chapter VII to follow;

that is to say, all Chapter VII resolutions should have a determination under Article 39, but not all determinations under Chapter 39 lead to Chapter VII resolutions. Two clear examples of this are UNSC Resolution 1976 (2011) and UNSC Resolution 1078 (1996), both of which contain determinations under Article 39 but no Chapter VII references or elements.[4] Article 39, therefore, is the 'portal' through which the Council must enter in order to access its Chapter VII powers and without such determination, any Chapter VII resolution would technically be a subversion of the law governing the Council;[5] indeed, it has been referred to as 'the single most important provision of the Charter'.[6]

Determination of a threat under Article 39

However, such explicit enumeration of the specific threat to the peace is not always given by the Council, leading to ambiguity, confusion and disarray. As such, certain resolutions refer to explicit determinations under Article 39, while others determine a threat to the peace either implicitly or not at all. These *explicit* determinations are unequivocal – they leave no room for doubt as to what the trigger of any subsequent Chapter VII action might be. Such determinations date back almost to the very origins of the Council itself in 1948 – and its first Chapter VII resolution – when the Council 'determine[d] that the situation in Palestine constitute[d] a threat to the peace within the meaning of Article 39 of the Charter of the United Nations'.[7]

Throughout the decades since, there have been numerous examples of explicit determinations from the 1950s,[8] 1960s,[9] 1970s,[10] 1980s,[11] 1990s[12] and even the early 21st century.[13] Moreover, once a determination has been made under Article 39, Council practice suggests that it would be necessary to reiterate this determination in any and all related resolutions, rather than simply referring back to the original resolution in which the determination can be found; that is to say, the determination of a threat under Article 39 is valid only for the single resolution in which it is made and not subsequent resolutions that make reference to it.[14]

A *closed* interpretation of resolutions, where meeting records, statements, comments and other peripheral material to a resolution are not used to interpret the meaning of a resolution[15] is generally in stark contrast to my wider approach to the work of the Council, which considers a resolution as benefiting from related material not necessarily included in the text of a resolution.[16] However, a narrow scope of interpretation with respect to a determination of the threat to the peace seems necessary; particularly where determinations are made in relation to *jus ad bellum*, '[t]he authorisation of the use of force by the Council cannot be presumed unless the Council's explicit intention is expressed'.[17] For example, in the military intervention in Libya, the phrase 'all necessary measures'[18] was tantamount to a green light for NATO to mobilise; UNSC Resolution 1441 on Iraq[19] featured no such terminology and therefore, according to the serving Secretary-General, 'from the charter point of view, it was illegal'.[20]

The imperative for an Article 39 determination prior to the invocation of Articles 41 or 42 is evidenced by Council practice itself: in the vast majority of cases, references have been made on each occasion where Article 39 determinations would be necessary, in addition to various Article 39 determinations that were not succeeded by explicit Chapter VII action. The following five illustrations clearly show that, while there has been a pattern in the behaviour of the Council on this point, there are at times various exceptions to the rule and the Council has not rigidly stuck to any specific routine, varying it slightly depending on the situations called for.

Angola

The case of Angola is perhaps the most straightforward of all; here, the Council made clear the reference to Article 39 in 1993 when first '[d]etermining that the . . . situation in Angola constitute[d] a threat to international peace and security in the region'.[21] The subsequent resolutions that span the years until 2002[22] all make reference to a threat to the peace that the Council has identified, thereby satisfying the criteria of Article 39. There is a clear pattern of reference to Article 39 determinations in every case where Chapter VII powers are invoked; this can be seen as the ideal standard to which the Council should adhere in all Chapter VII resolutions.

Somalia

Somalia first appeared on the agenda of the Security Council in 1992, when 'the continuation of [conflict and loss of human life] constitute[d], as stated in the report of the Secretary-General, a threat to international peace and security'[23] and a weapons and military embargo was imposed on Somalia under Chapter VII.[24] In the over two decades since, over 50 Chapter VII resolutions have emanated from the Council on subjects ranging from internal conflict to regional disputes to piracy and armed robbery at sea.[25] With the exception of four resolutions that refer to determinations made previously,[26] all Chapter VII resolutions – and even resolutions in relation to Somalia not issued under Chapter VII[27] – have reiterated explicit determinations under Article 39. However, determinations have not been forthcoming in every instance – there is slight deviation from the formula of an Article 39 determination leading to Chapter VII action in the case of Somalia.

Haiti

The first Chapter VII resolution to deal with Haiti came about in 1993, when a trade embargo was imposed by the Council following a determination of threat to the peace and subsequent explicit reference to the use of its Chapter VII powers.[28] Although Chapter VII resolutions dealing with the situation in Haiti are not as numerous as those dealing with Somalia, they are nevertheless equally consistent. Almost all of the Chapter VII resolutions that deal with the existence of a threat to peace and security in Haiti have explicit determinations made.[29] UNSC Resolution 861 (1993), however, makes no mention of a determination of a threat when referring to the lifting of elements of the trade embargo;

nonetheless, it serves to illustrate a different type of Chapter VII resolution of which the Council makes use.

As the General Assembly affirmed in UNGA Resolution 192,[30] Chapter VII resolutions 'can be revoked only by a decision of the Council and that any unilateral action in this regard would be in violation of the obligation assumed by member states under Article 25 of the Charter'.[31] In short, this principle of '*parallelism of competence*'[32] dictates that the Council, as the body to have imposed Chapter VII measures, shall also be the body to terminate those measures as and when it sees fit. Accordingly, a determination of a threat to the peace under Article 39 would not be necessary – and even run contrary to the meaning of a *parallelism of competence* resolution – as the lack of the threat that instigated the Chapter VII measures originally would be the very source of the decision to annul those measures in a *parallelism of competence* resolution; thus, resolutions such as UNSC Resolution 861 (1993) can legitimately exist as rule of law compliant Chapter VII resolutions without the need for prior Article 39 determinations.[33] However, this exemption from the norm is a narrow path that accommodates only the most limited of examples; indeed even extensions of a mission's mandate require a fresh determination of the threat posed, as evidenced by those of MINUSTAH[34] in 2010[35] and 2011.[36]

Until 2012, the sole exceptions to an otherwise consistent application of an Article 39 determination prior to Chapter VII action are Resolutions 1908[37] and 1927,[38] both increasing the number of troops deployed under MINUSTAH. It may be argued that these required a determination of their own, as the need for an increase in troops within the context of the perceived threat to peace should have been shown as justification for any increase in troop numbers. However, each of these resolutions, just as can be observed with Resolutions 878, 1356 and 1407 dealing with Somalia, contains a reaffirmation of previous resolutions in which determinations have been made.

The same concept applies to both Resolutions 2070[39] and 2119,[40] each extending the mandate of MINUSTAH. However, the use of the format of reaffirmation in lieu of new determinations is a departure for the Council from its own behaviour and suggested the start of a new trend; whereas extensions of the mandate in previous years had seen an explicit determination under Article 39,[41] resolutions 2070 and 2119 saw only the far weaker reference, 'Mindful of its primary responsibility for the maintenance of international peace and security under the Charter of the United Nations'.[42] There was no fresh determination, no reference to a threat and no reassessment of the determination as there had been in previous years, leading to the question as to what the reasoning behind and purpose of this shift in the Council's behaviour from existing practice. The case of Haiti, then, exemplifies an even larger departure from the standard seen in the case of Angola.

Afghanistan

The Council's issuance of resolutions dealing with the threat to the peace in Afghanistan is not only another example where the Council has repeatedly made determinations under Article 39 before invoking Chapter VII,[43] but where the use of *parallelism of competence* is highlighted. UNSC Resolution 1388 in 2002, where sanctions imposed under Chapter VII against Ariana Afghan Airlines were lifted[44] using a mirror Chapter VII resolution is a minor example of this, but it is Council practice during recent years, where resolutions on Afghanistan have become less frequent, that Council behaviour exemplifies the need for and use of *parallelism of competence.*

Since 2009 the Council has adopted the habit of issuing two resolutions every year on Afghanistan – one under Chapter VII renewing the mandate of the ISAF[45] and another, not taken under Chapter VII, renewing the mandate of UNAMA.[46] This reflects the origins, and indeed the nature, of each of the projects.[47] While the latter's establishment was supported by UNSC Resolution 1401 (2002), which was not issued under Chapter VII, ISAF was unequivocally, and necessarily, formalised through a Chapter VII resolution. It therefore follows that UNAMA mandate renewals are not taken under Chapter VII,[48] whereas ISAF mandates must always be renewed under Chapter VII,[49] with an eye to the threat to the peace that exists, despite the fact that both UNAMA and ISAF are dealing with the same threats in the same country.

Sudan

The majority of Council resolutions dealing with the Sudan, including the conflict in Darfur, comply with the bi-partite formula of a standard Chapter VII resolution – both the determination and explicit reference to Chapter VII exist.[50] As in previous examples, there are examples where Article 39 determinations are made without subsequent Chapter VII invocation[51] and where the parallelism of competence doctrine lies behind instances in which Chapter VII is legitimately invoked without prior determination of the threat to the peace.[52]

However, there are examples where this is not the case, in contrast to the examples of Haiti and Afghanistan. The establishment of the United Nations Interim Security Force for Abyei (UNIFSA), for example, emerged from a resolution taken under Chapter VII;[53] therefore, any resulting extension of the duration or scope of the mandate should, by virtue of the principle of parallelism of competence, also be issued under Chapter VII. Such was not the case; while each of the subsequent resolutions to UNSC Resolution 1990 included a determination of the threat to the peace, in accordance with Article 39,[54] there was no reference to Chapter VII. This raises the question as to why the Council felt it necessary to deal with the mandate of UNISFA in a way different to MINUSTAH, as already discussed above, and other peacekeeping missions such as UNMIL[55] and UNOCI.[56]

Patterns in Council practice

Thus it seems that there exists, in the majority of cases, a determination of threats to the peace prior to, and even in the absence of subsequent, Chapter VII action, particularly in recent years where the practice of the Council appears to have incorporated elements of transparency in ensuring that all States are clearly aware of the obligations of and procedural path to Chapter VII. Even in the case of Iraq – where among the plethora of Chapter VII resolutions on Iraq passed between the years 1990 and 2003[57] only four determinations were made under Article 39[58] – the last decade has seen a significant improvement in the number of determinations in Chapter VII resolutions relating to Iraqi affairs.[59] This is, though, one half of the formula for Chapter VII action, the other being the explicit reference to measures being taken under Chapter VII itself, which will now be addressed.

Explicit reference to Chapter VII

In addition to the previous chapter's discussion of what constitutes a threat to the peace, there is also disagreement on whether certain resolutions can be classed as constituting a Chapter VII resolution at all. In *The Procedure of the UN Security Council*, Bailey and Daws present a list of 129 Chapter VII resolutions from 1946 through 1995;[60] however, the Global Issues Research Group of the Foreign and Commonwealth Office counts 17 Chapter VII resolutions between the years of 1946-1989 and 104 Chapter VII resolutions between 1990 and 1995 – a total of 121 and, perhaps surprisingly, eight less than Bailey and Daws.[61]

This cannot simply be attributed to mathematical error, but reflects two key elements of Chapter VII resolutions. First, it exposes the fluid interpretations of Council resolutions, which are open to different perspectives depending on the reader; such space for intellectual manoeuvring may be appropriate for political and diplomatic situations that encourage a broad interpretation allowing for later negotiation or clarification. One might imagine equivocal language, inconclusive clauses and abstract notions in the manifestos of a political party or pledges of a political candidate that are later spun to reveal an element of hollowness; however, such obscurity has no place in the legal sphere that is frequently criticised for overemphasis and intricate attention to the most miniscule of legal intricacies and avoidance of loopholes. Secondly, it displays a certain failure on the part of the Council itself to abide by the specificity demanded of it by the Charter.

Nonetheless, it would appear that the Council has increasingly shifted its behaviour from one of opacity in its resolutions to one of increased clarity and specificity. Whether in response to the criticism of States such as South Africa, which in 2007, accused the Security Council of having 'resorted to Chapter VII of the Charter as an umbrella for addressing issues that may not necessarily pose a threat to international peace and security, when it could have opted for alternative provisions of the Charter to respond more appropriately, utilizing other provisions of the same Charter'[62] or due to an increased awareness of the need to implement elements of the rule of law in its behaviour to increase legitimacy on the world stage, there has been a marked shift in the depth of explanatory provisions of resolutions.

The anatomy of a Chapter VII resolution

Since 1990, authorising resolutions has typically included three elements: a determination in accordance with Article 39; the statement 'acting under Chapter VII'; and an explicit decision to authorise member states to use force. Such was the case with authorisations regarding Iraq,[63] Bosnia,[64] Somalia,[65] Haiti,[66] Rwanda,[67] the Democratic Republic of Congo,[68] Albania,[69] Central African Republic,[70] Sierra Leone,[71] Kosovo,[72] Timor-Leste,[73] Afghanistan,[74] Côte d'Ivoire,[75] Liberia[76] and Chad.[77] However, this has not always been, nor does it continue to be, the case; historically, Simma notes, there has not been a tendency to explicitly refer to action taken under Chapter VII using an unequivocal phrase in the vein of 'acting under Chapter VII of the Charter of the United Nations'[78] until the end of the Cold War.[79]

Although in the teething years of the Security Council explicit reference to 'Chapter VII' was not made,[80] there were nonetheless numerous references to the relevant Articles of Chapter VII or the explicit threat to the peace that was being dealt with, if only to give some audit trail of the process by which the Council has reached its conclusion: UNSC Resolution 54 (1948) '[d]*etermines* that the situation in Palestine constitutes a threat the peace within the meaning of Article 39 of the Charter . . . [and] *Orders* the Governments and authorities concerned, pursuant to Article 40 . . . to desist from further military action . . .'.[81] Indeed, the UN approval for military intervention in the Korean War of 1950 came about in UNSC Resolution 83 (1950), which simply '*determined* that the armed attack upon the Republic of Korea by forces from North Korea constitute[d] and breach of the peace'[82] and where no explicit mention of the term 'Chapter VII' or Article 42 of the Charter was made despite it being implied in the language. However, evolution in the UN did not come only in the form of new member states, but also in the terminology used to authorise Council action and in 1968, UNSC Resolution 253 made the first use of the phrase 'acting under Chapter VII'.[83] Since this time, the use of the phrase to designate Chapter VII resolutions has been commonplace and yet there are numerous examples of the Council not providing clear Chapter VII status to a resolution that clearly should have been granted such status.

The fact that certain resolutions[84] are open to interpretation is an indictment of the process by which such decisions emanate from the Council chamber. The simple fact appears to be that resolutions should and must be specific and focused, announcing not only what the threat is but also whether the resolution has been issued under Chapter VII, and if so whether under Article 41 or 42 of the Charter. The negligence of the Council in doing so for *all* resolutions results in ambiguity for UN member states which forage for information and pore over the records of Council meetings. UN member states are able to rely far more solidly on a binding, clear Chapter VII resolution when fulfilling their obligations to abide by Council decisions and the more structured and limited the leeway given in any resolution, the more difficult they might find it to undermine or simply deny its implementation.[85]

Resolutions that are not explicitly binding may not be held as such by States; as Judge Hersch Lauterpacht has noted, '[a] resolution recommending . . . a specific course of action creates some legal obligation which . . . The state in consideration, while not bound to accept the recommendation, is bound to give it due consideration in good faith'.[86] An explicit Chapter VII leaves no room for interpretation and would affirm the need for abidance.

Dilution or digression?

Nonetheless, the Security Council has recently continued to blur the lines between resolutions adopted under Chapter VII and those not. Two recent cases where the Security Council has made use of Chapter VII language without explicit reference to Chapter VII itself are UNSC Resolution 2218 and UNSCR Resolution 2249. The former, in response to chemical attacks carried out by Syrian armed forces against its own citizens and civilians, '[d]etermines that the use of chemical weapons anywhere constitutes a threat to international peace and security'[87] and imposes obligations on the Syrian Arab Republic[88] Bar explicitly stating that the resolution is being taken under Chapter VII, this is the terminology of a Chapter VII resolution.

The ambiguity, however, lies most acutely in two distinct elements of these resolutions. The first of these elements is the *threat* of a further resolution under Chapter VII that would follow Syria's refusal or failure to implement the articles of UNSC Resolution 2218; the Council '[d]ecides, in the event of non-compliance with this resolution to impose measures under Chapter VII of the United Nations Charter',[89] thereby introducing a clear distinction between this resolution and a Chapter VII resolution, which would contain actions taken under Article 41 or 42 of the Charter. The inference is that if a Chapter VII resolution is to follow, then this cannot be a Chapter VII resolution and, therefore, lacks the gravity associated with the provisions of Articles 41 and 42 of the Charter. The second confusing element is the decision by the Council – given the terminology of a Chapter VII resolution as discussed – to 'underscore that Member States are obligated under Article 25 of the Charter of the United Nations to accept and carry out the Council's decisions'.[90]

This element clearly attempts to impose a legally binding obligation upon States – particularly Syria itself and its neighbours – to comply with the decisions of the Security Council on a par with a Chapter VII resolution. Indeed, one must question the reason for the insertion of this phrase; if a legally binding resolution is what the Council sought, surely a Chapter VII resolution would have offered this more easily.

UNSCR Resolution 2249 exhibits similar traits of a Chapter VII resolution, but stops short of explicitly stating that it was adopted under this Charter section. On the surface, the terminology used is almost identical to resolution 1973 which authorised NATO intervention in Libya in 2011: 'all necessary measures' being used rather than 'all necessary means'. Prior knowledge of Council terminology may allow states to pierce the legalese veil to understand this resolution to mean use of force, yet this does not negate the fact that the use of force is authorised under Article 42 of the UN Charter, which falls under Chapter VII.

Herein lies the key distinction: the missing reference in resolution 2249 to Chapter VII of the UN Charter, which grants the requisite legal authority to the use of force. From a purist's approach, without both a determination of the threat to the peace – Article 39 of the UN Charter – and an explicit reference to Chapter VII, military intervention would be illegal. Almost certainly, the inclusion of explicit references to international, refugee, humanitarian and human rights law were included following Sino-Russian criticism of the NATO campaign in Libya. Resolution 2249 rules out the possibility of regime change in Syria through its explicit preambular reference to the Geneva Communiqué; it further elaborates on a need for accountability of intervening states and sets definitive legal parameters; and it advocates a better respect for humanitarian and human rights law than was shown in Libya, where collateral damage was heavily criticised by international human rights organisations.

Other examples, too, illustrate the blurred lines between legally binding and non-legally binding resolutions throughout the history of the Security Council. Some commentators have noted that 'when the Security Council invoked Articles 25 and 49 in calling on states to carry out its decisions during the Congo peacekeeping efforts in 1960, it obviously regarded itself as acting under Chapter VII despite having made no express determination under Article 39'.[91] Decades later, the Council issued another resolution on the Congo that '*Determin*[*ed*] that the situation in the Democratic Republic of the Congo continues to pose a threat to international peace and security in the region' and where the Council made '[*d*]*emands once again* that Kisangani be demilitarized rapidly and unconditionally in accordance with Security Council resolution 1304 (2000) . . .'.[92] Once again, no reference to Chapter VII is made.

It has been suggested that '[t]his lack of formal clarity is sometimes a result of the political environment in which resolutions are negotiated. Pressures to include ambiguities or omit explicit references to Chapter VII in Council resolutions are sometimes accommodated in order to secure political agreement'.[93] John Bellinger suggests that the substitution of Article 25 for Chapter VII reveals the compromise that was necessary in reaching the unanimous approval of the resolution without diluting the legal basis attached to the Council's decisions.[94] As a political organ, it is understandable that the Council must balance the end with the means, particularly given, as some might argue, that 'the Security Council's role under the Charter is to further international peace and security and not the rule of law'.[95] In this vein, certain resolutions that all but mention Chapter VII – that is to say, include explicit reference to a threat to the peace and demand action of some sort – are not issued under Chapter VII, despite the fact that they are clearly intended to relay the same gravity and legal standing.[96] Other resolutions act under Chapter VII without first determining the precise threat to the peace, therein bypassing the 'portal' of Article 39 through which the Council must access its powers under Articles 41 and 42.[97]

A clear legal basis

Aside from the existence of phrases referring to the procedural requirements of Article 39 and the mention of Chapter VII, *Legal Certainty* requires that there be a legitimate, legally sound basis for the invocation of Chapter VII powers. There is a necessity for the Council to explain what exactly about the situation poses a threat to the international peace. Although the Council has been commendably forthcoming in attempting to increase the clarity and transparency of its decision-making with respect to explicitly stating when it is acting under Chapter VII through the determination of a threat to the peace, the decisions relating to what precisely such a threat comprises have been far less comprehensible, predictable, consistent and legally reasoned. While equality and predictability will be expanded upon later in the book, it is important to highlight some examples where there has been opacity in the process of determining a threat to the international peace.

There are several examples of instances where the Council has not expressly stated the nature of the threat that it conceived existed and where the threats themselves, even where explicitly stated, are tenuous. UNSC Resolution 733,[98] imposing an arms embargo on Somalia under Chapter VII in 1992 reiterated the same concerns that the Secretary-General had voiced previously in his report, which itself is cited only generally and without specificity; the resolution itself makes a generic reference to Chapter VII being necessary 'for the purposes of establishing peace and stability in Somalia'[99] but does not link the actions taken – namely the embargo – to the desired outcome – the establishment of peace and stability – or the 'consequences on stability and peace in the region'.[100] UNSC Resolution 733 was adopted following consultations but no public debate was instigated, shedding no further light on the nexus between the two; consequently, the exact reasoning behind the decision remains elusive and shows no signs of a legal basis.

There are doubts cast, also, on UNSC Resolution 841 on the subject of Haiti,[101] where economic sanctions were imposed on the country in an effort to ameliorate the humanitarian situation and bring about the return of President Aristide. The debate surrounding the imposition of economic sanctions in 1993 focused on the humanitarian crisis and the need to reinstate democracy; there was very little reference to any perceived threat to international peace. In fact, only Venezuela – one of three sponsors of UNSC Resolution 841[102] – made any explicit mention of the threat to the peace that formed the determination underscoring the sanctions taken under Chapter VII:[103] yet even this threat was non-descript, being linked tenuously to the 'substantial increase of hundreds of thousands of Haitians, in terrified flight to other countries'.[104]

The threat, then, according to the only representative to have verbalised it explicitly was the flight of refugees out of Haiti to other countries and not, as one might have supposed, the coup that ran contrary to democratically elected President Jean-Bertrand Aristide. This contrasts starkly the tone of the rest of the representatives speeches, which interpret the 'main purpose of the resolution [to be] an early political solution to the crisis in Haiti'[105] and believe that the goals of the sanctions are to 'bring the perpetrators of the coup d'état to the negotiating table in order to restore constitutional order in Haiti'[106] and 'to put pressure on those who stand in the way of a solution'.[107] Once more, those wishing to derive any semblance of structure or definition of the threat to the peace are left without any solid answers. Though these two examples date back over 20 years, as the remainder of this chapter has revealed, legal certainty has continued to evade Council resolutions since.

Conclusions

Determinations are made frequently under Article 39 and in most cases where Chapter VII is invoked there is a prior determination in accordance with the UN Charter, at least in recent years; however, the subsequent Chapter VII resolutions hides much of what exactly the actual threat perceived to be consists of. Coupled with the lack of transparency seen in chapter 4, where the reasoning behind a decision is not made by the Council, there is space for misunderstandings as to a clear definition of the threat and parameters and exactitudes that would allow all states – both those in attendance and those reading records – to understand fully where the threat lies are missing. Among other likelihoods, a volition on the part of the Council to stretch the definition of a threat to the peace in order to fit a political imperative is exhibited. This in turn has a serious effect on the equality of the law amongst UN member states, for where there is no clear definition of what a threat to the peace is in a given instance to where Chapter VII has been resorted, there can be no pattern emerging from Council behaviour; subsequently accusations of arbitrary behaviour and bias on the Council are levelled and even examples where Chapter VII is used inappropriately, insufficiently or excessively can be evidenced.

Notes

1 See Louis B Sohn, 'The UN system as authoritative interpreter of its law' in Oscar Schachter and Christopher C Joyner (eds), *United Nations Legal Order: Vol 1* (Cambridge University Press 1995) 169, 227.
2 UN Charter (1945) art 39.
3 ibid.
4 See also eg UNSC Res 867 (23 September 1993) UN Doc S/RES/867 and UNSC Res 862 (31 August 1993) UN Doc S/RES/862.
5 It is worth noting that a positive determination under art 39 does not immediately and automatically result in Chapter VII action, but merely provides the option to proceed further eg UNSC Res 1078 (9 November 1996) UN Doc S/RES1078.
6 US Secretary of State, 'Report to the President on the Result of the San Francisco Conference (1945)' in Jochen Frowein and Nico Krisch, 'Article 39' in Bruno Simma with others (eds), *The Charter of the United Nations: A Commentary* (Oxford University Press 2002) 718.
7 UNSC Res 54 (15 July 1948) UN Doc S/RES/54 preamble.
8 eg UNSC Res 82 (25 June 1950) UN Doc S/RES/82; UNSC Res 83 (27 June 1950) UN Doc S/RES/83; UNSC Res 84 (7 July 1950) UN Doc S/RES/84.

9 eg UNSC Res 161 (21 February 1961) UN Doc S/RES/161; UNSC Res 217 (20 November 1965) UN Doc S/RES/217.
10 eg UNSC Res 277 (18 March 1970) UN Doc S/RES/277; UNSC Res 418 (4 November 1977) UN Doc S/RES/418.
11 eg UNSC Res 502 (3 April 1982) UN Doc S/RES/502; UNSC Res 598 (20 July 1987) UN Doc S/RES/598; UNSC Res 611 (25 April 1988) UN Doc S/RES/611.
12 eg UNSC Res 864 (15 September 1993) UN Doc S/RES/864; UNSC Res 1234 (9 April 1999) UN Doc S/RES/1234.
13 See eg UNSC Res 1315 (14 August 2000) UN Doc S/RES/1315; UNSC Res 1590 (24 March 2005) UN Doc S/RES/1590; UNSC Res 1641 (30 November 2005) UN Doc S/RES/1641.
14 There are, of course, exceptions to this; for example, UNSC Res 169 (24 November 1961) UN Doc S/RES/169 para 6, relating to the Congo requested 'the Secretary-General to take all necessary measures to prevent the entry or return of . . . foreign military and paramilitary personnel and political advisors not under the United Nations Command' based on a recollection of resolution 143 (1960) in which the original determination under art 39 was made.
15 Alexander Orakhelashvili, 'The acts of the Security Council: meaning and standards of review' (2007) 11 *Max Planck Yearbook of United Nations Law* 143, 161.
16 Michael C Wood, 'The interpretations of Security Council resolutions' (1998) 2 *Max Planck Yearbook of United Nations Law* 73, 73–95.
17 See Orakhelashvili (n 15) 162.
18 UNSC Res 1973 (17 March 2011) UN Doc S/RES/1973 para 4.
19 UNSC Res 1441 (8 November 2002) UN Doc S/RES/1441.
20 'Iraq war illegal, says Annan' *BBC News* (16 September 2004).
21 UNSC Res 864 (15 September 1993) UN Doc S/RES/864, B preamble.
22 UNSC Res 1127 (29 August 1997) UN Doc S/RES/1127; UNSC Res 1173 (12 June 1998) UN Doc S/RES/1173; UNSC Res 1237 (7 May 1999) UN Doc S/RES/1237; UNSC Res 1295 (18 April 2000) UN Doc S/RES/1295; UNSC Res 1336 (23 January 2001) UN Doc S/RES/1336; UNSC Res 1348 (23 April 2001) UN Doc S/RES/1348; UNSC Res 1404 (18 April 2002) UN Doc S/RES/1404.
23 UNSC Res 733 (23 January 1992) UN Doc S/RES/733 preamble.
24 ibid para 5.
25 UNSC Res 751 (24 April 1992) UN Doc S/RES/751; UNSC Res 767 (24 July 1992) UN Doc S/RES/767; UNSC Res 775 (28 August 1992) UN Doc S/RES/775; UNSC Res 794 (3 December 1992) UN Doc S/RES/794; UNSC Res 814 (26 March 1993) UN Doc S/RES/814; UNSC Res 837 (6 June 1993) UN Doc S/RES/837; UNSC Res 886 (18 November 1993) UN Doc S/RES/886; UNSC Res 897 (4 February 1994) UN Doc S/RES/897; UNSC Res 923 (31 May 1994) UN Doc S/RES/923; UNSC Res 954 (4 November 1994) UN Doc S/RES/954; UNSC Res 1425 (22 July 2002) UN Doc S/RES/1425; UNSC Res 1474 (8 April 2003) UN Doc S/RES/1474; UNSC Res 1519 (16 December 2003) UN Doc S/RES/1519; UNSC Res 1558 (17 August 2004) UN Doc S/RES/1558; UNSC Res 1587 (15 March 2005) UN Doc S/RES/1587; UNSC Res 1630 (14 October 2005) UN Doc S/RES/1630; UNSC Res 1676 (10 May 2006) UN Doc S/RES/1676; UNSC Res 1724 (29 November 2005) UN Doc S/RES/1724; UNSC Res 1725 (6 December 2006) UN Doc S/RES/1725; UNSC Res 1744 (20 February 2007) UN Doc S/RES/1744; UNSC Res 1766 (23 July 2007) UN Doc S/RES/1766; UNSC Res 1772 (20 August 2007) UN Doc S/RES/1772; UNSC Res 1801 (20 February 2008) UN Doc S/RES/1801; UNSC Res 1811 (29 April 2008) UN Doc S/

RES/1811; UNSC Res 1814 (15 May 2008) UN Doc S/RES/1814; UNSC Res 1816 (2 June 2008) UN Doc S/RES/1816; UNSC Res 1831 (19 August 2008) UN Doc S/RES/1831; UNSC Res 1838 (7 October 2008) UN Doc S/RES/1838; UNSC Res 1844 (20 November 2008) UN Doc S/RES/1844; UNSC Res 1846 (2 December 2008) UN Doc S/RES/1846; UNSC Res 1851 (16 December 2008) UN Doc S/RES/1851; UNSC Res 1853 (19 December 2008) UN Doc S/RES/1853; UNSC Res 1863 (16 January 2009) UN Doc S/RES/1863; UNSC Res 1872 (26 May 2009) UN Doc S/RES/1872 (2009); UNSC Res 1897 (30 November 2009) UN Doc S/RES/1897; UNSC Res 1910 (28 January 2010) UN Doc S/RES/1910; UNSC Res 1916 (19 March 2010) UN Doc S/RES/1916; UNSC Res 1950 (23 November 2010) UN Doc S/RES/1950; UNSC Res 1964 (22 December 2010) UN Doc S/RES/1964; UNSC Res 1972 (17 March 2011) UN Doc S/RES/1972; UNSC Res 1976 (11 April 2011) UN Doc S/RES/1976; UNSC Res 2002 (29 July 2011) UN Doc S/RES/2002; UNSC Res 2015 (24 October 2011) UN Doc S/RES/2015; UNSC Res 2020 (22 November 2011) UN Doc S/RES/2020; UNSC Res 2036 (22 February 2012) UN Doc S/RES/2036; UNSC Res 2060 (25 July 2012) UN Doc S/RES/2060; UNSC Res 2072 (31 October 2012) UN Doc S/RES/2072; UNSC Res 2073 (7 November 2012) UN Doc S/RES/2073; UNSC Res 2077 (21 November 2012) UN Doc S/RES/2077; UNSC Res 2093 (6 March 2013) UN Doc S/RES/2093; UNSC Res 2111 (24 July 2013) UN Doc S/RES/2111; UNSC Res 2125 (18 November 2013) UN Doc S/RES/2125.

26 UNSC Res 878 (29 October 1993) UN Doc S/RES/878; UNSC Res 1356 (19 June 2001) UN Doc S/RES/1356; UNSC Res 1407 (3 May 2002) UN Doc S/RES/1407; UNSC Res 2111 (24 July 2013) UN Doc S/RES/2111.

27 eg UNSC Res 1976 (11 April 2011) UN Doc S/RES/1976; UNSC Res 2102 (2 May 2013) UN Doc S/RES/2102.

28 UNSC Res 841 (16 June 1993) UN Doc S/RES/841.

29 UNSC Res 873 (13 October 1993) UN Doc S/RES/873; UNSC Res 875 (16 October 1993) UN Doc S/RES/875; UNSC Res 917 (6 May 1994) UN Doc S/RES/917; UNSC Res 940 (31 July 1994) UN Doc S/RES/940; UNSC Res 1529 (29 February 2004) UN Doc S/RES/1529; UNSC Res 1542 (30 April 2004) UN Doc S/RES/1542; UNSC Res 1576 (29 November 2004) UN Doc S/RES/1576; UNSC Res 1601 (31 May 2005) UN Doc S/RES/1601; UNSC Res 1608 (22 June 2005) UN Doc S/RES/1608; UNSC Res 1658 (14 February 2006) UN Doc S/RES/1658; UNSC Res 1702 (15 August 2006) UN Doc S/RES/1702; UNSC Res 1743 (15 February 2007) UN Doc S/RES/1743; UNSC Res 1780 (15 October 2007) UN Doc S/RES/1780; UNSC Res 1840 (14 October 2008) UN Doc S/RES/1840; UNSC Res 1892 (13 October 2009) UN Doc S/RES/1892.

30 UNGA Res 34/192 (18 December 1979) UN Doc A/RES/34/192.

31 ibid para 9; this issue was put to rest by the Assembly in response to the unilateral decision of the UK in its letter of 12 December 1979 (UN Doc S/13688) to end mandatory sanctions on Southern Rhodesia imposed by the Council in UNSC Res 232 (16 December 1966) UN Doc S/RES/232 and UNSC Res 253 (29 May 1968) UN Doc S/RES/253.

32 Erika de Wet, *The Chapter VII Powers of the United Nations Security Council* (Hart Publishing 2004) 251.

33 See also UNSC Res 944 (29 September 1994) UN Doc S/RES/944, which terminates measures set out in resolutions UNSC Res 841 (1993), UNSC Res 873 (1993) and UNSC Res 917 (1994) in para 4. This, too, is a 'parallelism of competence' resolution.

34 United Nations Stabilization Mission in Haiti.

35 UNSC Res 1944 (14 October 2010) UN Doc S/RES/1944, preamble.
36 UNSC Res 2012 (14 October 2011) UN Doc S/RES/2012.
37 UNSC Res 1908 (19 January 2010) UN Doc S/RES/1908.
38 UNSC Res 1927 (4 June 2010) UN Doc S/RES/1927.
39 UNSC Res 2070 (12 October 2012) UN Doc S/RES/2070.
40 UNSC Res 2119 (10 October 2013) UN Doc S/RES/2119.
41 '*Determining* that the situation in Haiti continues to constitute a threat to international peace and security in the region, despite the progress achieved thus far', UNSC Res 1944 (14 October 2010) UN Doc S/RES/1944, preamble and UNSC Res 2012 (14 October 2011) UN Doc S/RES/2012, preamble (emphasis in original).
42 UNSC Res 2070 (12 October 2012) UN Doc S/RES/2070, preamble.
43 UNSC Res 1267 (15 October 1999) UN Doc S/RES/1267; UNSC Res 1333 (19 December 2000) UN Doc S/RES/1333; UNSC Res 1363 (30 July 2001) UN Doc S/RES/1363; UNSC Res 1386 (20 December 2001) UN Doc S/RES/1386; UNSC Res 1390 (16 January 2002) UN Doc S/RES/1390; UNSC Res 1413 (23 May 2002) UN Doc S/RES/1413; UNSC Res 1444 (27 December 2002) UN Doc S/RES/1444; UNSC Res 1510 (13 October 2003) UN Doc S/RES/1510; UNSC Res 1563 (17 September 2004) UN Doc S/RES/1563; UNSC Res 1623 (13 September 2005) UN Doc S/RES/1623; UNSC Res 1707 (12 September 2006) UN Doc S/RES/1707; UNSC Res 1776 (19 September 2007) UN Doc S/RES/1776; UNSC Res 1833 (22 September 2008) UN Doc S/RES/1833; UNSC Res 1890 (8 October 2009) UN Doc S/RES/1890.
44 UNSC Res 1388 (15 January 2002) UN Doc S/RES/1388.
45 International Security Assistance Force.
46 United Nations Assistance Mission to Afghanistan.
47 While UNAMA is a political mission proposed in to 'fulfil the tasks and responsibilities, including those related to human rights, the rule of law and gender issues, entrusted to the United Nations in the Bonn Agreement' (Report of the Secretary-General, 'The situation in Afghanistan and its implications for international peace and security' (2002) UN Doc A/56/875 para 97(a)), the ISAF was mandated to assist 'the Afghan Interim Authority in the maintenance of security in Kabul and its surrounding areas' (UNSC Res 1386 (20 December 2001) UN Doc S/RES/1386 para 3) in which participating Member States were authorised 'to take all necessary measures to fulfil its mandate' (UNSC Res 1386 (20 December 2001) UN Doc S/RES/1386 para 3).
48 See eg UNSC Res 1868 (23 March 2009) UN Doc S/RES/1868; UNSC Res 1917 (22 March 2010) UN Doc S/RES/1917; UNSC Res 1974 (22 March 2011) UN Doc S/RES/1974; UNSC Res 2041 (22 March 2012) UN Doc S/RES/2041; UNSC Res 2096 (19 March 2013) UN Doc S/RES/2096.
49 See eg UNSC Res 1943 (13 October 2010) UN Doc S/RES/1943; UNSC Res 2011 (12 October 2011) UN Doc S/RES/2011; UNSC Res 2069 (9 October 2012) UN Doc S/RES/2069; UNSC Res 2120 (10 October 2013) UN Doc S/RES/2120.
50 UNSC Res 1054 (26 April 1996) UN Doc S/RES/1054; UNSC Res 1070 (16 August 1996) UN Doc S/RES/1070; UNSC Res 1556 (30 July 2004) UN Doc S/RES/1556; UNSC Res 1564 (18 September 2004) UN Doc S/RES/1564; UNSC Res 1590 (24 March 2005) UN Doc S/RES/1590; UNSC Res 1591 (29 March 2005) UN Doc S/RES/1591; UNSC Res 1593 (7 April 2005) UN Doc S/RES/1593; UNSC Res 1627 (23 September 2005) UN Doc S/RES/1627; UNSC Res 1651 (21 December 2005) UN Doc S/RES/1651; UNSC Res 1663 (24 March 2006) UN Doc S/RES/1663; UNSC Res 1665 (29 March 2006) UN Doc S/RES/1665; UNSC Res 1672 (25 April 2006) UN Doc S/

RES/1672; UNSC Res 1679 (16 May 2006) UN Doc S/RES/1679; UNSC Res 1706 (31 August 2006) UN Doc S/RES/1706; UNSC Res 1709 (22 September 2006) UN Doc S/RES/1709; UNSC Res 1713 (29 September 2006) UN Doc S/RES/1713; UNSC Res 1714 (6 October 2006) UN Doc S/RES/1714; UNSC Res 1755 (30 April 2007) UN Doc S/RES/1755; UNSC Res 1769 (31 July 2007) UN Doc S/RES/1769; UNSC Res 1779 (28 September 2007) UN Doc S/RES/1779; UNSC Res 1784 (31 October 2007) UN Doc S/RES/1784; UNSC Res 1841 (15 October 2008) UN Doc S/RES/1841; UNSC Res 1891 (13 October 2009) UN Doc S/RES/1891; UNSC Res 1945 (14 October 2010) UN Doc S/RES/1945; UNSC Res 1982 (17 May 2011) UN Doc S/RES/1982; UNSC Res 1996 (8 July 2011) UN Doc S/RES/1996; UNSC Res 2035 (17 February 2012) UN Doc S/RES/2035; UNSC Res 2046 (2 May 2012) UN Doc S/RES/2046; UNSC Res 2063 (31 July 2012) UN Doc S/RES/2063; UNSC Res 2109 (11 July 2013) UN Doc S/RES/2109.

51 UNSC Res 1812 (30 April 2008) UN Doc S/RES/1812; UNSC Res 1828 (31 July 2008) UN Doc S/RES/1828; UNSC Res 1870 (30 April 2009) UN Doc S/RES/1870; UNSC Res 1881 (30 July 2009) UN Doc S/RES/1881; UNSC Res 1891 (13 October 2009) UN Doc S/RES/1891; UNSC Res 1935 (30 July 2010) UN Doc S/RES/1935; UNSC Res 1978 (27 April 2011) UN Doc S/RES/1978; UNSC Res 1997 (11 July 2011) UN Doc S/RES/1997; UNSC Res 2003 (29 July 2011) UN Doc S/RES/2003; UNSC Res 2024 (14 December 2011) UN Doc S/RES/2024; UNSC Res 2032 (22 December 2011) UN Doc S/RES/2032; UNSC Res 2047 (17 May 2012) UN Doc S/RES/2047; UNSC Res 2057 (5 July 2012) UN Doc S/RES/2057; UNSC Res 2063 (31 July 2012) UN Doc S/RES/2063; UNSC Res 2113 (30 July 2013) UN Doc S/RES/2113; UNSC Res 2126 (25 November 2013) UN Doc S/RES/2126.

52 UNSC Res 1372 (28 September 2001) UN Doc S/RES/1372, which terminated elements of Chapter VII resolutions UNSC Res 1054 (1996) and UNSC Res 1070 (1996).

53 UNSC Res 1990 (27 June 2011) UN Doc S/RES/1990.

54 UNSC Res 2024 (14 December 2011) UN Doc S/RES/2024; UNSC Res 2032 (22 December 2011) UN Doc S/RES/2032; UNSC Res 2047 (17 May 2012) UN Doc S/RES/2047; UNSC Res 2075 (16 November 2012) UN Doc S/RES/2075; UNSC Res 2104 (29 May 2013) UN Doc S/RES/2104; UNSC Res 2126 (25 November 2013) UN Doc S/RES/2126; UNSC Res 2156 (29 May 2014) UN Doc S/RES/2156; UNSC Res 2179 (14 October 2014) UN Doc S/RES/2179.

55 Established under Chapter VII by UNSC Res 1509 (19 September 2003) UN Doc S/RES/1509 and renewed under Chapter VII in UNSC Res 1626 (19 September 2005) UN Doc S/RES/1626, UNSC Res 1667 (31 March 2006) UN Doc S/RES/1667, UNSC Res 1712 (29 September 2006) UN Doc S/RES/1712, UNSC Res 1750 (30 March 2007) UN Doc S/RES/1750, UNSC Res 1777 (28 September 2007) UN Doc S/RES/1777, UNSC Res 1836 (29 September 2008) UN Doc S/RES/1836, UNSC Res 1885 (15 September 2009) UN Doc S/RES/1885, UNSC Res 1938 (15 September 2010) UN Doc S/RES/1938, UNSC Res 2008 (16 September 2011) UN Doc S/RES/2008, UNSC Res 2066 (17 September 2012) UN Doc S/RES/2066, UNSC Res 2116 (18 September 2013) UN Doc S/RES/2116, UNSC Res 2176 (15 September 2014) UN Doc S/RES/2176. Interestingly, the very first renewal of the mandate – S/RES/1561 (2004) – was not conducted under Chapter VII. Apart from this resolution, however, all renewal resolutions contained new determinations of a threat to the peace.

56 Established under Chapter VII by UNSC Res 1528 (27 February 2004) UN Doc S/RES/1528 and renewed under Chapter VII in the following: UNSC Res 1609

(24 June 2005) UN Doc S/RES/1609; UNSC Res 1652 (24 January 2006) UN Doc S/RES/1652; UNSC Res 1726 (15 December 2006) UN Doc S/RES/1726; UNSC Res 1739 (10 January 2007) UN Doc S/RES/1739; UNSC Res 1763 (29 June 2007) UN Doc S/RES/1763; UNSC Res 1765 (16 July 2007) UN Doc S/RES/1765; UNSC Res 1826 (29 July 2008) UN Doc S/RES/1826; UNSC Res 1880 (30 July 2009) UN Doc S/RES/1880; UNSC Res 1911 (28 January 2010) UN Doc S/RES/1911; UNSC Res 1924 (27 May 2010) UN Doc S/RES/1924; UNSC Res 1933 (30 June 2010) UN Doc S/RES/1933; UNSC Res 1962 (20 December 2010) UN Doc S/RES/1962; UNSC Res 1981 (13 May 2011) UN Doc S/RES/1981; UNSC Res 2000 (27 July 2011) UN Doc S/RES/2000; UNSC Res 2062 (26 July 2012) UN Doc S/RES/2062; UNSC Res 2112 (30 July 2013) UN Doc S/RES/2112; UNSC Res 2162 (25 June 2014) UN Doc S/RES/2162. With the exception of UNSC Res 1981 (2011) all these resolutions contained new determinations of a threat to the peace.

57 A total of 59 resolutions.

58 UNSC Res 660 (2 August 1990) UN Doc S/RES/660; UNSC Res 687 (3 April 1991) UN Doc S/RES/687; UNSC Res 688 (5 April 1991) UN Doc S/RES/688; UNSC Res 1137 (12 November 1997) UN Doc S/RES/1137. It is also noteworthy that between 1997 and the invasion of Iraq by multi-national forces in 2003, there was no determination of a threat under art 39.

59 UNSC Res 1483 (22 May 2003) UN Doc S/RES/1483, UNSC Res 1511 (16 October 2003) UN Doc S/RES/1511, UNSC Res 1518 (24 November 2003) UN Doc S/RES/1518, UNSC Res 1546 (8 June 2004) UN Doc S/RES/1546, UNSC Res 1637 (8 November 2005) UN Doc S/RES/1637, UNSC Res 1723 (28 November 2006) UN Doc S/RES/1723, and UNSC Res 1790 (18 December 2007) UN Doc S/RES/1790 are Chapter VII resolutions that have clear, express determinations of a threat to the peace under Article 39; UNSC Res 1472 (28 March 2003) UN Doc S/RES/1472, UNSC Res 1476 (24 April 2003) UN Doc S/RES/1476, UNSC Res 1490 (3 July 2003) UN Doc S/RES/1490, and UNSC Res 1762 (27 June 2007) UN Doc S/RES/1762 are Chapter VII resolutions that do not make mention of any determination. UNSC Res 1859 (22 December 2008) UN Doc S/RES/1859, UNSC Res 1905 (21 December 2009) UN Doc S/RES/1905, UNSC Res 1956 (15 December 2010) UN Doc S/RES/1956, UNSC Res 1957 (15 December 2010) UN Doc S/RES/1957, UNSC Res 1958 (15 December 2010) UN Doc S/RES/1958 are also Chapter VII resolutions that do not make mention of a determination of threat to the peace; however, they are example of 'parallelism of competence', ie necessarily issued under Chapter VII to revoke a previous Chapter VII decision, such as the Oil for Food programme.

60 Sidney Bailey and Sam Daws, *The Procedure of the UN Security Council* (Oxford University Press 1998) 271.

61 Global Issues Research Group, 'Research analysts memorandum: summary of UN Security Council Resolutions, 1946–1998' (Foreign and Commonwealth Office 1999).

62 UNSC Verbatim Record (8 January 2007) UN Doc S/PV.5615.

63 UNSC Res 678 (29 November 1990) UN Doc S/RES/678; UNSC Res 1483 (22 May 2003) UN Doc S/RES/1483; UNSC Res 1511 (16 October 2003) UN Doc S/RES/1511.

64 UNSC Res 770 (13 August 1992) UN Doc S/RES/770; UNSC Res 787 (16 November 1992) UN Doc S/RES/787; UNSC Res 816 (31 March 1993) UN Doc S/RES/816; UNSC Res 820 (17 April 1993) UN Doc S/RES/820; UNSC Res 836 (4 June 1993) UN Doc S/RES/836; UNSC Res 908 (31 March 1994) UN Doc S/RES/908; UNSC Res 1031 (15 December 1995) UN Doc S/

RES/1031; UNSC Res 1088 (12 December 1996) UN Doc S/RES/1088; UNSC Res 1174 (15 June 1998) UN Doc S/RES/1174; UNSC Res 1575 (22 November 2004) UN Doc S/RES/1575.

65 UNSC Res 794 (3 December 1992) UN Doc S/RES/794; UNSC Res 1744 (21 February 2007) UN Doc S/RES/1744.

66 UNSC Res 875 (16 October 1993) UN Doc S/RES/875; UNSC Res 940 (31 July 1994) UN Doc S/RES/940; UNSC Res 1529 (29 February 2004) UN Doc S/RES/1529.

67 UNSC Res 929 (22 June 1994) UN Doc S/RES/929.

68 UNSC Res 1080 (15 November 1996) UN Doc S/RES/1080; UNSC Res 1484 (30 May 2003) UN Doc S/RES/1484; UNSC Res 1671 (25 April 2006) UN Doc S/RES/1671.

69 UNSC Res 1101 (28 March 1997) UN Doc S/RES/1101; UNSC Res 1114 (19 June 1997) UN Doc S/RES/1114.

70 UNSC Res 1125 (6 August 1997) UN Doc S/RES/1125.

71 UNSC Res 1132 (8 October 1997) UN Doc S/RES/1132.

72 UNSC Res 1244 (10 June 1999) UN Doc S/RES/1244.

73 UNSC Res 1264 (15 September 1999) UN Doc S/RES/1264.

74 UNSC Res 1386 (20 December 2001) UN Doc S/RES/1386; UNSC Res 1510 (13 October 2003) UN Doc S/RES/1510.

75 UNSC Res 1464 (4 February 2003) UN Doc S/RES/1464; UNSC Res 1528 (27 February 2004) UN Doc S/RES/1528.

76 UNSC Res 1497 (1 August 2003) UN Doc S/RES/1497.

77 UNSC Res 1778 (25 September 2007) UN Doc S/RES/1778.

78 See eg UNSC Res 955 (8 November 1994) UN Doc S/RES/955 on Rwanda; UNSC Res 1267 (15 October 1999) UN Doc S/RES/1267 on Afghanistan; UNSC Res 1037 (15 January 1996) UN Doc S/RES/1037 on Croatia; UNSC Res 1967 (19 January 2011) UN Doc S/RES/1967 on the Cote D'Ivoire; UNSC Res 1973 (17 March 2011) UN Doc S/RES/1973 on Libya. All of these contained this explicit phrase.

79 Bruno Simma with others (eds), *The Charter of the United Nations: A Commentary* (Oxford University Press 2002) 584.

80 See eg UNSC Verbatim Record (22 August 1947) UN Doc S/PV.138, 2175, where UNSC Res 27 (1947) on the Indonesian question made reference to provisional measures in the same line as article 40 without explicit reference to Chapter VII; in UNSC Verbatim Record (14 May 1970) UN Doc S/PV.1538, UNSC Verbatim Record (14 May 1970) UN Doc S/PV.1540(OR), and UNSC Verbatim Record (15 May 1970) UN Doc S/PV.1541 the same was believed of resolution 279 (1970) on the withdrawal of Israeli forces from Lebanon.

81 UNSC Res 54 (15 July 1948) UN Doc S/RES/54 paras 1–2 (original emphasis).

82 UNSC Res 83 (27 June 1950) UN Doc S/RES/83; see also UNSC Res 84 (7 July 1950) UN Doc S/RES/84 (original emphasis).

83 UNSC Res 253 (29 May 1968) UN Doc S/RES/253, preamble.

84 As far back as 1947, the US argued that UNSC Res (1947) was tantamount to provisional measures under art 40 of the Charter. See UNSC Verbatim Record (22 August 1947) UN Doc S/PV.138, 2175; see also, more recently in 1970, the interpretations of Syria (UNSC Verbatim Record (12 May 1970) UN Doc S/PV.1538 paras 120–21), Poland (UNSC Verbatim Record (14 May 1970) UN Doc S/PV.1540(OR) para 13) and Colombia (UNSC Verbatim Record (15 May 1970) UN Doc S/PV.1541 para 8), where provisional measures were deemed to have been taken in UNSC Res 280 (1970) despite the absence of specific wording reflecting it.

85 See eg Thomas M Franck, *Fairness in International Law and Institutions* (Clarendon Press 1995) 1–46; David Armstrong, Theo Farrell and Helene

Lambert, *International Law and International Relations* (Cambridge University Press 2012) 113–14.
86 *South-West Africa – Voting Procedure* (Advisory Opinion) [1955] ICJ Rep 67 (Separate Opinion of Judge Lauterpacht) 118–19.
87 UNSC Res 2118 (27 September 2013) UN Doc S/RES/2118 para 1.
88 ibid para 4.
89 ibid para 21.
90 ibid preamble.
91 Frederic L Kirgis Jr, 'The Security Council's first fifty years' (1995) 89(3) *American Journal of International Law* 506; see also E M Miller, 'Legal aspects of the United Nations action in the Congo' (1961) 55 *American Journal of International Law* 1, 4.
92 UNSC Res 1376 (9 November 2001) UN Doc S/RES/1376, preamble (emphasis in original).
93 Security Council Report, 'Security Council action under Chapter VII: myths and realities' (23 June 2008) 5.
94 John Bellinger, 'The Security Council Resolution on Syria: is it legally binding?' *Lawfare Blog* (28 September 2013).
95 Vaughan Lowe and others (eds), *The United Nations Security Council and War: The Evolution of Thought and Practice since 1945* (Oxford University Press 2010) 36.
96 See eg UNSC Res 1376 (9 November 2001) UN Doc S/RES/1376 on the Democratic Republic of the Congo (DRC).
97 See eg UNSC Res 1737 (27 December 2006) UN Doc S/RES/1737 on Iranian nuclear proliferation, where the Council was '[a]*cting* under Article 41 of Chapter VII of the Charter of the United Nations' without prior mention of art 39 or a specific threat to the peace (emphasis in original).
98 UNSC Res 733 (23 January 1992) UN Doc S/RES/733.
99 ibid para 5.
100 ibid preamble.
101 UNSC Res 841 (16 June 1993) UN Doc S/RES/841.
102 UNSC Verbatim Record (16 June 1993) UN Doc S/PV.3238 at 3–5.
103 ibid 11.
104 ibid. Pakistan also makes mention of the threat to the peace in passing, ibid 14, as does China, ibid 20.
105 China, ibid 21. See also, Canada (ibid 6); France (ibid 9); Pakistan (ibid 15); Brazil (ibid 18); USA (ibid 18).
106 France, ibid.
107 USA, ibid 19.

6 Equality before the law

Introduction

Equality before the law is at the core of both General Assembly[1] and Security Council[2] rule of law activities to support development and the promotion of international standards, particularly in post-conflict societies. At the national level, it is a cross-cutting theme that includes gender equality, self-determination and numerous other elements that fall outside the immediate scope of the current discussion around Security Council, which operates on an entirely different plane. This is not to deny or undermine the importance of the Council's promotion of the component at the domestic level, rather to emphasise the focus of this book upon a discussion and analysis of state behaviour and the behaviour of the Council on the supranational plane. There are, nonetheless, similarities in the conceptualisation of equality in the Council's decision-making process, relating to the way in which states must be viewed. An apt analogy once presented by Professor Alejandro Lorite Escorihuela referred to states as *triangles*; extending this analogy, before the Council, states should be viewed simply as three-sided, without further attention as to features such as size, colour, or how perpendicular the sides are.

States must therefore be equal in the eyes of the Council, and reactions by the Council to threats against the international peace must be seized in an equal manner, without prejudice, preference, or distinction. To impose different standards upon states would be unequal; what equality can be said to exist if some threats are left unaddressed by the Council when comparable situations have been addressed in other countries? An unequal decision-making process is also highlighted by contradictions in the standards applied to states by the Council, holding some accountable for actions or violations in which that others surreptitiously or flagrantly engage. Equality before the law is therefore the impartial seizure of a threat to the international peace and the imposition of equally applicable international standards upon all states by the Council.

The mechanism for equality before the law currently exists at the Council, which has *kompetenz kompetenz* insofar as its own workload and focus of attention is concerned; the Council also has the power to convene both at the request of any member of the Security Council[3] and urgently to respond in real-time to threats.[4] In essence, the Council may direct its efforts freely to whichever cause it deems necessary under the wide scope of authority granted by the UN Charter and its rules of procedure – there are no procedural obstacles to an equal seizure of affairs at the Council level and, in theory at least, equality of states is an easily achievable goal.

Council responses to conflicts

However, the existence of de jure equality before the law does not immediately remove the possibility of a different justice model prevailing de facto.[5] Despite the potential for the Council to grant bespoke, rapid and effective responses to each potential threat to the peace owing to the ability to meet at a moment's notice and take legally binding decisions implementing both non-military and armed force measures, the reality at times fails to live up to such expectations. It has been alleged that the Council is lethargic in responding to some incidents, whereas others are granted the full attention and force of the Council.[6]

Is Syria about Libya?

The March 2011 Syrian government crackdowns on civilian protesters first appeared as a topic for Council discussion not – as one might expect – as a stand-alone issue, but rather on the periphery of an existing Council meeting in April 2011 on the Middle East situation focused on the Palestinian question.[7] Despite deep concern over 'the Government's brutal crackdown on political protests . . . result[ing] in more than 200 deaths'[8] at the time, unequivocal condemnation of the violence against and killing of peaceful demonstrators[9] and calls for the Syrian authorities to 'renounce the use of force against demonstrators'[10] by three of the P5 members, it was deemed by Russia 'unacceptable [for] any external interference in Syrian affairs'[11] to take place. A public debate was held later that month,[12] intimating that the Council might have begun to address the situation in Syria as a potential threat to the international peace separate from the Middle East question as a whole; nonetheless, this did not come to fruition and the Syrian situation remained addressed within the general theme of the Middle East question for a year,[13] with the first statement by the Council condemning the situation in Syria[14] emerging under the aegis of the situation in the Middle East.

Indeed, even when presented in February 2012 with credible information that 'the death toll . . . often exceeds 100 civilians per day . . . [and] the total number of people killed so far [was] certainly well more than 7,500 . . . [with] 25,000 refugees . . . [and b]etween 100,000 and 200,000 people internally displaced',[15] little was done by the Council to intercede in the situation owing to a stalemate between the P5 members. Against this backdrop, the only consensus that could be reached was the implementation of a six-point proposal, brokered by former UN Secretary-General Kofi Annan in his capacity as Joint Special Envoy for the UN and League of Arab States.[16] In the year between Syria first appearing on the Council's agenda in April 2011 and the first Council resolution in April 2012, two vetoed Chapter VII resolutions[17] were tabled. Undermining the

Council's capacity to respond in real-time in contrast to the Assembly, it was the latter that on 19 December 2011 overwhelmingly adopted a resolution cosponsored by 61 states condemning 'the continued grave and systematic human rights violations by the Syrian authorities . . . [and calling] upon the Syrian authorities to immediately put an end to all human rights violations . . . and . . . an immediate end to all violence in the Syrian Arab Republic',[18] while the Council had yet to implement any binding resolutions and had itself only officially managed to break its silence on the situation in Syria through a presidential statement three months earlier.

Frankfurt has posited that '[t]hose who are concerned with equality aim at outcomes that are in some pertinent way indistinguishable . . .';[19] this can be interpreted not as an expectation that the facts themselves should be indistinguishable, but rather that the response should be such. Indeed, it would be misguided to suggest that the situation in Syria is exactly the same as the facts of Libya and, without addressing the deep-rooted political, ethnic and geographical characteristics of each country and its conflict it would be remiss to attempt such a comparison, which indeed divided the Council members during discussions on the situation in Syria. While Russia identified that '[t]he situation in Syria cannot be considered in the Council separately from the Libyan experience',[20] the US defended 'strong Council action on Syria . . . [which] is not about military intervention . . . or Libya'.[21] Clearly, calls for restraint and reflection on the Libyan experience by the Council was key to Russia's hesitation to intervene in Syria in the same way as Libya.[22]

However, the intersection of the situations in both countries becomes relevant to this component of equality within the framework of the rule of law when addressing how the Council responded to each potential threat; this is particularly true when in the case of Libya, less than a year passed between the first discussion of the situation at the Council[23] in February 2011 and the declaration of liberation of Libya by the new National Transitional Council,[24] including the passing of a Chapter VII resolution[25] authorising NATO military involvement in the subsequent Operation Unified Protector, officially ending on 31 October 2011.[26] In contrast, this same period of time – a year – was how long elapsed between the situation in Syria reaching the agenda of the Council and its first resolution on the matter; of course, over three years later, the situation is not yet resolved and there has not been a single Chapter VII resolution emerging from the Council despite the use of chemical weapons in Syria, the standing total of over 4.8 million refugees[27] and hundreds of thousands of deaths.[28]

Despite this severe disparity in the length of time that was taken in dealing with each situation, the situation in Libya appears to have been afforded far more attention by the Security Council. In fact, in 2011 the subject of Libya was tabled as an individual subject for discussion twenty-three times[29] and of the four Chapter VII resolutions on Libya in 2011[30] it took a mere four days from the Under-Secretary-General's briefing on 22 February 2011 to reach unanimous consensus for a Chapter VII resolution[31] imposing an arms embargo on the country,[32] travel ban on key figures of the Gaddafi regime[33] and asset freeze on the Gaddafi family,[34] in addition to referring the situation to the prosecutor of the International Criminal Court, a previously contentious issue.[35]

Although the situation in Syria has been discussed numerous times since the beginning of the conflict in 2011,[36] with fourteen resolutions being passed – mostly relating to military observers and UNSMIS[37] – there have been no sanctions imposed, no criminal accountability and no asset freezes on the Assad regime in the same manner of the Gaddafis. In contrast to Ibrahim Dabbashi, the current UN representative for Libya who renounced allegiance to the Gaddafi regime early on in the Libyan conflict before Gaddafi was toppled, the Syrian representation to the UN remains occupied by Bashar Jaafari, a loyalist of the Assad regime and frequent speaker at the Council itself. The lack of such sanctions has facilitated the payment of tens of millions of dollars of contracts to those closely associated with the Assad regime, including his wife and close associates;[38] since the UN is under no obligation to abide by the terms of state or regional sanctions regimes but rather only those of the UN itself, the aid has continued to flow to individuals and organisations within Syria currently subject to EU and US sanctions.[39]

This referral to the ICC in the case of Libya is remarkable for the identification by the Council that the 'widespread and systematic attacks [that took] place in the Libyan Arab Jamahiriya against the civilian population may amount to crimes against humanity';[40] the far more moderately worded resolutions[41] than that of UNSC Resolution 1970 calling for a cessation of violence in Syria have been consistently vetoed[42] or watered down[43] for the purposes of passing through the Council. This is despite protestations by members of the Security Council at the 'especially horrific campaign . . . [of] indiscriminate violence . . . [and] abhorrent brutality';[44] allegations of war crimes by the Office of the High Commissioner for Human Rights,[45] the Human Rights Council[46] and various NGOs;[47] the apparent breach of International Humanitarian Law;[48] and an investigative UN Mission conclusion 'that chemical weapons have been used in the ongoing conflict between the parties in the Syrian Arab Republic'.[49]

According to the UN's own 2015 OCHA Syria report,[50] 13.5 million people are in need of humanitarian assistance, of which children account for 6 million; meanwhile, the Directorate-General for European Civil Protection and Humanitarian Aid Operations (ECHO)[51] has deemed the situation in Syria the largest humanitarian crisis since the Second World War. Nonetheless, since its initial stalemate over the subject, the Council has moved ever-slowly and cautiously on the matter of the Syrian civil war, initially hesitant as a political body to make any bold statements apart from condemnation of attacks by terrorists or on diplomatic premises.[52]

Council action in analogous situations

Efficacy and swiftness is, in general, typical of the behaviour of the Council, as one might expect from the powers to act it is granted unrestrained by the necessity of a framework of forward planning and its self-regulating rules of procedure. In the case of Kosovo, the process from the first Chapter VII resolution calling for steps to achieve a peaceful solution and imposing an arms embargo[53] to authorisation for NATO intervention to secure the withdrawal of Yugoslav forces from Kosovo[54] took barely over a year; similarly, despite being on the agenda of the Council for many years – with the first resolution issued in 1997[55] – the Council's response to the internal conflict in the Central African Republic[56] intensified even before[57] the assessment of the Under Secretary-General/Special Adviser on the Prevention of Genocide that 'there [was] a risk of genocide in this country'[58] when the violence was noted to have intensified. The conflict in the Democratic Republic of Congo is arguably the deadliest since the Second World War;[59] the Council dedicated the same number of meetings to the situation[60] and adopted 12 decisions between 2011 and 2014[61] and has consistently addressed the threat through over 40 Chapter VII resolutions since the Great War of Africa broke out in 1998 – more than two a year. Most recently, perhaps, when conflict erupted in South Sudan, barely a month passed before the Council bolstered peacekeeping forces in the country through a Chapter VII resolution.[62]

The Syrian example, therefore, seems to be an exception to a pattern of rapid response. The failure of the Council adequately to address the threat and its resulting impact on global peace and security, as well as humanitarian affairs highlights the impact of a rapid, efficacious and appropriate response to conflict.

Equality in international standards towards nuclear threats

One of the principal obstacles to equality before the law at the Council is its treatment of nuclear capacities of states, which varies widely. Of the eight known nuclear-weapon states[63] and Israel, which maintains ambiguity over its possession or lack thereof,[64] and the remaining 190 states parties to the Non-Proliferation Treaty (NPT),[65] the Democratic People's Republic of Korea (DPRK) that has been singled out by the Council in multiple rounds of sanctions.[66] Moreover, of the eight nuclear-power states, only the P5 members have signed[67] or ratified[68] the treaty, leaving India and Pakistan not only as the sole two known nuclear powers not to have acceded to or ratified the NPT[69] but also one of the few states not to have done so[70] alongside the ambiguously reticent Israel and South Sudan – the newest country in the world. All other UN members have signed the NPT.

The case of the Democratic People's Republic of Korea

The DPRK initially signed the Non-proliferation Treaty on 12 September 1985, before announcing it would withdraw on 12 March 1993 as a result of the resumption of joint US/South Korean 'Team Spirit' exercises and IAEA demands to open military sites to inspection.[71] Almost immediately, three P5 members issued a statement declaring that '[s]ince the NPT is an essential element of international peace and security, DPRK withdrawal from the NPT would constitute a serious threat to regional and international stability',[72] prompting the Council to pass UNSC Resolution 825[73] 'reaffirming the crucial contribution which progress in non-proliferation can make to the maintenance of international peace and security'[74] and calling upon the DPRK to reconsider its announcement. Despite suspending its decision to withdraw from the NPT, over the following year there was reluctance on the part of the DPRK to allow intervention in what it deemed sovereign affairs[75] and it finally withdrew its membership from the IAEA in 1994 and, save for a deal brokered with the US,[76] would have led to the withdrawal of the DPRK from the NPT[77] had it not been for the moratorium announced in the Agreed Framework. In 2003, however, the DPRK decided conclusively to withdraw from the NPT[78] and has since not rejoined despite concerted efforts and significant pressure by the Council and its individual members.

After the first ballistic missile tests by the DPRK in 2006, although the Council stopped short of a Chapter VII resolution, it nonetheless condemned the launch of ballistic missiles and demanded that it suspend all activities related to its ballistic missile programme.[79] Three days after the DPRK launched its missiles into the Sea of Japan, India undertook its first test[80] of its Agni-III Intermediate-range ballistic missile with a more than 3,000km range and a payload weight of 1.5 tons;[81] there was no Council condemnation, or even mention, of this launch at the Council meeting of 15 July 2006, despite direct reference during the discussion of UNSC Resolution 1540's prohibition of weapons and their delivery.[82] The Council's first Chapter VII resolution on the DPRK[83] was issued in response to its decision to carry out an underground nuclear test later that year and, in addition to condemning the nuclear test itself[84] imposed an obligation on the DPRK to rejoin the NPT.[85]

UNSC Resolution 1874,[86] following another DPRK nuclear test in 2009, reiterated much of the language and demands of its predecessor, again imposing the obligation on the DPRK to accede to a treaty it had decided to withdraw from;[87] as Joyner highlights, 'the Council's demand that the DPRK re-join the NPT is the only example . . . of the Security Council demanding that a state re-accede to a treaty from which that state had duly withdrawn according to the treaty's terms'.[88] Despite the irregularity of the measure, which has not been seen before or since the DPRK example, this call for a return to the NPT has been reiterated against the DPRK as recently as 2013,[89] and mentioned in 2016.[90] As penance for non-compliance, UNSC Resolution 2270 imposed the toughest sanctions yet on the DPRK, including a discretionary embargo on any item except for food and medicine and total bans on foreign investment or sales of fuel.

India and Pakistan

While the Council has been adamant for the DPRK to maintain its adherence to the NPT, there has been no such reaction to the nuclear statuses of India and Pakistan. Despite the apparent threat highlighted by the IAEA,[91] there has been no serious denouncement of India or Pakistan for their nuclear possession, attempts to construct a nuclear weapon or proliferation of delivery methods through missile and other technology. Notwithstanding the predictable protestations by both states,[92] UNSC Resolution 1172,[93] issued against India and

Pakistan in the wake of their 1998 nuclear tests, is a relatively weak resolution in comparison to the forceful nature of the Council's reaction to the DPRK: it was not adopted under Chapter VII, it did not call for the dismantling of their existing weaponry, it did not impose any obligations or stipulations to join the NPT and condemned only the tests themselves, rather than the fact that either state had acquired nuclear weaponry. Far from condemning the test in 1974, which took place after the NPT came into force, 'the United States in June 1974 proceeded to ship an instalment of previously approved uranium fuel to India's Tarapur reactor . . . [concluding] that the Indian test did not violate any agreement with the United States'[94] and France 'through its Atomic Energy Commission, sent a congratulatory message to the chairman of the Indian Atomic Energy Commission'.[95]

UNSC Resolution 1540 was passed in response to the threat of illicit procurement of nuclear and nuclear delivery weaponry by non-State actors; however, despite a network of Pakistani agents[96] selling clandestine nuclear information and components to numerous states including the DPRK, Iran and Libya,[97] allegedly with the complicity of Pakistani authorities,[98] Pakistan has continued on its path to nuclear delivery proliferation with tests on nuclear-capable missile systems on a regular basis.[99] While Pakistan's two research reactors currently run on low-enriched uranium, which poses no weapons threat, highly Enriched Uranium remained in Pakistan until 2010 at least.[100] Civilian nuclear programmes, too, have remained unaffected by the leak of information by the Khan network, with three currently operating nuclear reactors[101] in Pakistan, a fourth on the cusp of completion, a further five due by 2020, and the supply of Chinese nuclear reactors to Pakistan in 2013. in addition to a recent $6.5bn loan for the construction of twin nuclear power stations in Karachi.[102]

Such deals are in contradiction to the Guidelines[103] of the Nuclear Suppliers Group,[104] of which China is a member, which state that 'suppliers should not authorize the transfer of enrichment and reprocessing facilities if the recipient is not Party to the NPT';[105] Pakistan has never signed the NPT and therefore, although the Guidelines are not legally binding, China's defiance of the 'fundamental principles'[106] of an organisation created to counter the proliferation of nuclear weapons undermines its position when addressing nuclear proliferation elsewhere, notably on the Security Council. Despite findings by the United States Congress that '[w]hile U.S. and Pakistani officials continue to express confidence in controls over Pakistan's nuclear weapons, continued instability in the country could impact these safeguards'[107] and Pakistan's outright refusal[108] of US demands to commence negotiations to accede to the Fissile Material Cut-off Treaty (FMCT), which bans production of fissile material suitable for use in the manufacture of nuclear weaponry, no repercussions have followed.

Neighbouring India has similarly made no efforts to participate in the NPT[109] and only gradually accepted opening its nuclear facilities to the International Atomic Energy Agency (IAEA).[110] Despite over 20 instances of ballistic missile testing since 2006 alone[111] there has been no equal pressure on India to dismantle its nuclear programme, to desist from missile testing or to comply with legislative encroachment of the Council on the international legal field by signing the NPT.[112] Moreover, India has signed nuclear deals with numerous states, including most of the P5 members – France,[113] the US,[114] the Russian Federation[115] and the UK,[116] as well as ongoing negotiations on a bilateral Civil Nuclear Agreement with others.[117] India's pursuit of increased nuclear technology cannot be argued to be purely for pacific reasons;[118] not only did the Russian Federation deliver its second nuclear-powered submarine to India in 2012,[119] the P5 member is alleged to have 'continued to be the main supplier of technology and equipment to India's . . . naval nuclear propulsion programs'.[120] India leads even some P5 Council Members in terms of the breadth of their nuclear capabilities.[121]

India's proliferation of weaponry is in direct and blatant conflagration of UNSC Resolution 1540[122] – a Chapter VII resolution – issued long before its most recent tests were carried out,

> [a]ffirming that proliferation of nuclear, chemical and biological weapons, as well as their means of delivery [defined for the purpose of this resolution only as missiles, rockets and other unmanned systems capable of delivering nuclear, chemical, or biological weapons, that are specially designed for such use] constitutes a threat to international peace and security . . .[123]

In addition to the Council members of US,[124] Russian Federation[125] and China[126] continuing to flout this affirmation and concurrent Pakistani nuclear development, India has been repeatedly bolstered by Council member state support for its pacific nuclear and defensive weapon delivery programmes. Although there have been calls for both to ratify the Comprehensive Nuclear Test Ban Treaty (CTBT), neither has done so to date.

Conclusions

The Council appears to set independent standards both with respect to conflicts and other threats to the peace such as nuclear proliferation. However, in some situations, it would appear, the Council appears more forthcoming in its efforts to direct attention and quell incidents of violence or potential threats to the peace than others, and such consensus is not immediately forthcoming in all situations. Syria simultaneously highlights the difficulties of an adequate response to conflict and those of political motivations that appear to be behind the decision-making process.[127] While there can be no definitive means of measuring equality of the Council's attention to perceived threats to the international peace, a clear indication is the amount of time expended, effort exerted and decisions taken in response to any given issue.

During a 2010 discussion on the rule of law at the Council level, emphasis was made on the necessity for the Council to hold itself to the same standards it imposes upon states. The Russian Federation identified that 'in adhering to standards of international law in its activity, [the Council] sets an example by complying with the law'.[128] However, not only have Council members failed to adhere to the same standards they impose on other states, there has been no explanation for the seemingly contradictory stances the Council has taken in, on the one hand, the Indian and Pakistani situations and, on the other, the case of the DPRK. It remains unclear in what way the aspirations of India and Pakistan to procure and expand both civilian and military capacities within the framework or nuclear powers and the very same of the DPRK might differ. Nonetheless, the two situations have been approached by the Council in wildly different manners. The insistence on incrementally tighter sanctions against the DPRK, its vilification by the Council for actions that have been carried out with impunity by other states and the imposition of standards upon the DPRK that are not imposed on other states, including Council members themselves, surely points towards an unequal application of the laws emerging from the Council.

Notes

1 See eg UNGA Res 61/39 (18 December 2006) UN Doc A/RES/61/39; UNGA Res 62/70 (8 January 2008) UN Doc A/RES/62/70; UNGA Res 63/128 (15 January 2009) UN Doc A/RES/63/128.
2 See eg UNSC Presidential Statement 15 (2003) UN Doc S/PRST/2003/15; UNSC Presidential Statement 2 (2004) UN Doc S/PRST/2004/2; UNSC Presidential Statement 32 (2004) UN Doc S/PRST/2004/32; UNSC Presidential Statement 28 (2006) UN Doc S/PRST/2006/28.
3 UNSC Provisional Rules of Procedure (1946) UN Doc S/96/Rev.7, r 2.
4 See UNSC Verbatim Record (20 August 2013) UN Doc S/PV.7020 (2013); UN Press Release, 'Ukraine in emergency meeting, calls on Security Council to stop military intervention by Russian Federation' (1 March 2014).
5 See eg Rachel Kleinfeld, 'Competing definitions of the rule of law' in Thomas Carothers (ed), *Promoting the Rule of Law: In Search of Knowledge* (Carnegie Endowment for International Peace 2006) 38.
6 See eg Pakistan, UNSC Verbatim Record (27 August 2008) UN Doc S/PV.5968 (Resumption 1) 24.
7 UNSC Verbatim Record (21 April 2011) UN Doc S/PV.6520.
8 US ibid 13.
9 UK ibid 15.
10 France ibid 21.
11 Russia ibid 27.
12 UNSC Verbatim Record (27 April 2011) UN Doc S/PV.6524.
13 See eg UNSC Verbatim Record 6562 (23 June 2011) UN Doc S/PV.6562; UNSC Verbatim Record 6590 (26 July 2011) UN Doc S/PV.6590; UNSC Verbatim Record (3 August 2011) UN Doc S/PV.6598; UNSC Verbatim Record (12 March 2012) UN Doc S/PV.6734; UNSC Verbatim Record 6650 (9 November 2011) UN Doc S/PV.6650).
14 UNSC Presidential Statement 16 (2011) UN Doc S/PRST/2011/16.
15 UNSC Verbatim Record (28 February 2012) UN Doc S/PV.6725, 2.
16 UNSC Res 2042 (14 April 2012) UN Doc S/RES/2042.
17 UNSC Draft Res (4 October 2011) UN Doc S/2011/612; UNSC Draft Res (4 February 2012) UN Doc S/2012/77.
18 UNGA Res 66/176 (24 February 2012) UN Doc A/RES/66/176, para 1.
19 Harry Frankfurt, 'Equality and respect' (1997) 64(1) *Social Research* 3, 9.
20 Russia, UNSC Verbatim Record (4 October 2011) UN Doc S/PV.6627, 4.
21 US ibid 8.

22 Russia ibid 4.
23 UNSC Verbatim Record (22 February 2011) UN Doc S/PV.6486.
24 'NTC declares liberation of Libya' *Al Jazeera* (24 October 2011).
25 UNSC Res 1973 (17 March 2011) UN Doc S/RES/1973.
26 UNSC Res 2009 (16 September 2011) UN Doc S/RES/2009 para 20 repealed the authorisation to use 'all necessary measures' in UNSC Res 1973 (2011).
27 As of 16 August 2016 (Source: UNHCR, Government of Turkey) http://data.unhcr.org/syrianrefugees/regional.php#_ga=1.82479254.1649110338.1472719329 (last accessed 11 November 2016).
28 Although the UN has ceased updating its official figures, other sources point to this number. The exact number is extremely divisive. For an excellent analysis, see Adam Taylor, '200,000 dead? Why Syria's rising death toll is so divisive' *Washington Post* (3 December 2014).
29 UNSC Verbatim Record (22 February 2011) UN Doc S/PV.6486; UNSC Verbatim Record (25 February 2011) UN Doc S/PV.6490; UNSC Verbatim Record (26 February 2011) UN Doc S/PV.6491; UNSC Verbatim Record (17 March 2011) UN Doc S/PV.6498; UNSC Verbatim Record (24 March 2011) UN Doc S/PV.6505; UNSC Verbatim Record (28 March 2011) UN Doc S/PV.6507; UNSC Verbatim Record (4 April 2011) UN Doc S/PV.6509; UNSC Verbatim Record (3 May 2011) UN Doc S/PV.6527; UNSC Verbatim Record (4 May 2011) UN Doc S/PV.6528; UNSC Verbatim Record (9 May 2011) UN Doc S/PV.6530; UNSC Verbatim Record (31 May 2011) UN Doc S/PV.6541; UNSC Verbatim Record (15 June 2011) UN Doc S/PV.6555; UNSC Verbatim Record (27 June 2011) UN Doc S/PV.6566; UNSC Verbatim Record (28 July 2011) UN Doc S/PV.6595; UNSC Verbatim Record (30 August 2011) UN Doc S/PV.6606; UNSC Verbatim Record (16 September 2011) UN Doc S/PV.6620; UNSC Verbatim Record (26 September 2011) UN Doc S/PV.6622; UNSC Verbatim Record (26 October 2011) UN Doc S/PV.6639; UNSC Verbatim Record (27 October 2011) UN Doc S/PV.6640; UNSC Verbatim Record (31 October 2011) UN Doc S/PV.6644; UNSC Verbatim Record (2 November 2011) UN Doc S/PV.6647; UNSC Verbatim Record (2 December 2011) UN Doc S/PV.6673; UNSC Verbatim Record (22 December 2011) UN Doc S/PV.6698.
30 UNSC Res 1973 (17 March 2011) UN Doc S/RES/1973; UNSC Res 2009 (16 September 2011) UN Doc S/RES/2009; UNSC Res 2016 (27 October 2011) UN Doc S/RES/2016.
31 UNSC Res 1970 (2011), passed with no abstentions.
32 ibid para 9.
33 ibid para 15.
34 ibid para 17.
35 This was the first referral to the ICC without abstentions; the only other, on 31 March 2005 in UNSC Res 1593 on Sudan featured abstentions by Algeria, Brazil and, more importantly, China and the US, both of which are P5 members and neither of which are signatories to the Rome Statute.
36 UNSC Verbatim Record (27 April 2011) UN Doc S/PV.6524; UNSC Verbatim Record (3 August 2011) UN Doc S/PV.6598; UNSC Verbatim Record (31 January 2012) UN Doc S/PV.6710; UNSC Verbatim Record (4 February 2012) UN Doc S/PV.6711; UNSC Verbatim Record (12 March 2012) UN Doc S/PV.6734; UNSC Verbatim Record (21 March 2012) UN Doc S/PV.6736; UNSC Verbatim Record (14 April 2012) UN Doc S/PV.6751; UNSC Verbatim Record (21 April 2012) UN Doc S/PV.6756; UNSC Verbatim Record (30 August 2012) UN Doc S/PV.6826; UNSC Verbatim Record (26 September 2012) UN Doc S/PV.6841; UNSC Verbatim Record (18 April 2013) UN Doc S/PV.6949; UNSC Verbatim Record (16 July 2012) UN Doc S/PV.7000; UNSC Verbatim Record

(20 August 2013) UN Doc S/PV.7020; UNSC Verbatim Record (25 October 2013) UN Doc S/PV.7049; UNSC Verbatim Record (22 February 2014) UN Doc S/PV.7116; UNSC Verbatim Record (22 May 2014) UN Doc S/PV.7180; UNSC Verbatim Record (14 July 2014) UN Doc S/PV.7216.

37 United Nations Supervision Mission in Syria.

38 Nick Hopkins and Emma Beals, 'UN pays tens of millions to Assad regime under Syria aid programme' *The Guardian* (29 August 2016).

39 Nick Hopkins and Emma Beals, 'How Assad regime controls UN aid intended for Syria's children' *The Guardian* (29 August 2016).

40 UNSC Res 1970 (26 February 2011) UN Doc S/RES/1970 preamble.

41 See the statement by the UK on UNSC Draft Res S/2012/77 (2012) in UNSC Verbatim Record (4 February 2012) UN Doc S/PV.6711, 7; see also, statement by the US on UNSC Draft Res S/2012/77 (2012) 5.

42 Both China and Russia voted negatively on UNSC Draft Res S/2011/612 (2011), UNSC Draft Res S/2012/77 (2012) and UNSC Draft Res S/2012/538 (2012).

43 Both UNSC Res 2118 (2013) and UNSC Res 2139 (2014) condemn and demand, using terminology of Chapter VII, but fail to include the necessary criteria for Chapter VII as discussed previously and do not take action under art 41 or 42 of the Charter. They were also to results of several rounds of negotiations on the wording.

44 US, UNSC Verbatim Record (4 February 2012) UN Doc S/PV.6711 at 5. See also the condemnation of the representatives of the UK, France and others at 3 ff.

45 'Mass executions in Syria may amount to war crimes, senior UN official warns' *UN News Centre* (16 January 2014).

46 OHCHR, 'Preliminary report of the High Commissioner on the situation of human rights in the Syrian Arab Republic' (14 June 2011) UN Doc A/HRC/17/CRP.1 at 3 ff.

47 Amnesty International, 'Deadly reprisals: deliberate killings and other abuses by Syria's armed forces' (June 2012); Human Rights Watch, 'In cold blood: summary executions by Syrian security forces and pro-government militias' (10 April 2012).

48 Jean-Marie Henckaerts and Louise Doswald-Beck, *Customary International Humanitarian Law: Vol 1* (Cambridge University Press 2005) 3, 25, 37–40.

49 UNGA, 'United Nations Mission to Investigate Allegations of the Use of Chemical Weapons in the Syrian Arab Republic: Final report' (12 December 2013) para 108.

50 2016 Humanitarian Needs Overview (October 2015) https://www.humanitarianresponse.info/en/system/files/documents/files/2016_hno_syrian_arab_republic.pdf (last accessed 11 November 2016).

51 ECHO Factsheet: Syria Crisis (May 2016) https://ec.europa.eu/echo/files/aid/countries/factsheets/syria_en.pdf (last accessed 11 November 2016).

52 2011 saw three unofficial documents emerge from the Council, all press statements: UN Press Release, 'Security Council press statement on embassy attacks in Damascus' (12 July 2011); UN Press Release, 'Security Council press statement on attacks against diplomatic premises in Syria' (15 November 2011); UN Press Release, 'Security Council press statement on terrorist attacks in Damascus, Syria' (23 December 2011).

53 UNSC Res 1160 (31 March 1998) UN Doc S/RES/1160.

54 UNSC Res 1244 (10 June 1999) UN Doc S/RES/1244.

55 UNSC Res 1125 (6 August 1997) UN Doc S/RES/1125.

56 Although external forces in the CAR play a role in the conflict, it is technically termed an intra-State dispute, in much the same way as there are allegations of neighbouring countries exerting pressure on the internal conflict in Syria.

57 UNSC Res 2088 (24 January 2013) UN Doc S/RES/2088 and UNSC Res 2121 (24 January 2013) UN Doc S/RES/2121 both refer to the extension or updating of the mandates of BINUCA; UNSC Res 2127 (5 December 2013) UN Doc S/RES/2127 is a Chapter VII resolution demanding swift implementation of transitional agreements (para 5), deploring the limited progress made (para 6) and authorising French military intervention in the country (para 50).
58 UNSC Verbatim Record (22 January 2014) UN Doc S/PV.7098, 5.
59 See Amber Peterman, Tia Palermo and Caryn Bredenkamp, 'Estimates and determinants of sexual violence against women in the Democratic Republic of Congo' (2011) 101 *American Journal of Public Health* 1060, 1060; an estimated 5.4 million people have died as a result of the conflict in the DRC since 1998, 50% of whom have been children, see International Rescue Committee, 'Measuring mortality in the Democratic Republic of Congo' (2007) 7.
60 Security Council Report, 'Security Council Statistics in 2013' (31 January 2014): the Council discusses the DRC in eight meetings each in 2011, 2012 and 2013.
61 UNSC Res 1991 (28 June 2011) UN Doc S/RES/1991; UNSC Res 2021 (29 November 2011) UN Doc S/RES/2021; UNSC Presidential Statement 11 (2011) UN Doc S/PRST/2011/11; UNSC Res 2053 (27 June 2012) UN Doc S/RES/2053; UNSC Res 2076 (20 November 2012) UN Doc S/RES/2076; UNSC Res 2078 (28 November 2012) UN Doc S/RES/2078; UNSC Presidential Statement 22 (2012) UN Doc S/PRST/2012/22; UNSC Res 2098 (28 March 2013) UN Doc S/RES/2098; UNSC Presidential Statement 11 (2013) UN Doc S/PRST/2013/11; UNSC Presidential Statement 17 (2013) UN Doc S/PRST/2013/17; UNSC Res 2136 (30 January 2014) UN Doc S/RES/2136; UNSC Res 2147 (28 March 2014) UN Doc S/RES/2147; UNSC Presidential Statement 22 (2014) UN Doc S/PRST/2014/22.
62 UNSC Res 2304 (12 August 2016) UN Doc S/RES/2304.
63 All five P5 members – Russia, China, the US, the UK and France – possess nuclear weaponry, in addition to Pakistan, India and the DPRK.
64 Israel was believed to have between 60–85 nuclear weapons with 65–85 predicted in 2020 according to the US Defense Intelligence Agency (DIA), 'A primer on the future threat: the decades ahead: 1999–2020' (1999) 38, reproduced in Rowan Scarborough, *Rumsfeld's War: The Untold Story of America's Anti-Terrorist Commander* (Regnery 2013); the CIA believed as early as 1974 that 'Israel already has produced nuclear weapons', Central Intelligence Agency, 'Prospects for further proliferation of nuclear weapons' (1974) 2. See also eg Leonard S Spector and Jacqueline R Smith, *Nuclear Ambitions: The Spread of Nuclear Weapons 1989–1990* (Westview Press 1990); Nuclear Non-proliferation Project, 'Nuclear proliferation Status Report July 1992' (1992); Hans M Kristensen and Robert S Norris, 'Global nuclear weapons inventories, 1945–2013' (2013) 69 *Bulletin of the Atomic Scientists* 75.
65 Treaty on the Non-proliferation of Nuclear Weapons (1970).
66 UNSC Res 1695 (15 July 2006) UN Doc S/RES/1695; UNSC Res 1718 (14 October 2006) UN Doc S/RES/1718; UNSC Res 1874 (12 June 2009) UN Doc S/RES/1874; UNSC Res 2087 (22 January 2013) UN Doc S/RES/2087; UNSC Res 2094 (7 March 2013) UN Doc S/RES/2094.
67 France and China acceded in 1992.
68 Russia ratified the treaty in 1970; the UK ratified in 1968; the US ratified in 1970.
69 The DPRK acceded in 1985 before withdrawing in 2003.
70 93 states are signatories and 190 states have acceded.
71 'Letter dated 12 March 1993 from the Minister for Foreign Affairs of the Democratic People's Republic of Korea addressed to the President of the Security Council' (12 March 1993) UN Doc S/25405 Annex.

72 'Letter dated 1 April 1993 from the Representatives of the Russian Federation, the United Kingdom of Great Britain and Northern Ireland and the United States of America addressed to the President of the Security Council' (2 April 1993) UN Doc S/25515 Annex.
73 UNSC Res 825 (11 May 1993) UN Doc S/RES/825.
74 ibid preamble.
75 See eg numerous letters from the DPRK: 'Letter dated 21 February 1994 from the Permanent Representative of the Democratic People's Republic of Korea to the United Nations addressed to the Secretary-General' (23 February 1994) UN Doc S/1994/204; 'Letter dated 21 March 1994 from the Permanent Representative of the Democratic People's Republic of Korea to the United Nations addressed to the Secretary-General' (21 March 1994) UN Doc S/1994/319; 'Letter dated 22 March 1994 from the Permanent Representative of the Democratic People's Republic of Korea to the United Nations addressed to the Secretary-General' (22 March 1994) UN Doc S/1994/327; 'Letter dated 24 March 1994 from the Permanent Representative of the Democratic People's Republic of Korea to the United Nations addressed to the Secretary-General' (24 March 1994) UN Doc S/1994/337; 'Letter dated 25 March 1994 from the Permanent Representative of the Democratic People's Republic of Korea to the United Nations addressed to the Secretary-General' (25 March 1994) UN Doc S/1994/344; 'Letter dated 29 March 1994 from the Permanent Representative of the Democratic People's Republic of Korea to the United Nations addressed to the Secretary-General' (29 March 1994) UN Doc S/1994/358.
76 Agreed Framework between the United States of America and the Democratic People's Republic of Korea (21 October 1994).
77 UNSC Presidential Statement 64 (1994) UN Doc S/PRST/1994/64: 'The Security Council takes note of the decision of the DPRK in the Agreed Framework to remain a party to the Treaty on the Non-proliferation of Nuclear Weapons'.
78 For the full text of the withdrawal see 'The Statement of the Government of the Democratic People's Republic of Korea date 10 January 2003' in 'Letter dated 24 January 2003 from the Permanent Representative of the Democratic People's Republic of Korea to the United Nations addressed to the President of the Security Council' (24 January 2003) UN Doc S/2003/91 Annex II.
79 UNSC Res 1695 (15 July 2006) UN Doc S/RES/1695 paras 1–2.
80 Indian Ministry of Defence Press Release, 'Agni III take off successful' (9 July 2006) *Press Information Bureau* http://pib.nic.in/newsite/erelease.aspx?relid=18775 (last accessed 11 November 2016).
81 Indian Ministry of Defence Press Release, 'Agni III launched successfully' (12 April 2007) *Press Information Bureau* http://pib.nic.in/newsite/erelease.aspx?relid=26817 (last accessed 11 November 2016).
82 US, UNSC Verbatim Record (15 July 2006) UN Doc S/PV.5490 at 4.
83 UNSC Res 1718 (14 October 2006) UN Doc S/RES/1718.
84 ibid para 1.
85 ibid para 3.
86 UNSC Res 1874 (12 June 2009) UN Doc S/RES/1874.
87 ibid paras 5–6.
88 Daniel Joyner, 'The Security Council as a legal hegemon' (2012) 43 *Georgetown Journal of International Law* 225, 250.
89 UNSC Res 2094 (7 March 2013) UN Doc S/RES/2094 paras 3–4. This is particularly irrational when coupled with the fact that also in May 2009, India tested its nuclear-capable Agni-II ballistic missile, but once was left off the Council agenda despite discussions on the same topic – nuclear non-proliferation – in relation to the DPRK.

90 UNSC Res 2270 (2 March 2016) UN Doc S/RES/2270.
91 International Atomic Energy Agency, *Illicit Nuclear Trafficking: Collective Experience and the Way Forward* (IAEA 2008) 265.
92 UNSC Verbatim Record (6 June 1998) UN Doc S/PV/3890, 28 ff.
93 UNSC Res 1172 (6 June 1998) UN Doc S/RES/1172.
94 George Perkovich, *India's Nuclear Bomb: The Impact on Global Proliferation* (California University Press 2002) 184.
95 ibid 183.
96 International Atomic Energy Agency, *Illicit Nuclear Trafficking: Collective Experience and the Way Forward* (IAEA 2008) 103.
97 ibid.
98 Rob Crilly, 'AQ Khan claims Benazir Bhutto ordered nuclear sale' *The Telegraph* (London 17 September 2012); James Astill, 'Musharraf knew I was selling secrets, says nuclear scientist' *The Guardian* (London 4 February 2004).
99 Pakistan has tested its Babur nuclear capable cruise missile in 2005, 2007, 2009 and 2011. Babur (Hatf-VII), tested in 2012, is capable of carrying nuclear and conventional weaponry, in addition to possessing stealth technology. Hatf IX (Nasr) was last tested in late 2013: Pakistani Inter Services Public Relations Press Release, 'No. PR179/2013-ISPR' (5 November 2013).
100 See eg Matthew Bunn, 'Securing the bomb 2010: securing all nuclear materials in four years' (1 April 2010) 28.
101 The Karachi Nuclear Power Plant (live in 1971) and two at the Chasma Nuclear Power Plant (live in 2000 and 2011).
102 Farhan Bokhari and James Crabtree, 'China strengthens Pakistan ties with $6.5bn loan for nuclear power' *Financial Times* (London 1 January 2014).
103 IAEA 'Guidelines for the Export of Nuclear Material, Equipment and Technology' Series, published under IAEA Doc INFCIRC/254/Rev.xxx Part 1.
104 IAEA 'The Nuclear Suppliers Group: Its Origins, Role and Activities' (4 December 2012) INFCIRC/539/Rev.5 at 1.
105 IAEA 'Communication Received from the Permanent Mission of the United States of America to the International Atomic Energy Agency regarding Certain Member States' Guidelines for the Export of Nuclear Material, Equipment and Technology' (12 November 2012) INFCIRC/254/Rev.11/Part 1a para 6(a)(i).
106 ibid para 1.
107 Paul Kerr and Mary Beth Nikitin, 'Pakistan's nuclear weapons' *Congressional Research Service* (Washington 1 August 2016).
108 Kamran Yousaf, 'Pakistan rules out talks on nuclear programme freeze' *The Express Tribune* (Islamabad 18 May 2016).
109 It remains a non-member of the NPT and continues to vote against relevant clauses in General Assembly resolutions that stress the need for nuclear States to accede see eg voting against UNGA Res 67/59 (3 December 2012) UN Doc A/RES/67/59, para 2; UNGA Verbatim Record (3 December 2012) UN Doc A/67/PV.48, 21.
110 Although six nuclear reactors were brought under safeguards of the IAEA between 1971 and 1994, the *Agreement Between the Government of India and the IAEA for the Application of Safeguards to Civilian Nuclear Facilities* was only approved in 2008 by the IAEA Board of Governors, a decade after the most recent nuclear weapons test, and aimed to gradually bring in a total of 14 reactors under Agency safeguards. See, Mohamed ElBaradei, 'Introductory Statement to the Board of Governors' (Vienna 1 August 2008).
111 Agni I was tested in October 2007, November 2010, December 2011, July 2012 and November 2013; Agni II was tested in May 2009, November 2009, May 2010, September 2011, August 2012 and April 2013; Agni III was tested

in July 2006, April 2007, May 2008, February 2010, September 2012 and December 2013; Agni IV was tested in November 2011, September 2012 and January 2014; Agni V was tested in April 2012, September 2013 and January 2015. Agni VI is currently in development.

112 In fact, somewhat contradictorily, the P5 members have furnished India with components, nuclear weaponry and even technical knowledge through cooperation on the construction of nuclear technology throughout the period that the P5 members have been reducing their nuclear cache.

113 'Nicholas Sarkozy and Manmohan Singh in nuclear deal' *BBC News* (London 6 December 2010).

114 'US–India: Civil Nuclear Cooperation', US Department of State.

115 Most recently, Russia announced it would build 16 nuclear reactors in India, in addition to the existing two in the process of construction in Tamil Nadu. See, 'Russia signs India nuclear reactor deal' *BBC News* (London 12 March 2010).

116 Nicholas Watt, 'Britain to allow export of civil nuclear technology to India' *The Guardian* (London 28 July 2010).

117 Including South Korea in 2011, Canada in 2012 and Australia in 2012.

118 On land, India has test-launched at least two strategic missiles on numerous occasions since the start of the decade: the Agni IV was launched three times – in 2011, 2012 and 2013 – and is capable of achieving a range of 4,000km while carrying a nuclear warhead weighing one tonne; the Agni V missile was tested in 2012 and 2013 and, an intercontinental ballistic missile, is capable of carrying nuclear payloads to a range of more than 5,000 km. Following the success of the Agni-V missile, the Indian Defence Ministry plans to soon test the more than 6,000 km range Agni-VI with the goal of eventually constructing a 10,000km range inter-continental Ballistic missile. These tests were and continue to be carried out against the backdrop of India's air force – the fourth largest in the world – containing three nuclear-weapon capable fleets, one of which, designed jointly by France and Britain, was nuclear-capable when deployed by those countries.

119 Gardiner Harris, 'World's biggest arms importer, India wants to buy local' *The New York Times* (New York 6 March 2014).

120 Central Intelligence Agency, 'Unclassified report to Congress on the acquisition of technology relating to weapons of mass destruction and advanced conventional munitions, 1 July through 31 December 2003' (2003) 9.

121 India has successfully achieved a nuclear triad: air-based, land-based and sea-based nuclear weapon deployment capacities. The US, Russia and China are all accepted as current nuclear triad powers; France and the UK, however, have phased out certain nuclear capabilities since the end of the Cold War and do not have deployable nuclear weaponry on all three fronts.

122 UNSC Res 1540 (28 April 2004) UN Doc S/RES/1540.

123 ibid.

124 The US maintained over 5000 nuclear warheads in 2010, down from over 30,000 in 1967 and has made concerted efforts to increase transparency and reduce the number of weapons held in its stockpile. Nonetheless, it continues to proliferate its missile systems capable of delivering nuclear payloads: Lockheed Martin Press release, 'Lockheed Martin-Built Trident II D5 Missile achieves a total of 148 successful test flights since 1989' (24 September 2013).

125 Despite a US–Russian treaty limiting the numbers of intercontinental ballistic missiles in their respective fleets, it plans to increase its strategic nuclear forces by 100% by 2020. See 'Russia to fully renew nuclear forces by 2020' *Russia Today* (Moscow 22 September 2014). Moreover, in March 2014, Russia tested its nuclear-capable RS-12M Topol missile in Kazakhstan. The US response

was simply that they had received proper notice, 'Russia test-fires ICBM amid tension over Ukraine' *Reuters* (Moscow 4 March 2014).

126 China has been elusive about its exact nuclear arsenal. However, it last publicly tested its nuclear-capable missile capabilities in January 2014 – the Dongfeng-31. See Minnie Chan, 'China's nuclear missile drill seen as warning to US not to meddle in region' *South China Morning Post* (23 January 2014).

127 See eg UK representative's assertion that Russia and China 'have chosen to put their national interests ahead of the lives of millions of Syrians', UNSC Verbatim Record (19 July 2012) UN Doc S/PV.6810, 3 and the counterclaim that the 'Pharisees [of Western Powers] have been pushing their own geo-political intentions', UNSC Verbatim Record (19 July 2012) UN Doc S/PV.6810, 8.

128 Russia, UNSC Verbatim Record (29 June 2010) UN Doc S/PV.6347, 22. See also Liechtenstein, UNSC Verbatim Record (29 June 2010) UN Doc S/PV.6347 (Resumption 1) 6, which remained 'convinced that the best way for the Security Council to promote international law and the rule of law is to lead by example'.

7 The predictability paradox

> I cannot believe that the Council, under any circumstances, would not assume its responsibility under the Charter of maintaining international peace and security. Nor can I believe that the Council would delay acting to put an end to a tragedy that endangers the lives of thousands of people and undermines the foundation of the edifice constructed by the world in order to avert the recurrence of violence and cruel wars.[1]

Introduction

Juxtaposed with the principle of equality before the law, is that of predictability in the Council's decision-making process. While the focus of the Council itself should be unbiased and the decisions avoid contradictory standards, decisions made without fully addressing the idiosyncratic and unique characteristics of each threat on an individual basis would be a misapplication of the principle of fairness, as well as highlighting an aura of arbitrary behaviour on the part of the Council.[2] In real world terms, this means that the Council *should* react to all potential threats to the peace, but should do so while identifying any differences between similar threats that might require a different approach to be introduced. This would be fair, but only predictable up to a point: that of the decision to intervene in some way, rather than the content or nature of the intervention. Although each case should be addressed on its individual merits – as highlighted previously, Syria is not Libya – states should nonetheless be able to predict the outcomes of their actions based on the Council's previous responses to analogous situations. It is for this reason that the DPRK may note hypocrisy in the Council's opposition to its nuclear programme.

States may be able to establish the extent and parameters of Council action based on the precedent of resolutions and other official actions in order to regulate their own actions in turn; but what country would readily accept a 'one-size-fits-all' solution by the Council, which might give the impression not only of lethargy or reluctance to address a threat but, perhaps more dangerously, limited resources at its disposal to react to different threats? It is an extremely thin line that the Council must be expected to walk, ensuring that it treats all threats equally and consistently, while also addressing the potential threat on an individual basis. Hence, a predictability paradox is created.

It would logically follow that if there was a consistent practice on the part of the Security Council to respond to certain threats in a particular manner – for example, certain violations of international human rights law – then states may have no basis upon which to claim ignorance or amnesty in the event that the Council took action against that violating state. Similarly, where certain actions have not historically been seized upon by the Council, a state may reasonably presume that such behaviour is acceptable. In short, a clear pattern of action should be evident to avoid allegation of arbitrariness and the undermining of a legal order that equally applies to all member states.

While this is a difficult standard to uphold for the Council, it is not excessively so, and ties into the component of transparency, where the work of the Council should be open and available to all interested parties. A bespoke approach may not immediately necessitate different approaches to similar threats; nonetheless, each threat must be taken on its merits. Accordingly, there should be an explanation as to why the Council has chosen to follow the same course charted previously, or an explanation as to why the situation at hand has dictated a departure from precedential norms – for example, how the DPRK poses a threat where India and Pakistan do not. Moreover, a clear legal basis must be evident in every situation as to why the Council has chosen to take action – or not – and what, if anything, differentiates this potential threat from other state actions that have not been perceived as such.

A clear pattern of action

Although in the vast majority of cases consensus is reached on the Council,[3] this does not immediately equate to impartiality or a lack of bias on the Council; if the fact that P5 members 'have mostly accompanied the consensus or the enabling majorities adopting the resolutions may be a product of their role as the pen holders on most Council agenda items',[4] as gatekeepers of the Council the accusation may be levelled that the predictability of Security Council resolutions can, at its most basic level, be said to correspond with the foreign policies of the voting states on the Council at any given time. States are more likely to vote in favour of resolutions that are compatible with their national interests and, conversely, more likely to vote against the passing of a resolution that is incompatible with such a trajectory; if only resolutions and discussions that conform to these policies are tabled, there is sure to be arbitrary behaviour. With this in mind, it is difficult to approach the Council as a monolithic entity that acts in unison on all counts and that shares all goals as one; frequently, it can be found that the principles that states defend through the use or threat of the veto shift dramatically and can even be interchanged between P5 members depending on the subject under discussion.

Respect for national sovereignty

As far back as 1993, China voiced its opposition to interfering in the domestic affairs of a state deeming the measures entailed within Council UNSC Resolution 841[5] on Haiti 'warranted only as a result of the unique and exceptional situation in Haiti, and therefore should not be regarded as constituting any precedent for the future'.[6] In fact, it was made quite clear that: '[t]he Chinese delegation, as its consistent position, does not favour the Security Council's handling matters which are essentially internal affairs of a Member State, nor does it approve of resorting lightly to such mandatory measures as sanctions by the Council'.[7] This stance suggests that there are principles upheld by the Chinese delegation on a non-arbitrary basis and that, as a rule, interference in the domestic situations of states should not be the immediate responsibility of the Security Council. This stance certainly appears to be shared by the Russian Federation in some respects and both the Russian Federation and China have displayed strong support for the principle of national sovereignty. Such support often determines when each makes use of the veto power to block Security Council resolutions and therefore, implicitly, when they acquiesce or agree to intervention under Chapter VII of the Charter.

In the case of Zimbabwe, the Russian Federation took the view that a draft resolution attempting to impose targeted sanctions and an arms embargo on the Mugabe regime in the aftermath of his re-election in 2008 'represent[ed] nothing but an attempt by the Council to interfere in the internal affairs of States, contrary to the Charter'.[8] China took a similar tack, stating that it 'has always believed that negotiation and dialogue are the best approach to solving problems on the international level'.[9] Similarly, during the debate on draft resolution S/2007/14[10] on the situation in Myanmar, China noted that the country was 'faced with a series of grave challenges relating to refugees, child labour, HIV/AIDS, human rights and drugs'.[11] Stating that no one would dispute that Myanmar was faced with a series of grave challenges, China found that similar problems existed in many other countries as well.[12]

It would seem, then – at least in the eyes of the Chinese representation – that the issues faced by Myanmar did not meet the threshold of a threat to peace and security, after having been examined within the wider scope of domestic troubles faced by comparable countries across the globe. The Russian Federation also shared this opinion, finding that Myanmar was not suitable for consideration by the Council.[13] This suggests non-arbitrary behaviour; both the Russian and Chinese delegations have examined the facts of the situation in Zimbabwe and Myanmar and reached the reasoned conclusion that the situation did not pose a threat to the region.

This stance was also the reasoning behind both Russia and China's decisions to veto three resolutions[14] relating to Syria. Russia, for its part, found that 'proposals for wording on the non-acceptability of foreign military intervention were not taken into account'[15] and emphasised that it 'simply cannot accept a document, under Chapter VII of the Charter of the United Nations, that would open the way for the pressure of sanctions and later for external military involvement in Syrian domestic affairs'.[16] China maintained this posture, advocating that the international community 'fully respect Syria's sovereignty, independence and territorial integrity'[17] and highlighting that 'sovereign equality and non-interference in the internal affairs of other countries are the basic norms governing inter-State relations enshrined in the Charter of the United Nations'.[18]

Both the Russian Federation and China faulted these resolutions for material omissions or generalisations, their 'unbalanced content [seeking] to put pressure on only one party'[19] and ignoring 'that the radical opposition no longer hides its extremist bent and is relying on terrorist tactics . . .';[20] conversely, the US, the UK and France advocated 'changing the situation on the ground for better',[21] invoking Chapter VII and threatening 'the only party with heavy weapons, the Syrian regime, with sanctions if it continued to use those weapons brutally against its own cities and citizens'.[22]

The views expressed by China and the Russian Federation on the subject of Syria – which 'consistently maintained that the future and fate of Syria should be independently decided by the Syrian people, rather than imposed by outside forces'[23] – mirror the stance held for decades that: 'the United States does not believe that the Security Council or the General Assembly should be in the business of inserting themselves into issues that the negotiating partners have decided will be addressed . . .'.[24] This commitment to the sovereignty and right to self-defence is, the US claims, at the foundation of its decision to use its veto powers on fourteen separate occasions since 1990 alone, all on 'The situation in the Middle East, including the Palestinian question' or 'The situation in the occupied Arab territories'.[25]

The meandering support of the P5 for territorial integrity and sovereignty is thus undermined by certain exceptions to the supposedly unshakeable values at the heart not only of the UN Charter but of the Council's self-proclaimed behaviour itself. The capacity of states to transpose their values so readily undermines the supremacy of the law and highlights the possibility of a double-standard on the Council. It would appear that all three P5 members of the US, China and the Russian Federation are willing momentarily to overlook the principles of sovereignty when the situation encroaches on their interests or the interests of allies, before reverting to an original stance of non-intervention. As the following sub-section will examine, humanitarian intervention has also been cited as a reason for the suspension of state sovereign rights.

Humanitarian intervention

While P5 states purport to be in favour of territorial integrity and sovereignty of states,[26] the reality is at times starkly different; humanitarian intervention has been cited as a valid reason to suspend the associated rights of state sovereignty, as the example of NATO intervention in Kosovo clearly highlights. Operation Allied Force proceeded on 24 March 1999 without any explicit, or implicit, Security Council authorisation, leading to condemnation by the Russian Federation of 'aggression against a sovereign State . . . which was undertaken in violation of the United Nations Charter and in circumvention of the Security Council'.[27]

Two days later, a Council resolution co-sponsored by Belarus and the Russian Federation[28] attempting to deem the 'use of force by NATO against the Federal Republic of Yugoslavia . . . a threat to international peace and security'[29] under Chapter VII failed to be adopted owing to a failure to reach the required majority in accordance with the Charter;[30] the bottom line – there was insufficient volition on the part of the Council members to condemn a breach of sovereignty. In fact, Council practice went even further; during discussions on the defeated resolution, NATO's unilateral response was deemed to be 'completely justified'[31] 'as an exceptional measure to prevent an overwhelming humanitarian catastrophe'[32] and actions that 'respond to Belgrade's violation of its international obligations under the resolutions which the Security Council has adopted under Chapter VII'.[33] Moreover, the subsequent resolutions that emanated from the Council[34] urging parties to cease violence passed with no negative votes[35] despite failing to mention the NATO transgression of the UN Charter.[36] The Council had openly accepted the military intervention of a third party, in clear contravention of the UN Charter.

With the NATO intervention having successfully bypassed the Council, avenues to circumvention were open to Council members that could not find support within the Council to pursue their own motivations either as a separate alliance or unilaterally. On 20 March 2003, against strong opposition from the three non-contributing members of the P5[37] and other UN members,[38] the US and allied countries, including the UK, intervened militarily in Iraq under the pretence of humanitarian reasons. Although an *ex post facto* Chapter VII resolution[39] can be argued to have gone some way in legitimising the intervention – if only by acknowledgement and omission of its condemnation along the lines of the Kosovo example – and another later 'recognising the specific authorities, responsibilities, and obligations under applicable international law of [the US and UK] as occupying powers under unified command',[40] the intervention remains one of the most controversial moves in recent Council history, harking back to an era during the Cold War stalemate when direct inter-state negotiations overshadowed and undermined the Council.[41]

Most recently, with Syria, too, there were ruminations of unilateral action in the aftermath of the reports of use of chemical weapons by the Assad regime. The US has consistently maintained that the use of these weapons was a 'red line' that Syria would not be permitted to cross without repercussions.[42] As such, it was, by the US government's own admission, '[i]n part because of the credible threat of U.S. military action, as well as constructive talks that [they] had with President Putin . . . [that t]he Assad regime has now admitted that it has these weapons, and even said they'd join the Chemical Weapons Convention, which prohibits their use'[43] – a unilateral show of force by the US, in circumvention of the Security Council, in conjunction with inter-State diplomacy away from the UN, led the way to the most realistic prospects of solving the crisis in Syria. Such military action clearly had no basis in the UN Charter and the threat of its use by a P5 member of the Security Council, just as with Kosovo and Iraq before it, undermines not only the legitimacy of the Council but also its adherence to the international rule of law. In reality, of course, there has been no end to the Syrian conflict and attacks – both chemical[44] and using prohibited weapons such as barrel bombs[45] – have continued indiscriminately. In fact, in contravention of the laws of war and the Geneva Conventions,[46] deliberate and targeted attacks on hospitals and other protected buildings have increased.[47]

Three courses of action have been displayed in recent decades on the part of the Security Council with respect to humanitarian intervention. The first, exemplified by NATO intervention in Kosovo and US/UK-led intervention in Iraq, is unilateral intervention in the absence of explicit Chapter VII Council mandates, unequivocally contrary to the UN Charter; the second, exemplified by the authorised NATO interventions in the Former Yugoslavia and Libya, is intervention for humanitarian reasons with an explicit Chapter VII resolution from the Council, acting in accordance with the procedure of the Charter; and the third, typified by the situation in Syria, is that of the Council failing to reach any agreement on the course forwards beyond rhetoric on the Council[48] owing to a lack of volition on the part of the Council members at the domestic level.

There cannot be said to exist a pattern of behaviour in the humanitarian intervention record of the Council; nor can it be argued that the Council has evolved in its approach from one of impunity to one of adherence to the rule of law, or vice versa, since there is no chronological evidence to support this claim. The Council chose to intervene in Bosnia/Herzegovina conflict from 1991 onwards,[49] then failed to do so in Rwanda prior to a genocide in 1994,[50] before acquiescing to NATO intervention in Kosovo without authorisation in 1999, legitimising the Iraqi invasion by multinational forces after the fact, intervening in Libya in 2011, while failing to do so in Syria until today. The Council's record of intervention on humanitarian grounds is seemingly peppered with inconsistencies.

Civilian nuclear programmes: an arbitrary standard?

The case of Iran's nuclear programme also highlights an arbitrary and unpredictable response by the Council. Iran has always maintained that its pursuit of nuclear technology is entirely for civilian purposes and non-militarily motivated as a result of both treaty and religious obligations.[51] To date, there has been no conclusive IAEA evidence of any nuclear weapons constructed or possessed by Iran; the stance taken by the IAEA, despite credible information that 'Iran has carried out activities that are relevant to the development of a nuclear explosive device'[52] is one of ambiguity – there is no evidence one way or the other.[53] Likewise, no intelligence points in that direction from US,[54] Israeli[55] and Russian[56] sources or factual evidence[57] that Iran is in pursuit of nuclear weaponry.

Nonetheless, since 2006, Iran has been subject to over 10 Security Council resolutions as a result of its nuclear activities and the US has made no effort to hide its conviction that it 'would still be a profound national-security interest of the United States to prevent Iran from getting a nuclear weapon'.[58] Iranian attempts to achieve civilian nuclear power are not newfound or recent ambitions at all[59] and were initially supported by both China[60] and Russia[61] before Beijing's[62] and Washington's[63] suspicions that Iran sought nuclear weapons despite the fact that 'it appears that the Natanz facility was designed to produce low-enriched uranium for nuclear power fuel, rather than weapons-grade uranium for a military programme'.[64] Even the 2002 announcement by the National Council of Resistance of Iran (NCRI) that Iran had hidden the existence of both the Natanz and Arak facilities[65] did not imply a violation of its safeguards agreement with the IAEA.[66]

Undeniably, there was no unequivocal evidence available to the Council itself that nuclear weaponry was the aim of the Iranian regime, even prior to the implementation of its first resolution on the matter, where 'Iran's nuclear activities and its history of concealment raise[d] pressing questions about whether Iran's programme is, as it claims, solely for civil purposes'.[67] It was this concealment that lay at the root of the adoption of UNSC Resolution 1696,[68] based on 'the view of the Security Council regarding the need for Iran to . . . clarify outstanding questions regarding its nuclear activities'[69] and 'the establishment of international confidence in the exclusively peaceful nature of Iran's nuclear programme'.[70]

In a departure from the standard formula for the adoption of Chapter VII resolutions discussed previously in this book, UNSC Resolution 1696 – despite being adopted 'under Article 40 of Chapter VII of the Charter of the United Nations in order to make mandatory the suspension required by the IAEA'[71] – fails to identify the threat to international peace under article 39 and therefore '[c]alls upon Iran without delay to take the steps required by the IAEA Board of Governors . . . [and d]emands, in this context, that Iran suspend all enrichment-related and reprocessing activities'[72] without legal basis or clarity. Even the IAEA indicated in its reports 'in November 2004, and again in September 2005, all the nuclear material in Iran has been accounted for . . . [and] the Agency has not seen any diversion of nuclear material to nuclear weapons or other nuclear explosive devices';[73] yet 'the history of concealment of Iran's nuclear activities . . . and resulting absence of confidence that Iran's nuclear programme is exclusively for peaceful purposes have given rise to questions that are within the competence of the Security Council'[74] and the alleged Iranian matter was referred to the Council in February 2006 for 'Iran's many failures and breaches of its obligations to comply with its NPT Safeguards Agreement'.[75]

UNSC Resolution 1696 is also in many ways self-contradictory. The NPT stipulates that '[n]othing in this Treaty shall be interpreted as affecting the inalienable right of all the Parties to the Treaty to develop research, production and use of nuclear energy for peaceful purposes without discrimination and in conformity with Articles I and II of this Treaty',[76] a standard that is referred to not only explicitly by the IAEA itself in its resolutions on Iran,[77] but also by the Security Council in its own resolutions[78] and discussions.[79] Articles I and II relate solely to the transfer or receipt of nuclear weapons or information on their construction respectively; there is no indication of any IAEA safeguards or criteria to be met, which in turn fall under Article III of the NPT.[80]

Thus, on the one hand, by reaffirming this principle in the preamble of UNSC Resolution 1696, the Council is actively supporting the NPT and its underlying aims, goals and allowances; on the other hand, the Council then demands that Iran suspend 'all enrichment-related and reprocessing activities, including research and development'.[81] This demand is based solely on the failure by Iran to comply with the IAEA safeguards – governed by Article III of the NPT – and the evaporation of confidence in Iranian sincerity in its declared pursuit of pacific nuclear technology – which is entirely subjective, speculative and contradictory to the intelligence of the international community; the Council undermines its own authority and interjects itself into the sovereign matters of a state as legally governed and permitted by an international treaty – the NPT – a matter over which it holds no jurisdiction.

One might argue that it is not the violation of the NPT itself that is the threat to the peace but rather the actions of Iran in allegedly attempting to build and maintain weapons of mass destruction and means of their delivery. However, this argument can easily be weakened by the allowances granted to both India and Pakistan – which have made no efforts to hide their animosity for one another[82] and can be argued to pose a risk to the stability of the region, as explored in the previous chapter – and which have had exceptions to international treaties made for them by P5 members.[83] Therefore, if the pursuit of nuclear weapons and delivery systems is a threat to the peace separate from the NPT, which the adoption of the matter by the Council suggests, then these states should be held accountable; this has not happened.

Under the Joint Comprehensive Plan of Action (JCPOA) – a deal brokered through international diplomacy but intricately linked to the work and sanctions of the Council through UNSCR 2231[84] – Iran today is subject to a 25-year programme of IAEA inspections, tied to relief on sanctions with – even once released – teetering precariously like the sword of Damocles ready for re-imposition at the slightest disobedience. It may begin testing up to 30 uranium centrifuge machines only eight years after the date of implementation of the JPAO – the third quarter of 2024 – and resolution 2231 is only due to be terminated in 2025, subject to the absence of any further imposition of UN sanctions on Iran. Only at this point can Iran begin expanding its uranium capacities using more efficient centrifuge machines, but would still not be permitted to enrich uranium close to weapons-grade levels. In fact, only in 2030 – 15 years after the implementation of the JCPAO – would Iran be permitted to expand its enrichment activities to more than one facility, restart certain spent fuel reprocessing activities, or build any plutonium reprocessing plants or heavy water reactors. The plan extends to the year 2040, at which point IAEA oversight of uranium ore concentration would lapse.

Iran is therefore barred from acquiring 'break-out' capabilities – the capacity of a state teetering over the edge of sufficient enrichment to cross over from having only enough for civilian purposes to one with weapons-grade enriched uranium. If this standard itself is what poses a threat to the peace, then such standard is also applied unequally through a brief examination of the current nuclear possessions of Japan, one of the main advocates for Council action against the DPRK.[85] At the most recent declaration in 2015, Japan held over 10 tonnes of non-irradiated separated plutonium on its soil[86] and a further thirty-seven tons in France and the UK,[87] in addition to going live with the Rokkasho reprocessing facility in late-2014.[88] These figures have increased over the past several years.[89] In total, Japan is estimated to have enough material to construct 5000 nuclear bombs[90] through weapons-grade plutonium, which is increasingly of concern, given the fact that Japan's civilian nuclear programme is based almost entirely on another source of nuclear power – enriched uranium. In light of this, it seems that the threat is not the acquisition of nuclear break-out capabilities, but rather that of *Iran* specifically acquiring such capabilities – a clear bias based apparently not on fact but on speculation.

Conclusions

The principle of avoidance of arbitrariness, combined with individuality of state situations, requires not only that the Council address the situation but also that it explain the reason for any departure from previous behaviour based on factual evidence. There has been no such presentation of facts by the Council; Iran posed no apparent threat to the international community and yet it was arbitrarily subjected to sanctions. Japan maintains that its nuclear programme is for pacific purposes and the international community has shown no considerable doubt over this;[91] Iran has claimed the same and has been subjected to numerous rounds of sanctions and has been the source of discussion at the Council and externally in diplomatic talks. Based upon the manner in which the Council has dealt with Japan or even Pakistan and India, it would be realistic to expect that Iran may predict that it would be dealt with in the same fashion. There have been no repercussions against any of these three; accordingly, the Iranian government – in tandem with the provisions of international treaties to which it is party – may note that there are no violations of international principles in its actions.

Moreover, the Council – and constituent member states – have respected the sovereignty and rights of Japan to peaceful nuclear progress, whereas in the case of Iran, unclear foundation for jurisdiction have given rise to the usurping of powers belonging to the ICJ and the trespassing on the rights of states under international law to extend its powers beyond the functions and authority granted in the UN Charter. Based upon this research and the notable disparity in response to threats around the world, it is seemingly evident that there is arbitrary behaviour and unpredictability in the Council's decision-making process.

Notes

1 Egypt, UNSC Verbatim Record (26 March 2003) UN Doc S/PV.4726, 13.
2 See eg Thomas M Franck, *The Power of Legitimacy Among Nations* (Oxford University Press 1990) 37–38.

3 Of all resolutions adopted since 2000, 93.5% have been adopted by consensus. See Security Council Report, 'In hindsight: consensus in the Security Council' (2013).
4 ibid.
5 UNSC Res 841 (16 June 1993) UN Doc S/RES/841.
6 China, UNSC Verbatim Record (16 June 1993) UN Doc S/PV.3238, 21 (on Resolution 841).
7 ibid.
8 UNSC Verbatim Record (11 July 2008) UN Doc S/PV.5933, 9.
9 ibid 13.
10 UNSC Draft Res (12 January 2007) UN Doc S/2007/14.
11 UNSC Verbatim Record (12 January 2007) UN Doc S/PV.5619, 3.
12 China (n 6) 3.
13 Russia, UNSC Verbatim Record (4 October 2011) UN Doc S/PV.6627, 6.
14 UNSC Draft Res (4 October 2011) UN Doc S/2011/612; UNSC Draft Res (4 February 2012) UN Doc S/2012/77; UNSC Draft Res (19 July 2012) UN Doc S/2012/538.
15 Russia (n 13) 5.
16 Russia, UNSC Verbatim Record (19 July 2012) UN Doc S/PV.6810, 8.
17 China, UNSC Verbatim Record (4 October 2011) UN Doc S/PV.6627, 5; see also China, UNSC Verbatim Record (4 February 2012) UN Doc S/PV.6711, 9.
18 China, UNSC Verbatim Record (19 July 2012) UN Doc S/PV.6810, 13.
19 ibid.
20 Russia (n 13) 4.
21 UK, UNSC Verbatim Record (19 July 2012) UN Doc S/PV.6810, 2.
22 US, ibid 10.
23 China (n 6) 13.
24 US, UNSC Verbatim Record (21 March 1997) UN Doc S/PV.3756, 5. See also, US, UNSC Verbatim Record (5 October 2004) UN Doc S/PV.5051, 2.
25 UNSC Draft Res (31 May 1990) UN Doc S/21326; UNSC Draft Res (17 May 1995) UN Doc S/1995/394; UNSC Draft Res (7 March 1997) UN Doc S/1997/199; UNSC Draft Res (21 March 1997) UN Doc S/1997/241; UNSC Draft Res (27–28 March 2001) UN Doc S/2001/270; UNSC Draft Res (14–15 December 2001) UN Doc S/2001/1199; UNSC Draft Res (20 December 2002) UN Doc S/2002/1385; UNSC Draft Res (16 September 2003) UN Doc S/2003/891; UNSC Draft Res (14 October 2003) UN Doc S/2003/980; UNSC Draft Res (25 March 2004) UN Doc S/2004/240; UNSC Draft Res (5 October 2004) UN Doc S/2004/783; UNSC Draft Res (13 July 2006) UN Doc S/2006/508; UNSC Draft Res (11 November 2006) UN Doc S/2006/878; UNSC Draft Res (18 February 2011) UN Doc S/2011/24.
26 See eg China, UNSC Verbatim Record (15 June 2009) UN Doc S/PV.6143, 5.
27 Russia, UNSC Verbatim Record (10 June 1999) UN Doc S/PV.4011, 7; see also China (n 6) 8, reiterating the same sentiment.
28 UNSC Draft Res (26 March 1999) UN Doc S/1999/328.
29 ibid preamble.
30 UN Charter (1945) art 27(3) states the need for an affirmative vote of nine members; UNSC Draft Res S/1999/328 gained three votes for and 12 abstentions.
31 US, UNSC Verbatim Record (26 March 1999) UN Doc S/PV.3989, 5.
32 UK (n 21) 7.
33 France, ibid. France's argument was that since previous resolutions has been adopted under Chapter VII (UNSC Res 1160 (1998), UNSC Res 1199 (1998) and UNSC Res 1203 (1998)), NATO intervention was legitimate.

34 UNSC Res 1239 (14 May 1999) UN Doc S/RES/1239; UNSC Res 1244 (10 June 1999) UN Doc S/RES/1244.
35 China abstained on both.
36 There is much authorship on the legality of the NATO intervention in Kosovo that was eventually found by The Independent International Commission on Kosovo to be 'illegal but legitimate', Independent International Commission on Kosovo, *The Kosovo Report: Conflict, International Response, Lessons Learned* (Oxford University Press 2000) 4. See also Bruno Simma, 'NATO, the UN and the use of force: legal aspects' (1999) 10 *EJIL* 1; Noam Chomsky, *The New Military Humanism: Lessons from Kosovo* (Pluto 1999); Mary Ellen O'Connell, 'The UN, NATO, and international law after Kosovo' (2000) 22(1) *Human Rights Quarterly* 57.
37 Russia, UNSC Verbatim Record (26 March 2003) UN Doc S/PV.4726 (Resumption 1) 26; China (n 6) 28; France, ibid.
38 A total of 67 non-Council member states requested to be invited to participate in the first discussion of the Council after the invasion of Iraq; criticism of the unilateral action was clear from all speakers. See eg Malaysia, UNSC Verbatim Record (26 March 2003) UN Doc S/PV.4726, 8, Algeria (ibid 10), Indonesia (ibid 19), South Africa (ibid 20) and Brazil (ibid 28).
39 UNSC Res 1472 (28 March 2003) UN Doc S/RES/1472.
40 UNSC Res 1483 (22 May 2003) UN Doc S/RES/1483, preamble. UNSC Res 1511 (16 October 2003) UN Doc S/RES/1511 further legitimised the occupying powers, reaffirming the temporary Coalition Provisional Authority, the interim administration and calling for a political timetable.
41 For example, the Cuban missile crisis of 1962 was averted due to an agreement between US President Kennedy and USSR leader Khrushchev with the assistance of UN Secretary-General U Thant, not the Council.
42 Barack Obama, 'Remarks by the President to the White House Press Corps' (Washington DC 20 August 2012): 'Remarks by President Obama and Prime Minister Reinfeldt of Sweden in Joint Press Conference' (Rosenbad 4 September 2013).
43 Barack Obama, 'Remarks by the President in Address to the Nation on Syria' (Washington DC 10 September 2013).
44 'Third report of the Organization for the Prohibition of Chemical Weapons-United Nations Joint Investigative Mechanism' (24 August 2016) UN Doc S/2016/738.
45 See eg Euan McKirdy and Bijan Hosseini, 'Syria barrel bomb attack: at least 16 killed at wake in Aleppo' *CNN* (28 August 2016) http://cnn.it/2fK3qEr (last accessed 13 November 2016).
46 First Geneva Convention art 23; Fourth Geneva Convention art 14(1).
47 See eg Emma Graham-Harrison, 'Aleppo hospitals are latest casualty in attacks by the Syrian regime' *The Guardian* (28 September 2016) http://bit.ly/2cCAIHz (last accessed 13 November 2016).
48 As previously discussed, resolutions UNSCR Res 2118 (2013) and UNSCR Res 2139 (2014) were not adopted under Chapter VII, despite being strongly worded. There is no threat of action to be taken under articles 40 and 41 of the UN Charter, which would be impossible without the acquiescence of Russia and China, both of which were the reason for the original omission of any Chapter VII language. In short, there seems not even the slightest chance of Chapter VII repercussions to the Syrian situation.
49 eg UNSC Res 713 (25 September 1991) UN Doc S/RES/713; UNSC Res 743 (21 February 1991) UN Doc S/RES/743; UNSC Res 757 (30 May 1992) UN Doc S/RES/757; UNSC Res 781 (9 October 1992) UN Doc S/RES/781;

UNSC Res 787 (16 November 1992) UN Doc S/RES/787; UNSC Res 816 (31 March 1993) UN Doc S/RES/816.

50 The ICTR was established *after* the genocides. See eg Roméo Dallaire, *Shake Hands with the Devil* (Arrow 2003) 142–47; Philip Gourevitch, *We Wish to Inform You That Tomorrow We Will Be Killed With Our Families* (Picador 2000). Following the massacre at a school on 6 April 1994, Chapter VII intervention was ruled out as 'not feasible, considering that no such force can be raised immediately' (Nigeria, UNSC Verbatim Record (21 April 1994) UN Doc S/PV.3368, 2) and UNSC Res 912 additionally reduced the UN Assistance Mission in Rwanda to just 270 men (UNSC Resolution 912 (21 April 1994) UN Doc S/RES/912). Genocide is mentioned in all but name for the first time in UNSC Resolution 918 (17 May 1994) UN Doc S/RES/918, at which point the death toll was already an estimated 500,000.

51 See eg Iran, UNGA Verbatim Record (17 September 2005) UN Doc A/60/PV.10, 8; 'Iran stopped nuclear weapons program as sinful – Rouhani' *Russia Today* (1 March 2014).

52 IAEA, 'Implementation of the NPT Safeguards Agreement and relevant provisions of Security Council resolutions in the Islamic Republic of Iran' (20 February 2014) GOV/2014/10, para 64.

53 ibid para 74.

54 See eg 'Remarks as delivered by James R Clapper, Director of National Intelligence to the Senate Select Committee on Intelligence' (Washington DC 29 January 2014), where the US did 'not know if Iran will eventually decide to build nuclear weapons'.

55 See eg Amos Harel, 'IDF chief to Haaretz: I do not believe Iran will decide to develop nuclear weapons' *Haaretz* (Tel Aviv 25 April 2012).

56 Jonathan Lis, 'Russia FM: Iran doesn't intend to attack Israel with nuclear weapons' *Haaretz* (Tel Aviv 11 October 2012).

57 See eg 'Iran's Bushehr plant joins national grid' *Press TV* (Tehran 4 September 2011).

58 Jeffery Goldberg, 'Obama to Iran and Israel: "As President of the United States, I don't bluff"' *The Atlantic* (Washington DC 2 March 2012).

59 Beginning in the 1950s, the nuclear programme was encouraged by US support through research reactors in 1967, cooperation with France in uranium enrichment in 1976 and renewed interest in nuclear power by Ayatollah Khomeini in 1984.

60 China was due to supply Iran with a miniature neutron source reactor and two power reactors. See Joseph Cirincione, Jon Wolfsthal and Miriam Rajkumar, *Deadly Arsenals: Nuclear, Biological, and Chemical Threats* (Carnegie Endowment for International Peace 2005) 303.

61 Russia signed an 'umbrella agreement for bilateral nuclear cooperation' with Iran in 1992. In 1995, further to agreeing completion of the Bushehr Nuclear Power Plant, 'Russia also offered in principle to supply Iran with a large research reactor, fuel fabrication facilities and a centrifuge enrichment plant'. See Gary Samore (ed), *Iran's Strategic Weapon Programmes: A Net Assessment* (Routledge 2005) 13.

62 ibid.

63 ibid 14.

64 ibid 14 ff.

65 'Remarks by Alireza Jafarzadeh on New Information on Top Secret Projects of the Iranian Regime's Nuclear Program' (Washington DC 14 August 2002).

66 Iran was not required to declare the facility until 180 days prior to introduction of any nuclear material to the facility under Code 3.1 of the Subsidiary Arrangements General Part of Iran's Safeguards Agreement.

67 UK, UNSC Verbatim Record (31 July 2006) UN Doc S/PV.5500, 4.
68 UNSC Res 1696 (31 July 2006) UN Doc S/RES/1696.
69 Russia, UNSC Verbatim Record (31 July 2006) UN Doc S/PV.5500, 5.
70 China, ibid 6.
71 UNSC Res 1696 (31 July 2006) UN Doc S/RES/1696, preamble.
72 ibid para 1.
73 IAEA, 'Implementation of the NPT Safeguards Agreement in the Islamic Republic of Iran' (27 February 2006) GOV/2006/15 para 53. See, also, IAEA, 'Implementation of the NPT Safeguards Agreement in the Islamic Republic of Iran' (8 June 2006) GOV/2006/38 para 18, where environmental samples previously taken from Iranian dual use materials were analysed and showed 'no indication of the presence of particles of nuclear material'.
74 IAEA, 'Implementation of the NPT Safeguards Agreement in the Islamic Republic of Iran' (2 September 2005) GOV/2005/77 para 2.
75 IAEA, 'Implementation of the NPT Safeguards Agreement in the Islamic Republic of Iran' (4 February 2006) GOV/2006/14, (g).
76 Treaty on the Non-Proliferation of Nuclear Weapons (1970) art 4.
77 See eg IAEA, 'Implementation of the NPT safeguards agreement and relevant provisions of United Nations Security Council resolutions in the Islamic Republic of Iran' (13 September 2012) GOV/2012/50, (f); IAEA, 'Implementation of the NPT safeguards agreement and relevant provisions of United Nations Security Council resolutions in the Islamic Republic of Iran' (18 November 2011) GOV/2011/69, (e); IAEA, 'Implementation of the NPT safeguards agreement and relevant provisions of Security Council resolutions 1737 (2006), 1747 (2007), 1803 (2008) and 1835 (2008) in the Islamic Republic of Iran' (27 November 2009) GOV/2009/82, (d); IAEA, 'Implementation of the NPT Safeguards Agreement in the Islamic Republic of Iran' (4 February 2006) GOV/2006/14, (c); IAEA, 'Implementation of the NPT Safeguards Agreement in the Islamic Republic of Iran' (2 September 2005) GOV/2005/77, (b); IAEA, 'Implementation of the NPT safeguards agreement in the Islamic Republic of Iran and related Board resolutions' (11 August 2005) GOV/2005/64, (g); IAEA, 'Implementation of the NPT safeguards agreement in the Islamic Republic of Iran' (29 November 2004) GOV/2004/90, (i); IAEA, 'Implementation of the NPT safeguards agreement and relevant provisions of United Nations Security Council resolutions in the Islamic Republic of Iran' (18 September 2004) GOV/2004/79, (f).
78 UNSC Res 1673 (27 April 2006) UN Doc S/RES/1673, preamble; UNSC Res 1696 (31 July 2006) UN Doc S/RES/1696, preamble; UNSC Res 1737 (27 December 2006) UN Doc S/RES/1737, preamble; UNSC Res 1747 (24 March 2007) UN Doc S/RES/1747, preamble; UNSC Res 1803 (3 March 2008) UN Doc S/RES/1803, preamble; UNSC Res 1929 (9 June 2010) UN Doc S/RES/1929, preamble.
79 See eg UNSC Presidential Statement 15 (2006) UN Doc S/PRST/2006/15; UNSC Verbatim Record (31 July 2006) UN Doc S/PV.5500, 4.
80 Moreover, Article IV of the NPT grants the right to participate in the 'fullest possible exchange of equipment, materials and scientific and technological information for the peaceful uses of nuclear energy'.
81 UNSC Res 1696 (31 July 2006) UN Doc S/RES/1696, para 2.
82 See Shayam Saran, 'Lecture at the India Habitat Centre' (New Delhi 24 April 2013).
83 The Agreement for the Cooperation between the Government of the United States of America and the Government of India concerning Peaceful Uses of Nuclear Energy (2005) had support from France, the UK and Russia and was a

step towards the landmark waiver of exemption for India in the Nuclear Supply Group, since it had signed neither the NPT nor the CTBT; China, as discussed previously, contravened the guidelines of the Nuclear Supplies Group in supplying Pakistan with nuclear energy in the absence of its acceptance of the NPT.

84 UNSC Res 2231 (20 July 2015) UN Doc S/RES/2231.

85 See eg 'Letter dated 4 July 2006 from the Permanent Representative of Japan to the United Nations addressed to the President of the Security Council' (5 July 2006) UN Doc S/2006/481, which led to a meeting on 14 October 2006 resulting in the adoption of UNSC Res 1718 (2006); 'Letter dated 5 April 2009 from the Permanent Representative of Japan to the United Nations addressed to the President of the Security Council' (5 April 2009) UN Doc S/2009/176 leading to UNSC Presidential Statement S/PRST/2009/7 (2009); 'Letter dated 25 May 2009 from the Permanent Representative of Japan to the United Nations addressed to the President of the Security Council' (25 May 2009) UN Doc S/2009/271, leading to resolution 1874 (2009); UNSC Verbatim Record (15 July 2006) UN Doc S/PV.5490, 2 ff; it has also taken part in the discussions on the Iranian regime actions taken (eg UNSC Verbatim Record (23 December 2006) UN Doc S/PV.5612) and supported the passing of resolutions against Iran eg UNSC Res 1737 (2006) and UNSC Res 1874 (2009).

86 IAEA, 'Communication Received from Japan Concerning Its Policies Regarding the Management of Plutonium' (28 August 2015) INFCIRC/549/Add.1/18 Annex B.

87 ibid; see also, eg Douglas Birch, R Jeffrey Smith and Jake Adelstein, 'Unarmed guards, bogus terror drills, and 96 tons of plutonium' *Foreign Policy* (Washington DC 10 March 2014).

88 This facility is estimated to be capable of nine metric tonnes of plutonium annually, equivalent to 2,000 nuclear weapons. See Jay Solomon and Miho Inada, 'Japan's nuclear plan unsettles US' *The Wall Street Journal* (New York 1 May 2013).

89 See eg IAEA, 'Communication Received from Japan Concerning Its Policies Regarding the Management of Plutonium' (3 October 2012) INFCIRC/549/Add.1/15, Annex B.

90 Robert Windrem, 'Japan has nuclear "Bomb in the Basement", and China isn't happy' *NBC News* (New York 11 March 2014).

91 There have been mild protestations by States such as the US and China, which have nonetheless failed to reach the Council.

8 Consistency with international human rights and humanitarian norms and standards

> '[I]t is essential, if man is not to be compelled to have recourse, as a last resort, to rebellion against tyranny and oppression, that human rights should be protected by the rule of law . . .'.[1]

Introduction

The issue of human rights at the Security Council comprises two elements – first, there is the consideration of human rights implications as substantive issues that affect the maintenance of international peace and security; that is to say that there are threats to the international peace and security that arise from human rights violations and concerns perpetrated against civilians either by their own governments or another, such as ethnic cleansing[2] or protection of civilians,[3] to which the Council must not turn a blind eye and which therefore instigate Council action. As UN Secretary-General Annan declared in 2000, 'no legal principle – not even sovereignty – can ever shield crimes against humanity. Where such crimes occur and peaceful attempts to halt them have been exhausted, the Security Council has a moral duty to act on behalf of the international community'.[4] These fall under a straightforward assessment of the threat to international peace and may potential instigate Council action under Chapter VII. I have discussed intervention for humanitarian reasons in the previous chapter, notably with reference to Syria, and as a result I will not enter into a lengthy discussion of Council intervention on humanitarian and human rights grounds in this chapter.

The second intersection of human rights with the rule of law at the Council level is more internalised and comes in the form of the Council's awareness and efforts to accommodate international human rights principles and standards in its own actions and decisions – those which do not focus primarily on responding to a human rights abuse per se. This component of the rule of law – compliance with international human rights norms – addresses whether the Security Council, first, should be and, secondly, feels itself bound by the principles of international human rights law in its decision-making process; this chapter attempts to identify what measures, if any, the Council takes to accommodate human rights concerns when taking a decision. Although it might be argued that many threats to the international peace touch on human rights issues – such as the proliferation of nuclear weapons,[5] international terrorism[6] or piracy[7] – this component of the rule of law examines whether the Council's response to such threats itself incorporates an alertness to human rights concerns. Such 'non-substantive' human rights issues may come about, for example, in situations where the Council imposes country-wide economic or targeted sanctions and where it decides to authorise military intervention or peacekeeping missions are established.[8]

In contrast to a response to a human rights violation by the Council – which requires a proactive response using legal and political machinery at its disposal under the Charter to violations of human rights perpetrated by governments and non-State actors – consistency with international human rights norms and standards is an intrinsic obligation to which the Council must adhere in the passing of resolutions. I intend to examine whether the Council shows compulsion to abide by international human rights law in its Chapter VII resolutions, evidenced by explicit statements either by states themselves in verbatim records or by the text of resolutions that are passed by the Council. Moreover, this component questions whether there is a pattern of compliance, or, in the event that human rights have not historically been considered by the Council in its decision-making process, a movement towards reform in its attitude and the gradual inclusion of human rights considerations when reaching a decision.

The case for applicability of human rights and humanitarian law to the Council

At a primitive level, it would immediately exemplify a double standard for the Council fail to incorporate the same standards to its own decision-making process that it advocates on a global basis through its Chapter VII powers in situations and areas where human rights concerns are deemed to exist. There are also compelling legal arguments that support the implementation of human rights considerations upon the Council's behaviour. In general, since its establishment in 1945, the UN has dedicated a large part of its work to human rights issues, not least with the Universal Declaration on Human Rights in 1948 and various international treaties and covenants, the enshrined principles of which have since passed into customary international law. It would therefore be remiss to argue that there is no basis upon which to argue that the Council should be held to maintain a standard of human rights in both its substantive and non-substantive human rights decisions.[9]

Previous standards for testing the Council's actions within the framework of international human rights law have taken *jus cogens* norms as the relevant benchmark,[10] in contrast to this research which expands to include wider human rights issues. *Jus cogens* norms relate to the most heinous of crimes that can be committed and are norms upon which all states are able to agree upon, having the widest base of support but an inverse, proportionately narrow scope; to gain the widest acceptance from states, it is only the highest-ranking, and least number of, crimes that can be outlawed. Furthermore, these are agreed upon by states in a customary manner – insofar as they are not enshrined in any text – and thus *jus cogens* is an insufficient code of conduct for two reasons: first, there is no concrete definition of what constitutes a *jus cogens* norm and, secondly, even those touted as being peremptory norms are a handful at best, continuing to grant the Council all but free reign in its actions and defeating the purpose of this research. As such, there are myriad violations of human rights law that can be perpetrated outside of the narrow scope of *jus cogens.*

This does not, however, immediately preclude the Council from an obligation to respect human rights law in its decision-making process. The applicability of rule of law components generally, which include the respect for human rights, has explicitly been highlighted by Secretaries-General not only in Annan's original 2004 enumeration of rule of law components,[11] but again in 2008, by Ban Ki-Moon, who reiterated that 'rules of international law apply *mutatis mutandis* to the Organization as they do to States'.[12] As is the case with other components of the rule of law, the first point of reference when examining the duties and responsibilities of the Council itself should be the Charter; '[t]he United Nations is a creation of international law, established by treaty, and its activities are governed by the rules set out in its Charter'.[13]

The Council is bound under the Charter to act 'in accordance with the Purposes and Principles of the United Nations',[14] of which both 'promoting and encouraging respect for human rights and for fundamental freedoms'[15] and the maintenance of peace and security 'in conformity with the principles of justice *and international law*'[16] both feature. Overarching both these principles, and the Charter itself, are the goals of the United Nations as an organisation, one of which is 'to establish conditions under which justice and respect for the obligations arising from treaties and other sources of international law can be maintained'.[17] It would be illogical and undermine the core principles of the UN as an organisation if the Council were to ignore international law in the decision-making process. It has even been postulated that, according to principles of *venire contra factum proprium*,[18] the Council is bound by estoppel to abide by the same human rights standards that it advocates.[19]

One may legitimately question why the UN Charter is silent on the existence of human rights if it was intended to apply as the main normative source for the work of the UN organs. The absence of extensive human rights protections in the Charter is most likely a result of the lack of consideration they were granted in the mid-20th century; for as valuable and integral as human rights are widely accepted to be both nationally and internationally today, 'when the UN Charter was drafted, human rights were at the international level still moral postulates and political principles only'.[20]

This stance is supported by the non-binding nature of the UDHR and the fact that it would be a further 20 years before legally binding international treaties like the ICCPR and ICESR would be adopted by states before entering into force a further decade later in 1976. Moreover, the UN is excluded from both the ICCPR and ICESCR, which focus on the actions and obligations of states rather than international organisations[21] and the UN is not party to the 1949 Geneva Conventions, the 1977 Additional Protocols or any other humanitarian law treaties due, officially, to the fact that the UN is not 'substantively in a position to become party to the 1949 Conventions, which contain many obligations that can only be discharged by the exercise of juridical and administrative powers which the Organization does not possess . . .'.[22] A differentiation must also be made between the accession of states to treaties relating to international human rights law or the imposition of customary international norms upon states and the exercise of power by those same states through the Council as a UN organ; it may be argued that states have obligations both domestically and internationally under international law that do not exist as an organ when deliberating or passing resolutions in their respective Council seats.[23]

In Council-mandated operations too, there have been developments in the applicability of human rights law; where individuals have been affected directly by Council-mandated action, there have been standards imposed upon UN personnel on the ground.[24] In the post-conflict environment of East Timor, the UN Transitional Administration in East Timor (UNTAET) – 'endowed [under Council resolution 1272 (1999)] with overall responsibility for the administration of East Timor empowered to exercise all legislative and executive authority, including the administration of justice'[25] – imposed upon 'all persons undertaking public duties or holding public office in East Timor . . . internationally recognized human rights standards'[26] of a wide variety, from the non-derogable to the non-legally binding;[27] in Kosovo, too, the UN Interim Administration in Kosovo (UNMIK) was under obligation to observe the same 'internationally recognized human rights standards'.[28] These standards are wide-ranging, comprehensive and based on legally binding international treaties; it would seem contradictory for peacekeeping operations to be required to comply with human rights law and principles when the organ that legitimises and authorises them itself fails to do so.

Extending, therefore, the thesis that the Council must be bound by the rule of law, UN organs must be held to the same standards that they attempt to promote, of which human rights is surely one. Rather than exempting the Council, the increased preponderance of international human rights law works in favour of the assertion that the Council should be held to the same standards as states; as human rights instruments have increased in number and scope – to which, of course, the UN itself has contributed in no small part – so too has the expectation that where the Council's decisions impact upon the rights and freedoms protected by those instruments has grown more acute. The Council, then, as an organ of the United Nations, has certain legal obligations to ensure that human rights are respected when making decisions. As early as 1950, this argument was being promoted by Lauterpacht[29] and there has been more recent growing support for the non-derogability of human rights in the Council procedure,[30] specifically that: 'when the rights of individuals are involved, *the application of human rights standards is a legal necessity*. Human rights now form *part of the concept of the international public order*'.[31]

Applying human rights to Council decisions

The Council itself has conceded that the rule of law should apply internally to the United Nations in a Council presidential statement from 2010, where it 'expressed its commitment to ensure that all UN efforts to restore peace and security themselves respect and promote the rule of law'.[32] Respect for human rights has generally been accepted to form part of the rule of law both domestically and internationally; it would, therefore, appear that a more explicit commitment and admission of the applicability of the rule of law to the Council, by extension from the UN, in its responsibility to maintain and restore the international peace cannot be made. However, the Council has not always granted such accord to the principles of human rights either as an issue that falls within its jurisdiction or as a concept that applies to it internally.

Throughout the late 20th century and continuing into the 21st, progress made in bringing human rights concerns to the fore have been undermined by lack of action. In addition to the massacres perpetrated by the Khmer Rouge in Kampuchea[33] between 1975 and 1979, the Council also neglected human rights violations in Congo in 1960, Burundi in 1972 and 1993, Bosnia Herzegovina in 1992, Rwanda in 1994, Kosovo in 1999, Sudan in 2000–2007, Sri Lanka in 2009, Syria from 2011 onwards and, most recently, both the situation in Ukraine and the renewed sectarian violence in Iraq in 2014. Most damningly, perhaps, is the explanation of this absence; as two scholars phrased it, 'the lack of political will, not lack of information, is at the core of the failures of the Security Council to address these and other abhorrent situations both timely and appropriately, or even to consider them at all'.[34]

Consequently, the protection of human rights externally by the Council cannot be said to have been exhaustive; the Council does acknowledge the need for consideration of the human rights effects of its decisions. In the post-Cold War landscape, there has been an increased applicability of human rights law to the actions of peacekeepers, missions and other entities mandated by the Council to operate on the ground;[35] yet the Council has never acknowledged that human rights should guide its response to a threat to the international peace. Rather, while the Council has shown that human rights – at least in certain cases – warrant a response by the Council,[36] and the groups and entities that direct these responses are bound by human rights law, there has been no explicit statement that such a response itself must be guided by principles of human rights.[37]

International human rights law is most relevant to Council responses to perceived threats to the peace and in this chapter the examination of integration of human rights standards into Council decisions will be conducted within the framework of this element. The authorisation or delegation of authority to intervene militarily also intersects with the applicability of international human rights and humanitarian law to the internal decision-making process of the Council; however, it does so to a lesser extent, as the conduct of peacekeepers has increasingly been regulated through various internal guidelines, rules and policies.[38] The conduct of military troops contributed to UN-mandated interventions is governed not only by international humanitarian law instruments,[39] but also the domestic jurisdictions of the contributing states themselves, which have an obligation to pursue prosecution for violations of human rights and humanitarian law.[40]

Prior to 1990 there is no evidence that the Council considered human rights within the framework of its decision-making process, which is unsurprising given the debate that raged over whether rights even fell within the scope of the Council's mandate at all.[41] There is no mention of human rights in the Council's Rules of Procedure and, notwithstanding Article 24(2) of the Charter, nor is there an obligation inherent in the text of any Chapter VII article that implies the Council must ensure that the effects of action taken under Articles 41 and 42 of the Charter adheres to human rights norms. As with the rise of the importance of human rights generally in the minds of UN Members and on the agendas of the Council and other UN organs, human rights appear to have been introduced by informal and organic means.

Article 41: humanitarian concerns regarding non-military intervention

As human rights began to take centre stage on the agenda of the Council after 1990, many commentators both inside the UN[42] and externally[43] criticised what appeared to be a 'human rights paradox' – namely that the reasons for imposition of sanctions have increasingly been the protection of human rights, when the imposition of sanctions themselves often have a detrimental effect:

> Sanctions can complicate the work of humanitarian agencies . . . [,] conflict with the development objectives of the Organization and do long-term damage to the productive capacity of the target country . . . [,] have a severe effect on other countries that are neighbours or major economic partners of the target country. . . [and] defeat their own purpose by provoking a patriotic response against the international community, symbolized by the United Nations, and by rallying the population behind the leaders whose behaviour the sanctions are intended to modify.[44]

The perils of hastily adopted and ill-planned sanction regimes were exemplified in 1990 with the imposition of economic sanctions on Iraq[45] as a result of its failure to comply with resolution 660 (1990),[46] ordering it to withdraw from the territory of Kuwait. These comprehensive sanctions resulted in a spike in infant mortality and morbidity,[47] child malnutrition and a deterioration in the standard of living, nutrition and health for the Iraqi people, especially with respect to access to drinking water, agriculture and the supply of electricity;[48] one Council member estimated that in 1995, '[s]even per cent of Iraq's population – about 1,300,000 people – [was] at risk, being hardest hit by the consequences of the sanctions regime'.[49] In fact, far from exerting pressure 'to secure compliance of Iraq with paragraph 2 of resolution 660 (1990)',[50] the sanction policy inhibited 'the importation of spare parts, chemicals, reagents, and the means of transportation required to provide water and sanitation services to the civilian population of Iraq',[51] thereby consolidating the Iraqi regime's power through its capacity to control distribution of bare necessities through a rationing system, granting the authorities further control over anti-government insurgence and expanding the existing corruption in the country.[52]

The impact of sanctions was a divisive issue amongst the Council members throughout the 1990s. Some, including Russia, China and France, argued that the humanitarian concerns raised by sanctions demanded they be reviewed,[53] while others, such as the UK and US, maintained that 'Iraq will remain subject to a regime of sanctions imposed under Chapter VII of the United Nations Charter until it complies fully with all the Security Council's relevant resolutions'[54] and that sanctions should even be augmented so long as the Iraqi authorities continued to refuse compliance with the numerous Council resolutions passed on the subject.[55] In fact, owing to the open-ended nature of resolutions such as 660 (1990), 661 (1990) and 678 (1990) and the fact that they were not rescinded subsequently, permanent members of the Council benefited from what has been referred to as a 'reverse veto'[56] over the termination of sanctions[57] – the capacity to use or threaten the use of the veto on any resolution that would put an end to existing sanctions. By 1994, deep into the sanctions regime that had been imposed on Iraq, it was clear that sanctions were not operating as intended: 'Iraqi authorities [had] enough money to maintain one of the largest armies and enough money to pay for military operations, whether to suppress the Marsh Arabs or to threaten Kuwait'.[58]

The Council members themselves had already recognised by the mid-1990s that sanctions could not be imposed in isolation of consideration for humanitarian concerns;[59] references to ensuring that humanitarian concerns were addressed prior to the imposition of sanctions were already emerging during discussions. The Russian Federation appears to have been the first to make mention, as early as 1994, that:

> thought must be given to the question *how sanctions may be aimed at political elites*, thereby reducing to a minimum the sufferings of broad strata of the population, including its most vulnerable categories . . . In other words, thought should be given to the fact that sanctions should not punish the most those who are perhaps least of all capable of righting the situation . . . and to *laying down clear humanitarian limits* in determining sanctions.[60]

Concrete efforts were made to assess and mitigate the humanitarian repercussions of the Council's sanctions regimes in 1995, with the commissioning of a report on the effect of sanctions on humanitarian conditions by the UN Department of Humanitarian Affairs (DHA)[61] and a study[62] conducted for the DHA with the objective of developing methods and indicators for assessment of humanitarian impact of sanctions. Nonetheless, it was not until the end of the decade that the Council abandoned paying lip service to the humanitarian situation in Iraq[63] and truly took stock of the failures resulting from its sanctions regime there.[64] A panel on humanitarian issues was established to 'assess the current humanitarian situation in Iraq and make recommendations to the Security Council regarding measures to improve the humanitarian situation in Iraq'.[65] The subsequent findings confirmed the protestations of agencies, states, NGOs and humanitarian groups which the Council already knew four years earlier[66] and arguably even as early as 1991:[67] '[e]ven if not all suffering in Iraq can be imputed to external factors, especially sanctions, the Iraqi people would not be undergoing such deprivations in the absence of prolonged measures imposed by the Security Council and the effects of the war'.[68] The Council was found, by its own established panel no less, to have verged on complicity with the regime in intensifying the horrific humanitarian situations in Iraq during the 1990s.

By 1995, the realisation was more widespread that the absence of humanitarian considerations can result in the detrimental outcome or by-product of a Council response such as sanctions, particularly in relation to vulnerable sections of society. In a letter to the President of the Security Council, the P5 members grouped together to support the proposal that 'further collective actions in the Security Council within the context of any future sanctions regimes should be directed to minimize unintended adverse side-effects of sanctions on the most vulnerable segments of targeted countries'.[69] Nonetheless, it took several years for the Council to implement this concept into practice. It was not until 1997, when debating the means of dealing with the situation in Sudan, that a note from the DHA[70] warning against the implementation of air sanctions under UNSC Resolution 1054[71] was heeded and the 90-day grace period given in the resolution elapsed without consequence. Both China and the Russian Federation were extremely hesitant to resort to the use of sanctions again in light of the concerns raised in Iraq and Haiti, with the latter noting that: '[t]he rash use of the sanctions instrument is not only destructive for the people of Sudan and the countries of the region, but creates a precedent which could do real damage to the Security Council's authority by giving the impression that the Council is not able to draw conclusions from past lessons'.[72]

A report by the Secretary-General two months later highlighted 'the likely negative humanitarian effects of the possible ban envisaged in UNSC Resolution 1070 (1996) and . . . the potential negative impact on the health situation'.[73] Whether as a result of humanitarian concerns or – more cynically – the threat of the use of a veto by the Russian Federation owing to economic concerns,[74] the flight ban on Sudan Airlines was not enforced. Similar investigations took place prior to the implementation of sanctions in Afghanistan,[75] Liberia[76] and Sierra Leone.[77]

The balance between humanitarian concerns and effective sanctions regimes was not perfected overnight and, despite the humanitarian crises that were risked as a result of the sanctions regime imposed by the Council, the frustration and disappointment that followed the failure of the Council to soften its stance even in the late 1990s was highlighted by the representative of France, which 'had hoped also that the Council, in the future exercise of its prerogatives, would continue to use very precise wording in its work in order to avoid situations in which people who are not directly responsible for the problems encountered might find themselves facing sanctions . . . but deem[ed] it unfortunate that this suggestion was not taken into account'.[78]

Indeed, criticism continued even to the turn of the century and the Council has been accused of adopting a policy where 'getting sanctions right has [often] been a less compelling goal than getting sanctions adopted'.[79] Such criticism of the humanitarian impact of comprehensive sanctions regimes and a drive to incorporate new techniques to make sanctions more effective at their goals to ensure compliance with its resolutions through non-military means led to several rounds of sanction reform reviews: in the years 1998–1999, the Interlaken Process focused on targeting financial sanctions;[80] in 1999–2000, the Bonn/Berlin Process tackled sanctions related to arms embargoes, travel and aviation;[81] in 2001–2003, the Stockholm Process[82] discussed UN Policy Options; in 2007, Greece sponsored a symposium on 'Enhancing the Implementation of UN Security Council Sanctions';[83] and in November 2015, a high-level review of UN sanctions built upon these processes.[84]

A lesson learnt?

In addition to these five rounds of sanctions review, the Council has also implemented its own reform efforts in the form of The Informal Working Group on General Issues of Sanctions – a temporary body established in 2000[85] – which was created to explore the sanctions process and propose amendments to the Council in how best to impose sanctions. When, in 2006, it submitted its recommendations, amendments to the design,[86] implementation,[87] monitoring[88] and working methods,[89] the Council significantly amended its approach to and content of sanctions, introducing targeted and smart sanctions to replace the blanket comprehensive sanctions employed in Haiti, Yugoslavia and Iraq. These newer forms of sanctions were also more bespoke to the countries upon which they were imposed.

Rather than adopting a *one size fits all* model of sanction regime, as the Council had previously been inclined to do, newer sanctions regimes integrated almost pinpoint-accurate measures such as commodity-specific sanctions pertinent to the country of sanction,[90] sanctions targeted to individuals and segmented sanction elements[91] that could be selected individually and tailored more accurately to ensure lower negative humanitarian and human rights impact upon civilians and increased pressure on the powerful elite that were the true targets of Council action. The ability of the Council to *mix and match* different components of sanctions allowed it to focus its sanctions regime on the sources of income for those in power or for those individuals that it wished to isolate, rather than effecting collateral damage on the scale of the Iraqi sanctions regime. Moreover, in various sanction regimes, assets that were deemed to be 'necessary for basic expenses, including payment for foodstuffs, rent or mortgage, medicines and medical treatment, taxes, insurance premiums, and public utility charges'[92] were exempt in a clear lesson learnt from the Iraq sanctions experience, which itself was overhauled[93] to account for the humanitarian situation following the Iraq War and finally replaced[94] in 2003 with a committee-led sanctions regime.

This practice of creating committees, panels or groups of experts and monitoring groups for all sanctions imposed is also a step towards increased transparency, fairness and institutional strength on the part of the Council. Eritrea and Somalia were subject to a simple sanction regime under UNSC Resolution 733[95] before the adoption of UNSC Resolution 751[96] created a committee to monitor the situation; the DRC's sanctions were also amended in 2003 from a simple arms embargo[97] to one under the supervision of both a committee and a group of experts;[98] Sudan's simple arms embargo[99] transitioned to sanctions under the watch of a committee and panel of experts;[100] and UNSC Resolution 1695[101] imposing non-proliferation sanctions on the DPRK was swiftly augmented to an arms embargo, asset freeze, non-proliferation and travel ban under the auspices of a committee in 2006.[102] In fact, since 2006 the Council has not imposed a sanctions regime without a corresponding committee at the very least.[103] Although these committees are established to monitor compliance with the sanctions regimes, their existence provides a much needed link between the situation on the ground and the Council through country reports that are filed.

Article 41: human rights concerns regarding non-military intervention

Notwithstanding the implementation of this measure, which may have added a degree of transparency and independence to the listing of individuals to be targeted, there remained human rights concerns with respect to the lists of individuals compiled. Due process rights are jeopardised by the procedure of the Council and the inability of individuals to contest their insertion on asset freeze and financial sanctions lists; under Article 25 of the Charter, states 'agree to accept and carry out the decisions of the Security Council'[104] and, in contrast to domestic jurisdictions where legal recourse may be available through domestic judicial channels in the event of an alleged breach of justice, there was initially no means of arguing one's innocence to the Council. In essence, once placed on the list, it was impossible to be removed without the express consent of the Council or the overseeing committee, a request for which had to come through the state of nationality or residency of the petitioner.

It was this 'resolve to ensure that sanctions are carefully targeted in support of clear objectives. . . [and that] fair and clear procedures exist for placing individuals and entities on sanctions lists and for removing them, as well as for granting humanitarian exemptions'[105] that led to the establishment of a Focal Point for Delisting requests, which allows direct access to the individual in question,[106] rather than the arduous path of applying through the state and is undoubtedly a step forward for the due process rights that may have been initially overlooked by the Council in their sanction regimes. The Council also created the Office of the

Ombudsperson – an independent and impartial review mechanism exclusively for delisting from the Al-Qaida sanctions list – in an effort to welcome 'improvements to the Committee's procedures and the quality of the Consolidated List and *expressing* its intent to continue efforts to ensure that procedures are fair and clear'.[107]

The Ombudsperson should 'perform [his] tasks in an independent and impartial manner and . . . neither seek nor receive instructions from any government'.[108] The Al-Qaeda and Taliban sanctions regime was first established in 1999[109] and has been subsequently amended numerous times since[110] but it was the concern over due rights process of individuals placed on the sanctions list that spurred the Council into action. Individuals who found themselves on the list were not subject to any judicial standards of trial prior to their inclusion[111] and there was no justification offered by the Council or other body for listing these individuals on the sanctions list, contrary to principles of *habeas corpus*, transparency and avoidance of arbitrariness.

A dearth of available case law and the lack of engagement in the decision-making process of the Ombudsperson undoubtedly impacts upon the fairness of the law and the right to a fair trial – if indeed this can be called a judicial process – for petitioners seeking to disengage themselves from any association with extremist, terrorist, or otherwise listed groups and individuals. Previous practice and cases are not made available for the preparation of petitioners' cases and counsel have no access to the jurisprudential history of the Ombudsperson or delisting decisions. The availability of such information is a basic principle of the right to a fair trial; although the Office of the Ombudsperson is not a judicial entity, the impact of the Council's decisions to list an individual or entity under the sanctions regime does have legal consequences at the domestic level of financial, mobility and other human rights impacts. The absence of access to these records leaves petitioners in a lacuna as to the fairness of the Ombudsperson mechanism; undoubtedly the inability for one to mount an effective defence is a severe violation of one of the most fundamental human rights issues: access to justice.

Thus, there is still work to be done to ensure that the Council complies with human rights fully in the process of establishing its sanctions regimes; in an apparent conflict of interest, the same committee entrusted with compiling and monitoring the sanctions list was the only body empowered to 'consider requests for exemptions from the measure imposed'[112] with no oversight. The inability of individuals to appeal their inclusion to the committee is what, in part, led to the landmark and controversial *Kadi*[113] and *Nada*[114] judgments in the EU Courts. The fundamental rights of Kadi – specifically the 'right to be heard, the right to respect for property and the principle of proportionality, and also the right to effective judicial review'[115] were found to have been violated by his inclusion on the sanctions list.[116]

In 2013 it was found by the ECJ that despite the establishment of the Office of the Ombudsperson, 'the procedure for delisting and *ex-officio* re-examination at UN level . . . do not provide to the person whose name is listed on the Sanctions

Committee Consolidated List . . . the guarantee of effective judicial protection'.[117] Although the European Court of Human Rights has previously held that 'in interpreting its resolutions, there must be a presumption that the Security Council does not intend to impose any obligation on Member States to breach fundamental principles of human rights',[118] in the *Nada* case it soon afterwards made it quite clear that: 'Resolution 1390 (2002) . . . [imposed] an obligation to take measures capable of breaching human rights'.[119] The legal interpretation, then, is that the Council does not *deliberately* breach human rights, but that it is capable of doing so nonetheless.

This interpretation is befitting to summarise the Council's approach to human rights; the Council's intentions and results are at times mismatched. While there may have been varying objectives of efforts towards reform, including strengthening capacities to administer the sanctions, increasing compliance and streamlining the design and implementation of embargoes and sanctions, the human rights impact of sanctions was undoubtedly one of the core elements for reflection; however, as respect for human rights increased in Council resolutions on sanctions, new challenges have arisen with which the Council has taken time to come to terms. Moreover, efficacy appears at times have declined. The subsequent shift in the Council's response – as a result of the implementation of some of the many recommendations and the increased concern for human rights and humanitarian issues in sanctioned countries – may have resulted in tamer results on the ground; it is not clear that sanctions have succeeded alone in altering the trajectory of troubled countries. In the Sudan,[120] Côte d'Ivoire[121] and Libya,[122] for example, sanctions were always coupled with the mobilisation of troops either in a protection or monitoring force[123] or military intervention capacity.[124] However, this may be a necessary forfeit on the part of the Council.

It is worth noting that sanctions are one of a number of tools at the disposition of the Council and, just as there are various types of sanctions that can be applied to a situation threatening the peace, so too the Council is not barred in any form from implementing sanctions in tandem with one or more other tools at its disposal either under Chapter VII, as was the case in Libya in 2011, or through international diplomacy, as was the case with Iran even more recently. Ultimately, the Council has correctly identified the necessity of ensuring that sanction measures take stock of human rights and humanitarian concerns; however, this does not mean that they are limited as to what course of action outside of a sanctions regime they may pursue.

Conclusions

What emerges from this study is that, at least over the past two decades, the Council appears actively to have searched to improve the human rights considerations in its decision-making process. The Council's record on the humanitarian impact of sanctions appears to have improved more than that of the human rights front; it is clear that the Council and its constituent members see an obligation to ensure that sanctions do not adversely affect the innocent individuals of a state subject to sanctions or embargoes. From refusing the assertion that human rights fell within under the responsibilities of the Council to maintain peace and security to a realisation and admission, not simply verbally in the course of resolutions debates, but through actions of the Council in establishing safeguards, committees and bodies to monitor and implement sanctions, the Council has moved a considerable distance in the space of several decades.

UNSC Resolution 2083[125] introduced the necessity for increased transparency as to how sanction lists are compiled; the Al-Qaida list now includes a narrative summary of reasons for the listing of individuals, groups, undertakings and entities included in the Al-Qaida Sanctions List. The Office of the Ombudsperson must also adhere to a strict time frame for dealing with all delisting requests[126] and the committee is obliged to decide within a 60-day window whether to delist the individual or entity.[127]

Similarly, the use of committees, panels of experts and other subsidiary bodies of the Council not only allow the Council members to receive more accurate and reliable information, but also display an increased willingness to achieve transparency and avoid arbitrariness in their actions. While the Council has perhaps not yet fully achieved this component of incorporating human rights fully into its decision-making process, in charting the course that it has taken over the past decades, it is clear that significant steps are being taken in the appropriate direction. However, there is still a great deal of headway to be made before total compliance with human rights by the Council can be claimed in its process. The Council's human rights and humanitarian intervention record is selective, as previously discussed, and with respect to its efforts to tackle the peripheral issues of human rights in post-conflict states it also lacks full engagement.

Moreover, as a result of inconsistencies between the official stances promulgated during meetings and the resulting action taken under its authority or delegation of powers, the Council risks losing moral authority and integrity. For instance, the Chinese stance for decades has been that 'the promotion of human rights and fundamental freedoms is a paramount purpose of the United Nations, no less important than the maintenance of international peace and security';[128] nonetheless, this did not prevent its recent vetoes, along with Russia, on issues that dealt with human rights in Zimbabwe,[129] Myanmar[130] or Syria.[131] Nor indeed did the respect for human rights shown by the US in pursuit of referrals to the ICC of the situations in Libya and Syria hinder its veto of resolutions condemning Israel for human rights issues[132] or Russian advocacy for human rights hinder its veto on the extension of an investigative mission to Georgia[133] and matters concerning minority rights in Ukraine.[134]

Even amidst calls by France[135] and Canada[136] to abolish the use of the veto when dealing with human rights issues, the Council continues to proceed on a selective basis with respect to both intervening in situations that involve violations of human rights and ensuring that human rights safeguards are enshrined in the documents resulting from its deliberations. Overall, the Council must seek to balance more effectively its duties as a UN organ in protecting and promoting human rights with the national political interests of the Members of which it is comprised, for the human rights of the peoples who rely on the Council for assistance and rescue should supersede all other concerns.

Notes

1 Universal Declaration of Human Rights (adopted 10 December 1948) UNGA Res 217 A(III) (UDHR) preamble.
2 See eg UNSC Res 819 (16 April 1993) UN Doc S/RES/819 and UNSC Res 836 (4 June 1993) UN Doc S/RES/836 on the humanitarian concerns of the Council in the Former Republic of Yugoslavia.
3 See UNSC Res 1894 (11 November 2009) UN Doc S/RES/1894 on compliance with international humanitarian, human rights and refugee law.
4 Report of the Secretary-General, 'We the peoples: the role of the United Nations in the twenty-first century' (2000) UN Doc A/54/2000 para 219.
5 See eg UNSC Res 984 (11 April 1995) UN Doc S/RES/984, adopting the stance that everything must be done to avoid nuclear war and prevent the proliferation of nuclear weaponry.
6 See eg UNSC Res 1267 (15 October 1999) UN Doc S/RES/1267 establishing the Al-Qaida and Taliban Committee.
7 See eg UNSC Res 1816 (2 June 2008) UN Doc S/RES/1816 authorising action against piracy in Somalia.
8 For a general introduction and discussion of the difference between human rights as substantive and incidental concerns of the Council see eg Bardo Fassbender, 'The role for human rights in the decision-making process' in Bardo Fassbender (ed), *Securing Human Rights? Achievements and Challenges of the UN Security Council* (Oxford University Press 2010) 88; Sidney D Bailey, *The UN Security Council and Human Rights* (Macmillan 1994); Jared Genser and Bruno Stagno Ugarte (eds), *The United Nations Security Council in the Age of Human Rights* (Cambridge University Press 2014).
9 See Mariano J Aznar-Gomez, 'A decade of human rights protection by the UN Security Council: a sketch of deregulation?' (2002) 13(1) *European Journal of International Law* 221.
10 Alexander Orakhelashvili, 'The acts of the Security Council: meaning and standards of review' (2007) 11 *Max Planck Yearbook of United Nations Law* 143, 178.
11 Report of the Secretary-General, 'The rule of law and transitional justice in conflict and post-conflict societies' (2004) UN Doc S/2004/616 para 6.
12 Report of the Secretary-General, 'Strengthening and coordinating United Nations rule of law activities' (6 August 2008) UN Doc A/63/226 para 27.
13 ibid.
14 UN Charter (1945) art 24(2).
15 ibid art 1(3).
16 ibid art 1(1) (emphasis added).
17 ibid preamble.
18 'No one may set himself in contradiction to his own previous conduct'. See Bryan A Garner (ed), *Black's Law Dictionary* (10th edn, Thomson West 1990) 1039. See also Bardo Fassbender, 'Human rights obligations and the UN Security Council' in Pieter H F Bekker, Rudolf Dolzer and Michael Waibel (eds), *Making Transitional Law Work in the Global Economy: Essays in Honour of Detlev Vagts* (Cambridge University Press 2010) 82.

19 See Malcolm N Shaw, *International Law* (Cambridge University Press 2003) 439. See also August Reinisch, 'Developing human rights and humanitarian law accountability of the Security Council for the imposition of economic sanctions' (2011) 95(4) *American Journal of International Law* 851.
20 Bardo Fassbender, 'The role for human rights in the decision-making process' (n 8) 79.
21 Art 48 of the ICCPR allows only states to accede to the treaty and even the language used in the texts, referring to 'State Parties', excludes entities that do not fit such a description.
22 'Legal Opinion of the Secretariat of the United Nations, Question of the Possible Accession of Intergovernmental Organizations to the Geneva Conventions for the Protection of War Victims' [1972] UN Juridical Yearbook 153 para 3.
23 For a more in-depth discussion of this issue see eg Bardo Fassbender, 'The role for human rights in the decision-making process' (n 8) 80–82.
24 'Secretary-General's Bulletin on the Observance by United Nations Forces of International humanitarian Law' (6 August 1999) ST/SGB/1999/13.
25 UNTAET 'Regulation No 1999/1 on the Authority of the Transitional Administration in East Timor' (27 November 1999) UNTAET/REG/1991/1 preamble.
26 ibid s 8.
27 ibid: 'Universal Declaration on Human Rights of 10 December 1948; International Covenant on Civil and Political Rights of 16 December 1966 and its Protocols; International Covenant on Economic, Social and Cultural Rights of 16 December 1966; Convention on the Elimination of All Forms of Racial Discrimination of 21 December 1965; Convention on the Elimination of All Forms of Discrimination Against Women of 17 December 1979; Convention Against Torture and other Cruel, Inhumane or Degrading Treatment or Punishment of 17 December 1984; International Convention on the Rights of the Child of 20 November 1989'.
28 UNMIK 'Regulation No 2000/59 Amending UNMIK Regulation No 1999/24 on the Law Applicable in Kosovo' (27 October 2000) UNMIK/REG/2000/59 para 1.3.
29 Hersch Lauterpacht, *International Law and Human Rights* (Stevens & Sons 1950) 159.
30 Henry G Schermers and Niels M Blokker, *International Institutional Law: Unity Within Diversity* (Nijhoff 2011) 824; Derek W Bowett, *The Law of International Institutions* (Stevens & Sons 1982) 366; Pierre-Marie Dupuy and Yann Kerbat, *Droit International Public* (Dalloz 2014) 143.
31 Ian Brownlie, 'The decisions of political organs of the United Nations and the rule of law' in Ronald St John Macdonald (ed), *Essays in Honour of Wang Tieya* (Nijhoff 1993) 102 (emphasis added).
32 UNSC Presidential Statement 11 (2010) UN Doc S/PRST/2010/11 at 2.
33 Now Cambodia.
34 Bruno Stagno Ugarte and Jared Genser, 'Evolution of the Security Council' in Jared Genser and Bruno Stagno Ugarte (eds), *The United Nations Security Council in the Age of Human Rights* (Cambridge University Press 2014) 27.
35 The human rights component of the UN Observer Mission in El Salvador (ONUSAL), established under UNSC Res 693 (1991) was first of its kind to be deployed; the UN Transitional Authority in Cambodia (UNTAC), established under UNSC Res 745 (1992) also featured a human rights component; Memorandums of Understanding (MoUs) such as that between the Department of Peacekeeping Operations (DPKO) and the Office of the High Commissioner for Human Rights (OHCHR) in November 1999 can enumerate how human rights elements within peacekeeping operations operate; human rights components of peacekeeping missions are viewed on a par with all other components, including

internal policy-making; the integration of human rights experts in an Integrated Mission Task Force (IMTF), established at the UN Headquarters in New York, is a prerequisite; there are usually express mandates by the Council requesting all parties, including peacekeepers, to protect and promote human rights; and the human rights obligations of a contributing state party to a mission apply to their citizens and staff extraterritorially.

36 UNSC Res 827 (25 May 1993) UN Doc S/RES/827 established the ICTY 'for the sole purpose of prosecuting persons responsible for serious violations of international humanitarian law' para 2; UNSC Res 955 (8 November 1994) UN Doc S/RES/955 established the ICTR 'for the sole purpose of prosecuting persons responsible for genocide and other serious violations of international humanitarian law' para 1; UNSC Res 1973 (17 March 2011) UN Doc S/RES/1973 authorised military intervention in Libya 'to protect civilians and civilian populated areas under threat of attack' para 4; UNSC Res 1975 (30 March 2011) UN Doc S/RES/1975 on Côte d'Ivoire included a decision by the Council to 'adopt targeted sanctions against those individuals . . . [who] commit serious violations of human rights and international humanitarian law' para 12; UNSC Res 2127 (5 December 2013) UN Doc S/RES/2127 on the Central African Republic condemned 'widespread human rights violations and abuses' para 17, and requested the establishment of 'an international commission of inquiry . . . to investigate reports of violations of international humanitarian law, international human rights law and abuses of human rights in CAR' para 24.

37 The Council has expressed its 'commitment to ensure that all UN efforts to restore peace and security themselves respect and promote the rule of law' (UNSC Presidential Statement 11 (2010) UN Doc S/PRST/2010/11 para 9) and the Representative of Lichtenstein has argued that the Council 'is legally bound by the applicable rules of the Charter and of international law' (UNSC Verbatim Record (29 June 2010) UN Doc S/PV.6347 (Resumption 1) 6) but the applicability of human rights to the Council decision-making process itself has never been put forward.

38 See principally UN Department of Peacekeeping Operations 'United Nations Peacekeeping Operations Principles and Guidelines' (March 2008) ('Capstone Doctrine'); UNGA 'Overview of the financing of the United Nations peacekeeping operations: budget performance for the period from 1 July 2004 to 30 June 2005 and budget for the period from 1 July 2006 to 30 June 2007' (24 February 2006) UN Doc A/60/696 para 6-21 ('Peace Operations 2010' reform strategy); UNGA 'Report of the Panel on United Nations Peace Operations' (21 August 2000) UN Doc A/55/305-S/2000/809.

39 *Legality of Use of Force (Yugoslavia v United States of America)* (Provisional Measures) [1999] ICJ Rep 1999 916 para 31.

40 This principle has been echoed in the criminal and military trials against soldiers perpetrating crimes against civilians. See eg *US v Frank J Ronghi*, 60 MJ 83 (ACMR, 2004); *R v Alexander Wayne Blackman and Secretary of State for Defence* [2014] EWCA Crim 1029. Conversely, in the wake of serious violations of prisoner rights by US soldiers at Abu Ghraib prison, minor sentences were handed down to the perpetrators in court martials; see 'Iraq prison abuse scandal fast facts' *CNN Library* (7 November 2014).

41 eg UNSC Res 286 (9 September 1970) UN Doc S/RES/286; UNSC Res 579 (18 December 1985) UN Doc S/RES/579; UNSC Res 161 (21 February 1961) UN Doc S/RES/161, B preamble; UNSC Verbatim Record (10 March 1961) UN Doc S/PV.944.

42 UNGA 'Supplement to an Agenda for Peace: Position Paper of the Secretary-General on the Occasion of the Fiftieth Anniversary of the United Nations'

(25 January 1995) UN Doc A/50/60 – S/1995/1 para 70: 'Sanctions, as is generally recognized, are a blunt instrument. They raise the ethical question of whether suffering inflicted on vulnerable groups in the target country is a legitimate means of exerting pressure on political leaders whose behaviour is unlikely to be affected by the plight of their subjects. Sanctions also always have unintended or unwanted effects'. See also Report of the Secretary-General, 'We the peoples: the role of the United Nations in the twenty-first century' (2000) UN Doc A/54/2000 at 50.

43 See eg Joy K Fausey, 'Does the United Nations' use of collective sanctions to protect human rights Violate its own human rights standards?' (1994) 10 *Connecticut Journal of International Law* 193; Nico Schrijver, 'The use of economic sanctions by the UN Security Council: an international law perspective' in Harry H G Post (ed), *International Economic Law and Armed Conflict* (Nijhoff 1994) 156.

44 UNGA 'Supplement to an Agenda for Peace: Position Paper of the Secretary-General on the Occasion of the Fiftieth Anniversary of the United Nations' (25 January 1995) UN Doc A/50/60 – S/1995/1 para 70.

45 UNSC Res 661 (6 August 1990) UN Doc S/RES/661.

46 UNSC Res 660 (2 August 1990) UN Doc S/RES/660.

47 See UNSC 'Report of the Second Panel established pursuant to the note by the President of the Security Council of 30 January 1999 (S/1999/100) concerning the current humanitarian situation in Iraq' (30 March 1999) UN Doc S/1999/356 Annex II; UNICEF 'Iraq child and maternal mortality surveys' (July 1999) http://fas.org/news/iraq/1999/08/irqscont.pdf (last accessed 11 November 2016).

48 See eg UNCHR Sub-commission on the Promotion and Protection of Human Rights 'Humanitarian situation of the Iraqi population, Sub-Commission on Human Rights Decision 2000/112' (18 August 2000) E/N.4/2000/L.11/Add.2.

49 Honduras, UNSC Verbatim Record (14 April 1995) UN Doc S/PV.3519 at 4.

50 UNSC Res 661 (6 August 1990) UN Doc S/RES/661 para 2.

51 UNICEF 'The status of children and women in Iraq: a situation report' (September 1995) 4.

52 See UNGA 'Situation of human rights in Iraq: note by the Secretary-General' (14 October 1999) UN Doc A/54/466 para 33: 'While the Government of Iraq has failed to use its existing resources well or to cooperate fully to take advantage of other available resources, the Government of Iraq has used some resources to enrich itself'.

53 Although UNSC Res 986 (1995) temporarily lifting the embargo on Iraqi oil exports passed unanimously, several states took the opportunity to make their views on the sanctions regime known, including China, the representative of which believed that 'the Council should proceed to discuss, at an early date, the lifting of the oil embargo against Iraq, on the basis of humanitarian considerations and in the light of Iraq's implementation of the resolutions, so as to truly and effectively ease the humanitarian situation in Iraq and alleviate the suffering inflicted on the Iraqi people by sanctions', China, UNSC Verbatim Record (14 April 1995) UN Doc S/PV.3519 at 3. Later, in 1997, it was only through negotiations at the Council that China agreed to vote for UNSC Res 1115 (1997): '[the Council] should consider gradually lifting sanctions against Iraq in order to alleviate its humanitarian difficulties. However, the resolution before us decides to suspect the review of sanctions against Iraq by the Council . . . and threatens to impose further sanctions. This is not fair . . . We have noted that considerable changes have been incorporated in the current resolution, with the deletion of new sanctions . . . For these reasons, the Chinese delegation voted in favour of the resolution before us', UNSC Verbatim Record (21 June 1997) UN Doc S/PV.3792 at 6. See also the explanation of vote by the Russia on UNSC Res 1129 (1997) in UNSC Verbatim

Record (12 September 1997) UN Doc S/PV.3817 at 4: 'while noting that both sides bear responsibility for the ongoing situation, we believe that it is exceedingly important to remedy the situation in the Committee on sanctions as regards the delivery of humanitarian goods to Iraq. Unfortunately, . . . this aspect is not reflected in the draft resolution, and for this reason we shall abstain in the voting'. China, France, Egypt, Kenya and Russia all abstained from voting on UNSC Res 1134 (1997), which set the stage for further sanctions.

54 UNSC Verbatim Record (14 April 1995) UN Doc S/PV.3519 at 11.

55 UNSC Verbatim Record (23 October 1997) UN Doc S/PV.3826 at 12: The US representative wished in UNSC Res 1129 (1997) to 'start the process [of further sanctions] by beginning the compilation of names, so if sanctions are imposed there will be no administrative delay . . . [and make] very clear to the Iraqi authorities that the next time they try to block UNSCOM's work the Council will impose sanctions against those individuals responsible for Iraqi failure to cooperate with UNSCOM'.

56 David D Caron, 'The legitimacy of the collective authority of the Security Council' (1993) 87 *American Journal of International Law* 552.

57 This open-endedness also formed the US legal basis, at least for a short period of time, behind the invasion of Iraq in 2003: 'Whereas United Nations Security Council Resolution 678 (1990) authorizes the use of all necessary means to enforce United Nations Security Council Resolution 660 (1990) and subsequent relevant resolutions and to compel Iraq to cease certain activities that threaten international peace and security, including the development of weapons of mass destruction and refusal or obstruction of United Nations weapons inspections in violation of United Nations Security Council Resolution 687 (1991), repression of its civilian population in violation of United Nations Security Council Resolution 688 (1991), and threatening its neighbors or United Nations operations in Iraq in violation of United Nations Security Council Resolution 949 (1994) . . . The President is authorized to use the Armed Forces of the United States as he determines to be necessary and appropriate in order to . . . enforce all relevant United Nations Security Council resolutions regarding Iraq', 'Authorization for Use of Military Force Against Iraq Resolution of 2002' 107th Congress (2001–2002) H J RES 114 ENR.

58 US, UNSC Verbatim Record (15 October 1994) UN Doc S/PV.3438 at 5; the UK voted in favour of both UNSC Res 1115 (1997) and UNSC Res 1134 (1997).

59 Although the 1990s saw the imposition of sanctions against Haiti and Yugoslavia, both of these were unique in their own way and pre-dated the review of sanctions regimes that began in the mid-1990s; for instance, sanctions on Haiti under UNSC Res 841 (16 June 1993) UN Doc S/RES/841 were imposed as a result of a coup, in the absence of existing post-conflict damage in the same vein as that of Iraq and rapidly followed by a military intervention a year later.

60 Russia, UNSC Verbatim Record (17 October 1994) UN Doc S/PV.3439 at 5 (emphasis added).

61 Claudia von Braunmühl and Manfred Kulessa, 'The impact of UN sanctions on humanitarian assistance activities: report on a study commissioned by the United Nations Department of Humanitarian Affairs' (Berlin: Gesellschaft für Communication Management Interkultur Training, December 1995).

62 Larry Minear and others, 'Towards more humane and effective sanctions management: enhancing the capacity of the United Nations system' (1998) Thomas J Watson Jr Institute for International Studies Occasional Paper No 31 https://sanctionsandsecurity.nd.edu/assets/110294/toward_more_humane_.pdf (last accessed 11 November 2016).

63 Discussions throughout the 1990s focused on the need for increased awareness and deference to humanitarian priorities; Italy voted in favour of UNSC

Res 986 (1995), but made it clear that while 'sanctions are, and remain, one of the most effective tools provided by the Charter of the United Nations to enforce compliance with international law, they should not lead to the extreme consequence of inflicting untold misery and starvation on an entire civilian population', UNSC Verbatim Record (14 April 1995) UN Doc S/PV.3519 at 2; the US 'shared the concern expressed by so many here that sanctions not strike an unintended target' and the UK 'Government has been concerned about the humanitarian situation in Iraq since 1991' ibid 11. Identification of a worsening humanitarian situation in Iraq was made clearly; see eg Russia, UNSC Verbatim Record (12 September 1997) UN Doc S/PV.3817 at 3: 'The situation has in fact become very serious. By the end of August, the medicine and other medical supplies being delivered to Iraq amounted only to 9.5 per cent of the target amount. In the areas of agricultural products, water supplies, electrical energy and education, when the Secretary-General's report was submitted, no supplies at all had reached the country. All of this is causing a worsening deterioration of the humanitarian situation in Iraq'.

64 Yet no definitive action was taken and even temporary measures were insufficient. See eg UNSC Verbatim Record (4 December 1997) UN Doc S/PV.3840 at 2.

65 NSC 'Note by the President of the Security Council' (30 January 1999) UN Doc S/1999/100 para 5.

66 France, UNSC Verbatim Record (14 April 1995) UN Doc S/PV.3519 at 12.

67 See 'Report to the Secretary-General on humanitarian needs in Kuwait and Iraq in the immediate post-crisis environment by a mission to the area led by Mr Martti Ahtisaari, Under-Secretary-General for Administration and Management, dated 20 March 1991' in UNSC 'Letter dated 20 March 1991 from the Secretary-General addressed to the President of the Security Council' (20 March 1991) UN Doc S/22366 Annex.

68 UNSC 'Report of the Second Panel established pursuant to the note by the President of the Security Council of 30 January 1999 (S/1999/100) concerning the current humanitarian situation in Iraq' (30 March 1999) UN Doc S/1999/356, Annex II para 45.

69 'Letter dated 13 April 1995 from the Permanent Representatives of China, France, Russia, The United Kingdom of Great Britain and Northern Island and the United States of America to the United Nations addressed to the President of the Security Council' (13 April 1995) UN Doc S/1995/300 at 2.

70 UN Department of Humanitarian Affairs 'Note from the Department of Humanitarian affairs concerning the possible humanitarian impact of the international flight ban decided in Security Council Resolution 1070 (1996)' (20 February 1997).

71 UNSC Res 1054 (26 April 1996) UN Doc S/RES/1054.

72 UNSC Verbatim Record (16 August 1996) UN Doc S/PV.3690 at 10. See also China, ibid 12; France, ibid 16.

73 UNSC 'Report of the Secretary-General pursuant to Security Council Resolution 1070 (1996)' (14 November 1996) UN Doc S/1996/940 para 18.

74 'Letter dated 19 December 1996 from the Permanent Representative of the Russian Federation to the United Nations addressed to the Secretary-General' (29 January 1996) UN Doc A/51/60, Annex at 2.

75 Office of the UN Coordinator for Afghanistan 'Vulnerability and humanitarian implications of UN Security Council Sanctions in Afghanistan' (December 2000) s 5 at 36.

76 UNSC 'Report of the Secretary-General in pursuance of paragraph 13(a) of resolution 1343 (2001) concerning Liberia' (5 October 2001) UN Doc S/2001/939 para 47.

77 UNSC Res 1132 (8 October 1997) UN Doc S/RES/1132 was passed only after the 'ECOWAS Committee of Five [had] given the United Nations Department of Humanitarian Affairs assurances that in implementing the current ECOWAS regional sanctions regime it does not intend to constrain humanitarian relief operations in Sierra Leone', UNSC Verbatim Record (8 October 1997) UN Doc S/PV.3822 at 8. Once introduced, an inter-agency mission comprising UN OCHA, UNICEF, UNHCR, WO, WFP and OSESG were tasked with the assessment of 'the humanitarian situation in Sierra Leone and measuring to what extent this situation has deteriorated under the UN sanctions and ECOWAS embargo, particularly in terms of the delivery of humanitarian assistance', Office of the Coordination of Humanitarian Affairs 'Inter-agency assessment mission to Sierra Leone: interim report' (17 February 1998) para 1.
78 UNSC Verbatim Record (23 October 1997) UN Doc S/PV.3826 at 10.
79 Canadian Foreign Minister Lloyd Axworthy. See David Cortright and George A Lopez, *The Sanctions Decade: Assessing UN Strategies in the 1990s* (Lynne Rienner 2000) 7.
80 See the Thomas J Watson Jr Institute for International Studies, 'Targeted financial sanctions: a manual for design and implementation: contributions from the Interlaken process' (2001).
81 Michael Brzoska (ed), 'Design and implementation of arms embargoes and travel and aviation related sanctions: results of the 'Bonn-Berlin process' (BICC 2001).
82 Peter Wallensteen, Carina Staibano and Mikael Eriksson (eds), 'Making targeted sanctions effective: guidelines for the implementation of UN policy options, results from the Stockholm process on the implementation of targeted sanctions' (Uppsala University 2003).
83 'Letter dated 12 December 2007 from the Permanent Representative of Greece to the United Nations addressed to the President of the Security Council' (13 December 2007) UN Doc S/2007/734 Annex.
84 Compendium: High Level Review of United Nations Sanctions, A/69/941-S/2015/432 (New York 2015).
85 UNSC 'Note by the President of the Security Council' (17 April 2000) UN Doc S/2000/319, later extended by UNSC 'Note by the President of the Security Council' (29 December 2005) S/2005/841.
86 UNSC 'Note by the President of the Security Council' (22 December 2006) UN Doc S/2006/997, Annex at 4.
87 ibid 5, 7.
88 ibid 6.
89 ibid 7, 9.
90 See eg charcoal in UNSC Res 2036 (22 February 2012) UN Doc S/RES/2036 and UNSC Res 2093 (6 March 2013) UN Doc S/RES/2093; timber in UNSC Res 1521 (22 December 2003) UN Doc S/RES/1521 and UNSC Res 1532 (12 March 2004) UN Doc S/RES/1532; and diamonds in UNSC Res 1173 (12 June 1998) UN Doc S/RES/1173, UNSC Res 1306 (5 July 2000) UN Doc S/RES/1306, and UNSC Res 1343 (7 March 2001) UN Doc S/RES/1343.
91 Travel bans, asset freezes, arms embargoes and commodity interdictions.
92 UNSC Res 1591 (29 March 2005) UN Doc S/RES/1591 para 3(g). See also UNSC Res 1718 (14 October 2006) UN Doc S/RES/1718 para 9(a), UNSC Res 1737 (27 December 2006) UN Doc S/RES/1737 para 13(a) and UNSC Res 1844 (20 November 2008) UN Doc S/RES/1844 para 4(a).
93 UNSC Res 1472 (28 March 2003) UN Doc S/RES/1472.
94 UNSC Res 1483 (22 May 2003) UN Doc S/RES/1483.
95 UNSC Res 733 (23 January 1992) UN Doc S/RES/733.

96 UNSC Res 751 (24 April 1992) UN Doc S/RES/751.
97 UNSC Res 1493 (28 July 2003) UN Doc S/RES/1493.
98 UNSC Res 1533 (12 March 2004) UN Doc S/RES/1533
99 UNSC Res 1556 (30 July 2004) UN Doc S/RES/1556.
100 UNSC Res 1591 (29 March 2005) UN Doc S/RES/1591.
101 UNSC Res 1695 (15 July 2006) UN Doc S/RES/1695.
102 UNSC Res 1718 (14 October 2006) UN Doc S/RES/1718.
103 Of the 15 current sanctions regimes, all have a committee established to oversee the stipulations of the relevant resolutions and sanction elements. These function to ensure that sanctions are carried out adequately and appropriately.
104 UN Charter (1945) art 25.
105 UNSC Presidential Statement 28 (2006) UN Doc S/PRST/2006/28 at 2. UNSC Res 1730 (19 December 2006) UN Doc S/RES/1730 preamble.
106 The basic procedures for the operation of the delisting request are publically available UNSC Res 1370 (18 September 2001) UN Doc S/RES/1370 Annex.
107 UNSC Res 1904 (17 December 2009) UN Doc S/RES/1904, preamble (emphasis in original).
108 ibid para 20.
109 UNSC Res 1267 (15 October 1999) (n 6).
110 See eg UNSC Res 1333 (19 December 2000) UN Doc S/RES/1333; UNSC Res 1390 (16 January 2002) UN Doc S/RES/1390; UNSC Res 1455 (17 January 2003) UN Doc S/RES/1455; UNSC Res 1526 (30 January 2004) UN Doc S/RES/1526; UNSC Res 1617 (29 July 2005) UN Doc S/RES/1617; UNSC Res 1735 (22 December 2006) UN Doc S/RES/1735; UNSC Res 1822 (30 June 2008) UN Doc S/RES/1822; UNSC Res 1904 (17 December 2009) UN Doc S/RES/1904; UNSC Res 1989 (17 June 2011) UN Doc S/ RES/1989; UNSC Res 2082 (17 December 2012) UN Doc S/RES/2082; UNSC Res 2083 (17 December 2012) UN Doc S/RES/2083.
111 The Committee of the Security Council dealing with sanctions against the Taliban established by UNSC Res 1267 was authorised to freeze funds and other financial resources in accordance with UNSC Res 1267 (15 October 1999) (n 6) para 4(b) without oversight and 'to designate the aircraft and funds or other financial resources referred to in paragraph 4' para 6(e).
112 ibid.
113 Case T-85/09, *Yassin Abdullah Kadi v European Commission and Others* [2010] ECR I-06351 (*Kadi II*); Joined Cases C-584/10 P, C-593/10 P and C-595/10 P, *European Commission and Others v Yassin Abdullah Kadi* [2013] (CFI, 23 July 2013).
114 *Nada v Switzerland* App no 10593/08 (ECtHR, 12 September 2012).
115 Joined Cases C-584/10 P, C-593/10 P and C-595/10 P, *European Commission and Others v Yassin Abdullah Kadi* [2013] (CFI, 23 July 2013) para 18.
116 This was later overturned in the *Kadi II* case.
117 Joined Cases C-584/10 P, C-593/10 P and C-595/10 P, *European Commission and Others v Yassin Abdullah Kadi* [2013] (CFI, 23 July 2013) para 133.
118 *Al-Jedda v The United Kingdom* App no 27021/08 (ECtHR, 7 July 2011) para 102.
119 *Nada v Switzerland* App no 10593/08 (ECtHR, 12 September 2012) para 172.
120 UNSC Res 1556 (30 July 2004) UN Doc S/RES/1556; UNSC Res 1591 (29 March 2005) UN Doc S/RES/1591; UNSC Res 1593 (7 April 2005) UN Doc S/RES/1593; UNSC Res 1945 (14 October 2010) UN Doc S/RES/1945.
121 UNSC Res 1572 (5 November 2004) UN Doc S/RES/1572; UNSC Res 1584 (1 February 2005) UN Doc S/RES/1584; UNSC Res 1643 (15 December 2005) UN Doc S/RES/1643; UNSC Res 1975 (30 March 2011) UN Doc S/ RES/1975; UNSC Res 2153 (29 April 2014) UN Doc S/RES/2153.

122 UNSC Res 1970 (26 February 2011) UN Doc S/RES/1970; UNSC Res 1973 (17 March 2011) UN Doc S/RES/1973; UNSC Res 2009 (16 September 2011) UN Doc S/RES/2009; UNSC Res 2146 (19 March 2014) UN Doc S/RES/2146.
123 See eg UNMIS and UNOCI.
124 UNSC Res 1973 (17 March 2011) UN Doc S/RES/1973.
125 UNSC Res 2083 (17 December 2012) UN Doc S/RES/2083 para 17.
126 The mandate of the Ombudsperson is outlined in UNSC Res 2083 (17 December 2012) UN Doc S/RES/2083, Annex II: information gathering (four months), dialogue (two months) and committee discussion (45 days).
127 ibid para 13.
128 UNSC Verbatim Record (5 August 1963) UN Doc S/PV.1053(OR) 13.
129 UNSC Draft Res (11 July 2008) UN Doc S/2008/447.
130 UNSC Draft Res (12 January 2007) UN Doc S/2007/14.
131 UNSC Draft Res (4 October 2011) UN Doc S/2011/612; UNSC Draft Res (4 February 2012) UN Doc S/2012/77; UNSC Draft Res (19 July 2012) UN Doc S/2012/538; UNSC 'Letter dated 16 January 2013 from the Permanent Representative of Guatemala to the United Nations addressed to the President of the Security Council' (21 January 2013) UN Doc S/2013/38.
132 UNSC Draft Res (13 July 2006) UN Doc S/2006/508; UNSC Draft Res (11 November 2006) UN Doc S/2006/878; UNSC Draft Res (18 February 2011) UN Doc S/2011/24.
133 UNSC Draft Res (14 June 2009) UN Doc S/2009/310.
134 UNSC Draft Res (15 March 2014) UN Doc S/2014/189.
135 France, UNGA Verbatim Record (7 November 2013) UN Doc A/68/PV.46 at 28.
136 Canada, UNSC Verbatim Record (27 August 2008) UN Doc S/PV.5968 (Resumption 1) 10.

9 Separation of powers and acting ultra vires

> The Council should stop encroaching on subjects falling squarely within the core competence of the Organization's other main organs, particularly the General Assembly and the Economic and Social Council, under the pretext of dealing with the security aspects of those subjects or by attempting to give a false impression that the subject matter under consideration gives rise to a threat to international peace and security. This issue stresses the importance of revisiting the relationship between the Security Council and the other principal organs of the Organization for the purposes of restoring the institutional balance between them that is clearly outlined in the Charter. In this regard, the International Court of Justice has a major role to play in settling any dispute that might arise between organs with respect to their mandates.[1]

Introduction

The separation of powers between branches of domestic governments – principally the executive, legislature and judiciary – cannot be directly transposed from constitutions the world over to the United Nations (UN) system; as discussed in Chapter 2, the UN Charter, while bearing many similarities to a constitution, does not function as one *par excellence*. Although there are critics of imposing a separation of powers to the UN system,[2] it is clear from the Charter itself in the mandates given to each of the constituent organs of the UN that each serves a distinct and deliberate purpose. The functions and powers of each of the UN organs are explicitly delineated in respective Chapters of the UN Charter; while each of the General Assembly,[3] Security Council[4] and Economic and Social Council[5] has the competence to adopt its own rules of procedure, there is a delicate balance of responsibilities that are distributed amongst the organs that form the United Nations: the ICJ is 'the principal judicial organ of the United Nations',[6] the General Assembly 'may discuss any questions or any matters within the scope of [the Charter]',[7] and the Council, as already established, has 'primary responsibility for the maintenance of international peace and security'.[8]

Bedjaoui proposes that the San Francisco conference resulted in the creation of a UN system that is governed by four overarching principles,[9] each of which supports the assertion that the separation of powers at the UN was fully intended from its earliest days: the *specialisation principle*, where each organ is endowed with a particular mission or set of tasks; a *non-subordination principle*, 'insomuch as each organ's special mission calls for an autonomy of conduct incompatible with dependence on another organ specializing in a different area';[10] *Kompetenz-Kompetenz*, reflecting the autonomy and self-proclaimed interpretation of Charter provisions; and a *coordination principle* that binds the work of the organs together. Accordingly, this principle of the separation of powers within the UN, can easily be extended to form the root of this component of the rule of law at the Council level.

Sources of support for the separation of powers

The Charter expressly works towards avoiding the duplication of efforts and discussions by separate organs: Charter Article 12, for example, states that '[w]hile the Security Council is exercising in respect of any dispute or situation the functions assigned to it in the present Charter, the General Assembly shall not make any recommendation with regard to that dispute or situation unless the Security Council so requests'.[11] The different mandates of the organs are reflected also in the extent to which they interact; although the Charter recognises five organs,[12] only the 'General Assembly or the Security Council may request the International Court of Justice to give an advisory opinion on any legal question',[13] reflecting the added value that coordination between the Assembly or the Council and the ICJ would impart. Juxtaposed with this, the Secretary-General, as the 'chief administrative officer of the Organisation'[14] may 'bring to the attention of the Security Council any matter which in his opinion may threaten the maintenance of international peace and security'[15] but has no such direct power to refer to the ICJ for advisory opinions.[16]

Similarly, there is division of labour even within the field of peaceful settlement of disputes between states; both the Council and the ICJ are authorised to deal with issues relating to inter-state disputes under the respective mandates of the Charter. However, whereas the Council is a political organ and deals with peaceful settlement of inter-state disputes within the framework of peace and security under Chapter VI,[17] the ICJ has jurisdiction over both advisory opinions and contentious cases – 'all cases which the parties refer to it and all matters specially provided for in the Charter of the United Nations or in treaties and conventions in force'.[18] The dissection of inter-state disputes into political and judicial matters is highlighted not only implicitly by these pithy mandates of each organ, but also explicitly in the Charter, which cautions the Council to 'take into consideration that legal disputes should as a general rule be referred by the parties to the International Court of Justice in accordance with the provisions of the Statute of the Court'.[19] Any deviation from this general norm would require compelling reasoning on the part of the Council.

The separation of powers within the United Nations has also been explicitly referred to by the ICJ itself in numerous cases including *Nicaragua*,[20] *Hostages*,[21] *Aegean Continental Shelf*,[22] *Armed Activities in the Congo*[23] and *Application of*

Genocide Convention.[24] In these cases it was shown that the seizure of a matter by the Council does not preclude its discussion within the court of the ICJ; indeed, '[t]he Council has functions of a political nature assigned to it, whereas the Court exercises purely judicial functions. Both organs can therefore perform their separate but complementary functions with respect to the same events'.[25] The ICJ took the same view when assessing whether to exercise jurisdiction in the Advisory Opinion sought by the General Assembly on the independence of Kosovo.[26] As each organ of the UN is bestowed with limited functions and specific powers, it would be absurd for the ICJ to enter into political discussions of a situation; equally, it must follow that for the Council to enter into judgments of legality of actions by states would achieve the same dearth of legitimacy. The ICJ's *Namibia* Advisory Opinion clearly affirmed the principle that the Security Council powers are bound by the standards of the Charter,[27] a stance later reiterated by a subsidiary organ of the UN Security Council itself – the ICTY.[28] The ICJ detailed even further its special relationship with the Council in the *Hostages* case, emphasising the distinct fields in which each must operate.[29]

Restrictions and explicit mandates such as these on the work of UN organs demonstrate the intentions of the drafters of the UN Charter to ring-fence powers and responsibilities to ensure not only an effective and efficient path towards achieving the goals, principles and purposes of the Charter, but also to avoid contradictory findings by UN organs that would undermine the integrity and authority of one of more of the organs; this inherent *lis alibi pendens*[30] element of the mandates given to organs under the UN Charter avoids the duplication of inconsistent decisions. There is further evidence from the statements of UN member states themselves during discussions on Council reform that strong support can be found for imposing boundaries to Council action both internally to the UN system and with respect to the extent of the existing powers it is mandated to exercise under the Charter.[31]

However, the Charter is deliberately broad in the discretion permitted to UN organs in the interpretation of its provisions; while there is a clear separation of both powers and responsibilities in the Charter, there is little in the way of ensuring their continued separation and avoiding the activities of one bleeding into the mandate of another. Proposals made by the Belgian delegation for UN organs to submit any interpretative disagreements to the ICJ[32] or the General Assembly[33] for analysis were rejected in 1945 and the UN was created with no specific mechanism for interpreting the provisions of the Charter[34] and the recognition that UN organs would interpret the respective applicable Charter provisions themselves.[35] Notwithstanding the ruling of the ICJ in the *Nuclear Weapons in Armed Conflict* case, this 'absence of [any specific legality-test clause] not only fails to offer protection against any excess of Charter powers but is conducive to it'.[36]

The Council's norm-setting

At the outset, it is key to establish the stark division between the capacity of the Council to create legal obligations upon UN member states through UN Charter

Article 25 and its foray into commenting upon or even ruling on the legality of actions by States unrelated to the Charter. Whereas the former grants the Council the unrivalled power immediately and spontaneously to alter the landscape of international law, both by forcing states to abide by its resolutions and by establishing a precedent for future action, the latter would place the Security Council – a political organ – squarely in the judicial role of weighing the actions of states against the international legal standard.

While the first is not only acceptable but forms part of the role of the Council, the latter would be a drastic change in the role of the Council for which it neither was designed not is competent to carry out; the Council may create and measure the actions of states against its own legal norms through its binding resolutions, but only incidental to its role in maintaining international peace and security – the 'progressive development of international law and its codification'[37] is a task for the General Assembly. Moreover, it may not rule on the legality or compliance of states with existing norms or principles of international law – this is the role of the ICJ.[38] This differentiation is exemplified by the fact that the both the Council and the ICJ may address the same matters simultaneously – as with the dispute between the US and Nicaragua – but divergently within their respective frameworks of responsibilities. The Council, however, has gradually begun encroaching on the territory of both the Assembly and the ICJ.

It cannot be disputed that the Council is empowered to make legislative decisions in response to threats to the international peace through the adoption of legally binding resolutions.[39] Indeed, the imposition of sanction regimes, authority for military intervention and the establishment of ad hoc international criminal tribunals are all examples of legislative powers at the disposal of the Council in response to specific threats. However, there is a key distinction between such *reactive* legislation, which is specific and parenthesised by timeframes for action, and *normative* legislation, which establishes law without time frames and without targeted methods and goals. As a result, legislative action can only legitimately emerge from the Council once, first, a specific to the threat to the peace has been determined by the Council and, secondly, the resolution is temporally limited to encompass exclusively the period of time required for addressing this threat. Laws of a general nature with indefinite durations are decidedly outside of the remit of the Council; the separation of powers, then, with respect to the Security Council, concerns not its capacity to legislate per se, but rather its adherence to the parameters of legislative power it has been granted by the Charter and ensuring that responding to threats of the international peace is not used as a gateway to effect permanent change in the norms of international law or domestic legislation.

The international tribunals: advancement of international law by proxy

The Council has always made full use of its *kompetenz kompetenz*, but has grown considerably bolder after 1990: for example, as mentioned previously the Council initially saw human rights as falling outside of its mandate where today it is central to its activities in peace and security. The use of Chapter VII in the creation of the ICTY and ICTR, as well as the referral to the ICC of situations in the Sudan and Libya are further examples. However, there still exists the risk that this self-interpretative mandate of the UN Charter may encroach on the mandates of sibling UN organs and that it has also shirked its responsibilities in some cases. This potential for a blurring in the separation of powers and excess of the Council's mandate under the Charter was hinted at early on the history of the United Nations; in 1947, the General Assembly was already recommending that 'organs of the United Nations . . . should, from time to time, review the difficult and important points of law within the jurisdiction of the International Court of Justice . . . including points of law relating to the interpretation of the Charter of the United Nations'.[40]

Nonetheless, the Council has not chosen to refer to the ICJ in interpreting its mandate or in deciding whether a matter falls within its remit, despite both the designated mandate of the ICJ to tackle issues of a judicial and legal nature and practical instances where the Court has over the course of the years exercised its right upon request of authorised UN organs to interpret the Charter on specific articles[41] and in general questions of law.[42] The lack of referral to the ICJ of questions relating to clarification of the limits of the Council cannot, then, be due to a lack of jurisdiction or experience, but attributable to other factors.[43] In defence of the Council, it can be evidenced that in the earliest stages of the UN's history, the Council had no need to seek clarification from the ICJ on the limits of its jurisdiction, as it originally abided by the demarcated Charter boundaries, recommending where appropriate that states 'immediately refer the dispute to the International Court of Justice in accordance with the provisions of the Statute of the Court'.[44] However, over the decades, the Council has increasingly deviated from this formula.

Since the mid-1960s the Council has grown increasingly bolder in its pronouncements on international legal matters, declaring governments and occupations illegal[45] and assigning legal liability to Parties[46] in some situations. Indeed, in a precursor to the ICTY, the ICTR and the Rome Statute, the Council advocated for the individual responsibility for war crimes in UNSC Resolution 794[47] affirming, in relation to Somalia, that 'those who commit or order the commission of such acts will be held individually responsible in respect of such acts'.[48] In so doing, the Council established a legal principle that had otherwise never been formally recognised and which later formed one of the bases for the Prosecutor of the ICTY to present evidence of *opinio juris* in the *Tadic* case[49] – individual responsibility for breaches of humanitarian law. The Council here clearly stumbles into the territory of other organs in developing international law, which has not been without concern by States.[50]

More than advancing the development of international law and creating international legal principles, which may well be argued as a by-product of the Council's work in promoting the international peace, the Council has in recent years stepped up its work as legislator. Concerns over the quasi-legislative resolutions of the Council risk undermining the legitimacy of the decisions of the Council.[51] Whereas the Council throughout the years has continued to encourage States to enact legislation and enforcement mechanisms themselves as means to counter certain threats, such as the illicit flow of arms in Africa,[52] the creation of the ICTY and ICTR as subsidiary bodies under Chapter VII marked the start of a new era in which the Council consolidated its role in norm-setting. The establishment itself of the tribunals may have been legally sound, but the Council's cavalier attitude towards its mandate and the knock-on effect this has had on principles of international law cannot be underestimated.

Orakhelashvili, relying on a statement of the ICTY itself,[53] argues that in creating

> the *ad hoc* criminal tribunals, the Council did not derogate from customary law, and the fact that the concept of crimes against humanity was linked to an armed conflict in *Tadíc* and to a discriminatory intent in *Akayesu* was due not to the intention of the Council to change or otherwise affect the composition of these crimes as recognized under general international law, but just to provide the ICTY and ICTR with the jurisdiction limited accordingly.[54]

Certainly, the ICTY was not intended to be 'empowered with – nor would the Council be [intended to be] assuming – the ability to set down norms of international law or legislate with respect to those rights';[55] the codification of customary law was therefore illegitimate. Nonetheless, the international humanitarian law that was thought to be 'impressively codified, well understood, agreed upon and enforceable'[56] was in fact significantly augmented by sources of law outside of the Geneva Conventions of 1949,[57] including 'international customary law which is not laid down in conventions':[58] the principle of *individual criminal responsibility* is included in part owing to the self-referential, circular reasoning that 'the Security Council has reaffirmed in a number of resolutions that persons committing serious violations of international humanitarian law . . . are individually responsible for such violations';[59] crimes against humanity had no written legal basis prior to the ICTY and were included owing to its recognition almost 50 years previously 'in the Charter and Judgment of the Nuremberg Tribunal, as well as in Law No. 10 of the Control Council for Germany';[60] and immunity from prosecution was removed from alleged perpetrators of crimes falling within the jurisdiction of the court based on 'comments received by the Secretary-General . . . [and] suggestions draw[ing] upon the precedents following the Second World War'.[61]

The creation or codification of hitherto unwritten law by the Council through its subsidiary organ of the ad hoc court was a rapid endeavour[62] that led some to reflect on whether '[p]erhaps more extensive legal studies could have been undertaken on various aspects of the Statute, such as the question of the principle of *nullum crimen sine lege* . . .'.[63] This was reiterated by Schabas, who noted 'an absence of any real guidance on the subject [of *mens rea*] in the applicable law of the [ICTY]'.[64]

The establishment of the ICTY was also ground-breaking in numerous respects. Primarily, it appears to be the first time that the expediency of action was explicitly acknowledged to trump the many benefits of a more inclusive process for the creation of an international criminal court. The Secretary-General highlighted at the outset of his report that:

> [t]he approach which, in the normal course of events, would be followed in establishing an international tribunal would be the conclusion of a treaty by which the States parties would establish a tribunal and approve its statute . . . [which] would have the advantage of allowing a detailed examination and elaboration of all issues pertaining to the establishment of the international tribunal. It also would allow the States participating in the negotiation and conclusion of the treaty fully to exercise their sovereign will . . .[65]

The establishment of the ICTY was, then, a departure from the traditional method of establishing a legal entity that held states accountable for their behaviour; with the exception of the ICJ, to which all UN member states are automatically party, there had never been a legal body established to preside over the behaviour of states without an accorded treaty to which accession is voluntary. The Secretary-General also made reference to fact that the General Assembly 'as the most representative organ of the United Nations, should have a role in the establishment of the international tribunal'.[66]

However, owing to the fact that some states may choose not to ratify any treaty establishing the ICTY, thereby circumventing its jurisdiction – as indeed, has happened with the ICC – and the considerable time that a treaty or Assembly deliberation would take – which 'would not be reconcilable with the urgency expressed by the Security Council in resolution 808 (1993)'[67] – a Chapter VII resolution was recommended: '[t]his approach would have the advantage of being expeditious and of being immediately effective as all States would be under a binding obligation to take whatsoever action is required to carry out a decision taken as an enforcement measure under Chapter VII'.[68] Kirgis also notes the legislative elements of the ICTY Statute, referring to them as 'directives to national governments'.[69]

The *Tadic* trial highlighted the impossibility of the ICTY reviewing its own establishment; at both the trial[70] and appellate[71] stages, the Court was found to have 'no authority to investigate the legality of its creation by the Security Council'.[72] Therefore, rather than referring to the ICJ to rule on the legality of the establishment of the ICTY, as originally suggested by the General Assembly in 1947 in relation to the interpretation of Charter provisions, it was left to the Secretary-General to declare that the 'establishment of the International Tribunal by means of a Chapter VII decision would be legally justified'.[73] Despite the Secretary-General's correct assertion that a Council 'determination of the existence of a threat to the peace, breach of the peace or act of aggression'[74] would be required for the establishment of the ICTY, it is the Secretary-General who contradictorily declares in his report that '[s]uch a decision would constitute a measure to maintain or restore international peace and security'[75] – a task clearly within the remit of the Council as primary maintainer of peace and security.

While the Council may delegate the '*action* required to carry out the decisions of the Security Council for the maintenance of international peace and security',[76] it is for the Council alone to 'decide what measures not involving the use of armed force are to be employed to give effect to its decisions'.[77] To delegate this task to the Secretary-General, who is ill-equipped to decipher the legal intricacies of Charter interpretation[78] – particularly in relation to the ICJ – is a gross blurring of the lines between organs and an *ultra vires* delegation of powers by the Council.

Furthermore, despite assurances from the Secretary-General that 'in assigning to the International Tribunal the task of prosecuting persons responsible for serious violations of the international humanitarian law, the Security Council would not be creating or purporting to "legislate" that law',[79] this was not borne out in reality. The principles created for the ICTY were replicated in the ICTR and the ICC statutes; Sadat notes that it 'is probably fair to say that the ICC would not have existed *but for* the successful creation and operation of the ICTY and ICTR'.[80] The Assistant Secretary-General for Legal Affairs has also noted that '[t]he contribution of the ICTY to the development of international criminal law has been significant',[81] a fact that is highlighted by ICTY decisions even forming part of the jurisprudence relied upon by the ICJ in the 2000 *Congo v Belgium* case.[82]

The Council has set precedents of international law under the guise of addressing threats to the international peace; as a result, the Council has created legal principles, which have been adopted by international courts as reliable evidence of *opinio juris*, and accordingly are now relied upon in international legal establishments such as the ICTY, ICTR and ICC. Weiss et al have noted, 'in a narrow sense [the ICTY and ICTR] have been successful not only in convicting and incarcerating a number of criminal defendants but also in engaging in a major rewriting of modern international criminal law'.[83]

The Council as direct legislator

The international criminal tribunals may have been the Council's introduction to legislating by proxy, but emboldened by this new-found power to legislate, it began towards the turn of the century to impose obligations of a generally applicable legal nature on states directly through Chapter VII resolutions, without the existence or determination of a specific threat to the international peace and with no temporal parameters. This direct legislation by the Council falls under what many commentators have termed '*ultra vires* action';[84] however, I have chosen to approach this differently, bringing it under the umbrella of the separation of powers.

The role of the Council as legislator runs contrary to the Charter for two principal reasons: first, as mentioned previously, the role of advancing international law falls within the remit of the Assembly. In addition to UNGA Resolution 67/1 on the rule of law, numerous Assembly resolutions developing international law have been adopted without vote, such as the 1970 Declaration on Principles of International Law concerning Friendly Relations[85] and the 1974 Definition of Aggression.[86] Secondly, it undermines the purposes and foundations of the Charter itself. When taken in isolation, legislative action by the Council may indeed be deemed *ultra vires* of its powers under the Charter; however, within the framework of the international rule of law and the international legal order against which the Council operates the Council encroaches upon other elements of the Charter, which flout the traditions and customs of international law – namely, the sovereign rights of states. Operating within the sphere of international law, states have obligations and rights outside of those imposed by their adherence to the UN Charter; that is to say that membership to the United Nations by states is itself an exercise in the sovereignty that underscores international law[87] and the sole jurisdiction over their domestic affairs.[88]

One may traditionally approach the separation of powers within the Charter, in much the same way as that of the domestic sphere, as comprising the core organs of the UN: functionally relevantly to this book's thesis the ICJ, the Assembly and the Council, which are loose transpositions of judiciary, legislative and executive branches. However, this omits an additional branch of power in the Charter that is uniquely idiosyncratic to the Charter: that of the sovereign state. Naturally, owing to the differences between domestic and international law – the vertical versus the horizontal– one would not find this additional branch of powers in national constitutions. Nonetheless, it lies at the foundation of the Charter.

This branch of *sovereign states*, the powers of which are sanctified on a par with the powers of the Council, the Assembly and the ICJ, is explicitly referred to in the Charter as being inviolable; with the exception of the application of *enforcement measures* under Chapter VII, '[n]othing contained in the [UN] Charter shall authorize the United Nations to intervene in matters which are essentially within the domestic jurisdiction of any state or shall require the Members to submit such matters to settlement under the present Charter'.[89] The only legitimate means for the Council to legislate, therefore, by virtue of a Chapter VII resolution authorising such enforcement mechanisms, which in turn as discussed earlier in this book must comply with the principles of legal certainty. Consequently, an illegitimate use of power by the Council in legislating outside of this narrow window[90] would be a violation not only of its powers under the Charter but of the rule of law itself.

Against this backdrop, for the Council to adopt the role of international legislator outside of the enforcement mechanisms of Chapter VII is, therefore, to encroach upon the sphere of international law itself – well outside of the UN Charter altogether – for not even the Assembly that is tasked with the advancement of international law under the Charter may obligate states to abide by non-customary norms of international law in the absence of general consent. The legislation of the Council in this manner circumvents entirely the concept of *opinio juris*, a core foundation of non-codified international law. Such legislation also disregards the separation of powers as outlined in the Charter, imposing legal obligations upon states that either regulate the domestic sphere of nations or binding their hands against action under their domestic constitutions.

International terrorism

Following the bombing of US embassies in Kenya and Tanzania in 1998 – claimed to have been perpetrated by operatives of Osama Bin Laden – the US began its crackdown against the Taliban in Afghanistan, who continued to 'provide bin Laden with safe haven and security, allowing him the necessary freedom to operate, despite repeated efforts by the United States to persuade the Taliban to turn over or expel him'.[91] While condemnation of international terrorism by the Council prior to 1999 was not unheard of, the Council had hitherto taken a piecemeal approach that was rarely invoked;[92] in fact, until 'the 1990s terrorism was dealt with almost entirely by the General Assembly, which approached the issue as a general problem of international law'.[93] In the aftermath of the attacks on the World Trade Centre in 2001, the Council paid far more acute attention to the threat of international terrorism which was deemed to 'constitute one of the most serious threats to international peace and security in the twenty-first century'.[94]

With indirect legislation on the front of human rights and humanitarian law having succeeded at the international tribunals, a further leap was taken in 2001 in imposing on states specifically outlined, but abstractly supported, legal obligations. Beginning with a general condemnation the day after the attacks, the Council called 'on the international community to redouble their efforts to prevent and suppress terrorist acts including by increased cooperation and full implementation of the relevant international anti-terrorist conventions and Security Council resolutions'.[95]

However, less than a month later, the Council emerged with detailed, legally binding, wide-reaching stipulations issued under Chapter VII, with which states were bound to comply. In contrast to the resolutions that established the ICTY and ICTR and other resolutions targeting the specific threats,[96] UNSC Resolution 1373[97] was extremely general in its scope, and presented more as an international treaty rather than the specific determination of a threat to the peace one might expect under Article 39 of the Charter:[98] the resolution lacked temporal limitation on the validity of the impositions, neglected to specify the exact situation that it aimed to address in an effort to reinstate peace and security[99] and failed to identify any subjects who were causing the threat to the international peace.[100] Indeed, despite numerous discussions prior to and in the wake of UNSC Resolution 1373[101] and one Assembly definition[102] there was no strictly agreed definition of terrorism, which was later to lead to some frustration on the part of several representatives.[103] UNSC Resolution 1373 made no mention of the Assembly definition of terrorism and it was not until 2004 that the Council made any attempt to define the act[104] despite the existence of twelve international conventions on the subject of terrorism at the time.[105]

Drawing heavily on the language and definition of the Assembly almost a decade earlier, no nexus is made between the two and the Council appears to ignore the seizure of the matter by the Assembly. Moreover, despite the lack of definition by the ICJ[106] or the Assembly,[107] either of which would arguably be better suited to the establishment of international legal definitions, UNSC Resolution 1373 was adopted without a definition of the act that it criminalised.[108] Accordingly, a blanket imposition of broad obligations[109] upon states and the requirement to report the steps taken[110] by states in compliance with these obligations were outlined in a manner reminiscent of the expansive sanctions regimes of the early 1990s.

Remarkably, not only did the resolution pass unanimously,[111] despite anticipation of opposition[112] to the far-reaching and overtly legislative nature of the content, but there was great praise for what was seen as 'one of the most important resolutions of [the Council's] history'.[113] Indeed, the 'unprecedented step of bringing into force legislation binding all states on the issue of combatting terrorism'[114] was seen in a positive light and, as a result, '[a]ll States now [had] the legal, as well as political and moral, obligation to act against it'[115] despite the fact that, first, there was no unanimously agreed definition of terrorism and, secondly, there was otherwise no legally binding obligation upon States to do so. On the one hand, the fact that the CTC did not intend to 'trespass onto the areas of competence of other parts of the United Nations system . . . [or] define terrorism in a legal sense'[116] was no more than mere lip service; in fact, its imposition of legally binding obligations without a clear framework of action of definition meant a distinct lack of legal clarity. On the other hand, the resolution imposed the obligation that '[n]ational efforts must . . . be welded into a global framework'.[117]

Moreover, although '[r]esolution 1373 (2001) drew on the language negotiated by all United Nations Members in the 12 conventions against terrorism',[118] the elimination of terrorism had not yet approached any level of general legal obligation outside the Council: there were still calls after the passing of UNSC Resolution 1373 that 'every State should ratify the existing 12 United Nations and international conventions against terrorism';[119] there were varying interpretations as to how exactly to tackle the issue of terrorism;[120] and accusations were levelled that 'fudging the definition of terrorism . . . is driven only by political ambitions for regional hegemony'.[121] At the time of the adoption of UNSC Resolution 1373, there was little agreement even on the definition of terrorism, much less any legal obligations on states to act in response to it; yet the Council maintained its right to press ahead with the Chapter VII resolution nonetheless, setting a dangerous precedent that was only later opposed by states. UNSC Resolution 1566 continued the legacy of legislating both in attempting to define terrorist acts[122] and in attempting to bind states under a Chapter VII resolution to general international law without temporal limitation.[123]

In 2014, in response to the threat posed by Daesh in Iraq and Syria, the Council has passed another legislative decision on terrorism under Chapter VII – UNSC Resolution 2178[124] – recalling UNSC Resolution 1373[125] and once more imposing legally binding obligations on states of a general nature and with indefinite duration. Perhaps most concerning about this resolution is reaffirmation 'that terrorism *in all forms and manifestations* constitutes one of the most serious threats to international peace and security';[126] whereas UNSC Resolution 1373's focus was confined to *international* terrorism, UNSC Resolution 2178 expands an already poorly-defined term even further, including the abstract notion of 'violent extremism'.[127] The Council's failure to define these terms, coupled with the obligation upon states to implement national legislation against their own citizens and individuals transiting through their territory, opens the door to an indefinite and arbitrary violation of individuals' rights. The omission of the international element also potentially allows for state crackdowns on internal dissidents and opposition to the government under the pretence of abidance by Council decisions to enforce the maintenance of international peace.

Nuclear non-proliferation

UNSC Resolution 1540 unequivocally built upon the legacy of UNSC Resolution 1373; the latter is recognised as paving the way for the 2004 resolution 'binding Security Council resolution on weapons of mass destruction, addressing non-State actors and terrorists'[128] and even 'to be part of what began with resolution 1373 (2001)'.[129] Although this resolution also passed unanimously, there was far more opposition by UN member states. On the most basic level, there was rejection of the 'justification for the adoption of this resolution under Chapter VII of the Charter'[130] and discussion over the duplication of work – that is to say that some states took the view that 'existing treaties . . . already prescribe most of the legislation that would cover proliferation by both State and non-State actors . . . [and] can be improved, if and where necessary, through negotiations among sovereign and equal States'.[131] Indeed, it could be argued that UNSC Resolution 1540 was superfluous in many respects, imposing 'obligations on United Nations member states and attempts to legislate on behalf of States . . . [even] where States have already accepted non-proliferation obligations under international treaties and other legal instruments'.[132]

Joyner is deeply critical of the Council for such actions, finding that 'the Security Council appears now to consider itself to possess ultimate and essentially unlimited legal authority – i.e. to represent something of a legal hegemon – by virtue of its UN Charter mandate to maintain and restore international peace and security'.[133] Particularly with respect to UNSC Resolution 1540, he argues that:

> . . . the Security Council has confused the proper scope of its enforcement powers under Chapter VII, with the proper scope of its long unused, limited lawmaking powers under Article 26, and has taken to itself by unilateral exercise of its Chapter VII powers a role which, under the Charter system, it is to share both with the General Assembly in the exercise of its Article 11(1) powers, as well as with the general membership of the United Nations.[134]

Both resolutions 1373 and 1540 were 'calculated, proactive forward-looking normative creations. In both cases the Security Council simply determined that an entire class of actions, which have been and which may be in the future committed potentially by any state, constitute a threat to international peace and security'.[135] This is the act of legislation that has been argued to exceed the mandate of the Council: general, temporally unlimited, legally binding rules for states.[136]

Of particular concern to states was the use of UNSC Resolution 1540 to fill in gaps of international law and 'remedy lacunae existing in the existing apparatus of multilateral legal instruments on disarmament and non-proliferation of weapons of mass destruction (WMD)'.[137] This 'increasing tendency of the Council . . . to assume new and wider powers of legislation on behalf of the international community, with its resolutions binding on all States'[138] was interpreted by many states to be unequivocally outside of the scope of the Council and led to concerns that 'the exercise of legislative functions by the Council, combined with recourse to Chapter VII mandates, could disrupt the balance of power between the General Assembly and the Security Council, as enshrined in the Charter'.[139] Further than this, states questioned 'whether the Security Council has the right to assume the role of prescribing legislative action by member states'[140] at all. Perhaps too late given the adoption of UNSC Resolution 1373 three years earlier, these questions of international law and the 'far-reaching legal and practical implications'[141] of UNSC Resolution 1540 on the international legal landscape and the precedent it set caused consternation to the Mexican representation

> . . . about the *proliferation of parallel regimes to those already established*, using channels outside the norms of existing treaties, but also about *the growing trend that the Security Council seeks to legislate*, particularly with regard to issues that have their own regime of rights and obligations, even if incomplete when it comes to non-State actors.[142]

Undeterred, despite a 'general view expressed in the Council's open debate that the Security Council cannot legislate for the world'[143] the Council – and its members – ignored accusations of excess of its Charter powers that were raised previously and any contravention of the Charter-assigned separation of powers. The Council is not tasked under the Charter with addressing gaps in international law – this is the role of the Assembly and, on a wider scale, the role of customary international law; nor indeed is it the role of the Council to bolster existing international treaties and conventions;[144] and the Council's use of Chapter VII simply to 'make [a resolution] legally binding in an unequivocal way and to send a strong political message'[145] is in clear contravention of its intended purpose under the Charter.[146] Nonetheless, as a result of UNSC Resolution 1540 each member state would 'need to review its laws and to determine what laws or regulations will be necessary to meet the resolution's requirements'.[147] National legislation of measures bringing states into compliance with the Council's resolution were obligatory, yet the Council members 'believe[d] that the resolution is not intrusive because it enables States to translate the obligations conferred by it into domestic law as they wish'.[148]

The use of Council power to impose such wide legal obligations on states was not seen to be *ultra vires* and, despite the fact that UNSC Resolution 1540 was recognised as 'contain[ing] provisions whose implementation would not include enforcement action',[149] it was nonetheless deemed 'appropriate to act under Chapter VII of the Charter'.[150] This, of course, is entirely opposed to the Council's powers under the Charter, which permit the imposition of legislation upon the domestic sphere of states only in 'the application of enforcement measures under Chapter VII'.[151] These landmark resolutions imposed a new legal order with respect to international terrorism, which – for better or worse and aside from any moral arguments that might have neutralised the adoption of UNSC Resolution 1540 from a political standpoint – imposed obligations upon states illegitimately and outside of the Charter's delineation of powers to the appropriate parties. It is this type of resolution 'not in response to a particular fact situation, and on an ongoing basis'[152] that caused consternation during debates in the run-up to resolutions 1422 and 1487 on the 'very questionable legal foundations'[153] of temporary immunity of peacekeepers from ICC prosecution.[154]

Resolutions such as UNSC Resolution 1696 are also *ultra vires* in their imposition. When taken in isolation as a right under the NPT, there is a convincing argument that the Council is within its powers to declare a threat to the international peace and force abidance by a Chapter VII resolution. The UN Charter outlines two articles that unambiguously place states in a position to follow the decrees of the Council: Article 25 delineates the obligation upon states to 'accept and carry out the decisions of the Security Council';[155] Article 103 imposes the hierarchical structure that Council resolutions 'trump' any state obligations under an international treaty.[156] However, in this particular case, it can be argued that the enshrined rights of the NPT of enrichment of nuclear material for peaceful means is a fundamental right of states separate to its codification in the NPT, having been successfully recognised by 190 nations.[157] Once this position is established, Article 103 of the Charter no longer remains relevant, since it relates exclusively to *obligations* upon states, rather than *rights* of states and the pursuit of a peaceful nuclear programme is distinctly the latter. The Council has, therefore, set a precedent for the violation of international law, placing itself above the inalienable right of Iran to pursue nuclear power peacefully.

However, the hegemony of which the Council is accused by both scholars and UN member states are resultant from the composition of the Council itself; in an example of the interconnectivity of rule of law components, the lack of equitable participation allows for a violation of the separation of powers and a Council acting *legibus solitus*. A hegemony of the P5 as a third of all UNSC members is, as the next chapter will examine, in theory proportionally representative of a third of all UN Members, when in reality as this section has examined there is great opposition to the decisions of the Council from the states parties purportedly represented. Such skewed representations of the will of the wider UN membership are perhaps the central flaw ripe for exploitation by the P5 and allow for the continuation of the criticised hegemony, encroachment upon the roles of other organs and ever-extension of Council power into the domestic sphere.

Conclusions

Throughout the course of its existence, there have been numerous voices criticising and warning the Council for its transgression beyond its Charter powers and 'dangerous tendency to undermine international law and erode [its] credibility'.[158] Nonetheless, the Council has persevered in its trajectory, despite internal criticism from Council Members and criticism from other UN member states. Sibling organs of the UN have been silent on the subject of encroachment and there has been no condemnation by the Assembly or the ICJ for Council actions conceivably within their jurisdiction. Legislation by the Council would have been inconceivable in the 1990s[159] yet was accepted almost without question in the aftermath of the highly emotional terrorist attacks in 2001. The unanimous adoption of both resolutions 1373 and 1540 may be seen to constitute state practice with respect to the interpretation of the Charter and the Council's powers thereunder;[160] however, it is key to note that notwithstanding the purported representative nature of the Council – the Council is formed of a mere 15 states out of almost 200 and that initial widespread state acceptance or acquiescence of the Council's legislative resolution in 2001 gradually shifted to stark warnings over the limits of Council powers with respect to the separation of powers: states were 'convinced that the starting point in reforming the Council's working methods is for the Council to refrain from exceeding the mandates entrusted to it under the Charter of the United Nations'.[161]

Nonetheless, with the exception perhaps of the renewal of UNSC Resolution 1422, these warnings have not borne fruit and the Council appears to have made little effort to move towards a less legislative role; rather, it has built upon its precedent by adopting resolutions such as 1737[162] and 1929,[163] both on the nuclear programmes in Iran and imposing legal obligations upon Iran to cooperate with the IAEA. The Council has also taken it upon itself to bind a states to a treaty under the guise of a threat to the international peace,[164] contrary to the principles of state sovereignty and the stipulations of the Vienna Convention on the obligations of third party states.[165] That the Council is not governed or monitored by its sibling organs does not except it from compliance with the strict stipulations and mandate of the UN Charter.[166]

The theory, however, belies the reality of affairs on the Council, which as an organ of the UN has not made any coherent efforts to move towards the symbiosis of powers within its parent system that the San Francisco drafters undoubtedly intended in the Charter; rather, it has chosen to itself increasingly fill gaps in international law in place of turning to the Assembly, create legal principles and precedent in the stead of the ICJ and encroach dramatically on the powers of UN member states, in direct confrontation with the underlying principles not only of the United Nations but of international law itself – state sovereignty. The Council does not believe that it acts ultra vires in legislating general international norms, which have no temporal boundaries. Indeed, in a similar political environment to that over a decade ago in 2001, where foreign terrorist organisations today pose a threat to the citizens and interests of Western states, the Council has not hesitated to pass a legacy of UNSC Resolution 1373 in UNSC Resolution 2178, placing legally binding obligations upon states that are general, poorly-defined and temporally indefinite. Moreover, in an even more concerning expansion of the powers seized under UNSC Resolution 1373, the Council has unequivocally crossed the boundaries set by Article 2(7) of the Charter in interfering in the domestic realm of sovereign states, namely terrorism on a domestic level.

Notes

1 Egypt, UNSC Verbatim Record (27 August 2008) UN Doc S/PV.5968 (Resumption 1) 3.
2 See eg Erika de Wet, *The Chapter VII Powers of the United Nations Security Council* (Hart 2004) 112.
3 UN Charter (1945) art 21.
4 ibid art 30.
5 ibid art 72(1).
6 ibid art 92.
7 ibid art 11.
8 ibid art 24.
9 Mohammed Bedjaoui, *The New World Order and The Security Council: Testing the Legality of Its Acts* (Nijhoff 1994) 12–13.
10 ibid 13.
11 ibid art 12.
12 ibid art 7(1).
13 ibid art 96.
14 ibid art 97.
15 ibid art 99.
16 Some have argued that reform of the ICJ should incorporate this element to extend the advisory jurisdiction of the ICJ; see eg Stephen M Schwebel, 'Preliminary rulings by the International Court of Justice at the instance of national courts' (1988) 28 *Virginia Journal of International Law* 495; Shabtai Rosenne, 'Preliminary rulings by the ICJ at the instance of National Court: a reply' (1989) 29 *Virginia Journal of International Law* 401. However, the Statute of the ICJ remains restrictive of requests for Advisory Opinions solely from 'whatever body may be authorized by or in accordance with the Charter of the United Nations to make such a request' (Statute of the International Court of Justice (1945) art 65) namely the Assembly and the Council under art 96 of the Charter.
17 See eg UN Charter (1945) art 33(2).
18 Statute of the International Court of Justice (1945) art 36(1).
19 UN Charter (1945) art 36(3).
20 *Military and Paramilitary Activities in and against Nicaragua (Nicaragua v United States)* (Jurisdiction and Admissibility) ICJ Rep 392, 433 (emphasis in original).
21 *United States Diplomatic and Consular Staff in Tehran* (Judgment) [1980] ICJ Rep 3 para 40.
22 *Aegean Sea Continental Shelf (Greece v Turkey)* (Request for the Indication of Interim Measures of Protection, Order of 11 September 1976) [1976] ICJ Rep 3 para 37.

23 *Armed Activities on the Territory of the Congo (Democratic Republic of Congo v Uganda)* (Request for the Indication of Provisional Measures, Order of 1 July 2000) [2000] ICJ Rep 111 para 36.
24 *Application of the Convention on the Prevention and Punishment of the Crime of Genocide (Bosnia and Herzegovina v Serbia and Montenegro)* Provisional Measures [1993] ICJ Rep 3 para 33.
25 *Military and Paramilitary Activities in and against Nicaragua (Nicaragua v United States)* (Jurisdiction and Admissibility) ICJ Rep 392 para 95.
26 *Accordance with International Law of the Unilateral Declaration of Independence in Respect of Kosovo* [2010] (Advisory Opinion) ICJ Rep 403 para 40.
27 *Legal Consequences for States of the Continued Presence of South Africa in Namibia (South West Africa) notwithstanding Security Council Resolution 276 (1970)* (Advisory Opinion) [1971] ICJ Rep 16.
28 *Tadic case* (Decision by Appeals Chamber) IT-94-1-AR72 (2 October 2000) para 28. For further discussion see Alexander Orakhelashvili, 'The acts of the Security Council: meaning and standards of review' (2007) 11 *Max Planck Yearbook of United Nations Law* 143.
29 *United States Diplomatic and Consular Staff in Tehran* (Judgment) [1980] ICJ Rep 3 para 40.
30 'Dispute elsewhere pending'.
31 See eg Iran, UNSC Verbatim Record (27 August 2008) UN Doc S/PV.5968 (Resumption 1) 12 (2008); Russia, UNSC Verbatim Record (12 January 2007) UN Doc S/PV.5619 at 6.
32 United Nations Conference on International Organization (UNCIO) Vol 13 (1945) 657.
33 United Nations Conference on International Organization (UNCIO) Vol 8 (1945) 394.
34 United Nations Conference on International Organization (UNCIO) Vol 3 (1945) 709–10.
35 ibid.
36 See Bedjaoui (n 9) 9.
37 UN Charter (1945) art 13.
38 See eg *Alleged Violations of Sovereign Rights and Maritime Spaces in the Caribbean Sea (Nicaragua v Colombia)* (Application instituting Proceedings) General List No 155 [2013] 22.
39 Daniel Joyner, 'The Security Council as a legal hegemon' (2012) 43 *Georgetown Journal of International Law* 225, 226.
40 UNGA Res 171 (II) (1947) UN Doc A/RES/2/171 preamble.
41 eg *Certain Expenses of the United Nations (Article 17, paragraph 2, of the Charter)* (Advisory Opinion) [1962] ICJ Rep 151; *Admission of a State the United Nations (Charter, Art 4)* (Advisory Opinion) [1948] ICJ Rep 57.
42 See eg *Legal Consequences for States of the Continued Presence of South Africa in Namibia (South West Africa) notwithstanding Security Council Resolution 276 (1970)* (Advisory Opinion) [1971] ICJ Rep 16; *Reparation for Injuries Suffered in the Service of the United Nations* (Advisory Opinion) [1942] ICJ Rep 174.
43 For further discussion see Bedjaoui (n 9) 15–21.
44 UN Doc S/RES/22 (1947) referred to the UK-Albanian dispute over damage to UK shops in the Straits of Corfu, which was settled at the ICJ in the *Corfu Channel Case* (Judgment) [1949] ICJ Rep 4.
45 UNSC Res 216 (12 November 1965) UN Doc S/RES/216 para 2; UNSC Res 276 (30 January 1970) UN Doc S/RES/276 para 2.
46 UNSC Res 687 (3 April 1991) UN Doc S/RES/687.
47 UNSC Res 794 (3 December 1992) UN Doc S/RES/794.

48 ibid 5.
49 *Tadic Case* (Decision by Appeals Chamber) IT-94-1-AR72 (2 October 2000) para 133.
50 Iran, UNSC Verbatim Record (27 August 2008) UN Doc S/PV.5968 (Resumption 1) 12.
51 See eg Austria, ibid 17.
52 UNSC Res 1209 (19 November 1998) UN Doc S/RES/1209 para 2.
53 *Tadic Case* (Decision by Appeals Chamber) IT-94-1-AR72 (2 October 2000) para 296.
54 Alexander Orakhelashvili, 'The impact of peremptory norms on the interpretation and application of United Nations Security Council Resolutions' (2005) 16(1) *European Journal of International Law* 59, 80.
55 Venezuela, UNSC Verbatim Record (25 May 1993) UN Doc S/PV.3217 at 7.
56 US, UNSC Verbatim Record (22 February 1993) UN Doc S/PV.3175 at 11.
57 This is explicitly mentioned as the basis for art 2 of the ICTY Statute, but no other codified international law is referred to in the Statute.
58 UNSC 'Report of the Secretary General pursuant to Paragraph 2 of Security Council Resolution 808 (1993)' (3 May 1993) UN Doc S/25704 para 33. Such sources of law include the 1907 Hague Convention (IV) Respecting the Laws and Customs of War on Land and the Regulations annexed thereto and the 1948 Convention on the Prevention and Punishment of the Crime of Genocide.
59 ibid para 53.
60 ibid para 47.
61 ibid para 55. See also Ivan Simonvic, 'The role of the ICTY in the development of international criminal adjudication' (1999–2000) 23 *Fordham International Law Journal* 440, 457–58.
62 France, UNSC Verbatim Record (25 May 1993) UN Doc S/PV.3217 at 11.
63 Japan, UNSC Verbatim Record (25 May 1993) UN Doc S/PV.3217 at 24. See also Brazil, UNSC Verbatim Record (22 February 1993) UN Doc S/PV.3175 at 6–7.
64 William Schabas, '*Mens rea* and the International Criminal Tribunal for the Former Yugoslavia' (2002–03) 37 *New English Law Review* 1015, 1017.
65 UNSC 'Report of the Secretary General pursuant to Paragraph 2 of Security Council Resolution 808 (1993)' (3 May 1993) UN Doc S/25704 para 19.
66 ibid para 21.
67 ibid.
68 ibid para 23. See also Ralph Zacklin, 'Some major problems in the drafting of the ICTY Statute' (2004) 2 *Journal of International Criminal Justice* 361.
69 Frederic L Kirgis Jr, 'The Security Council's first fifty years' (1995) 89(3) *American Journal of International Law* 506, 524.
70 *Tadic Trial* (Decision on the Defence Motion on Jurisdiction) IT-94-I-T (10 August 1995).
71 *Tadic case* (Decision by Appeals Chamber) IT-94-1-AR72 (2 October 2000) para 20.
72 *Tadic Trial* (Decision on the Defence Motion on Jurisdiction) IT-94-I-T (10 August 1995) para 5.
73 UNSC 'Report of the Secretary General pursuant to Paragraph 2 of Security Council Resolution 808 (1993)' (3 May 1993) UN Doc S/25704 para 24.
74 ibid para 22.
75 ibid.
76 UN Charter (1945) art 48 (emphasis added).
77 ibid art 41.

78 While the legal analysis may have come from the Office of Legal Counsel, the most appropriate forum for the discussion of the legality of the establishment of international tribunals is the ICJ.
79 UNSC 'Report of the Secretary General pursuant to Paragraph 2 of Security Council Resolution 808 (1993)' (3 May 1993) UN Doc S/25704 para 29.
80 Leila Nadya Sadat, 'The legacy of the ICTY: the International Criminal Court' (2002–03) 37 *New English Law Review* 1073, 1074 (emphasis in original).
81 Ralph Zacklin, 'The failings of Ad Hoc International Tribunals' (2004) 2 *Journal of International Criminal Justice* 541, 542.
82 *Arrest Warrant of 11 April 2000 (Democratic Republic of the Congo v Belgium)* (Judgment) [2002] ICJ Rep 3 para 58.
83 Thomas G Weiss and others, *The United Nations and Changing World Politics* (Westview Press 2012) 198.
84 See Eric Rosand, 'The Security Council as "global legislator": ultra vires or ultra innovative?' (2004) 28(3) *Fordham International Law Journal* 542; Björn Elberling, 'The *ultra vires* character of legislative action by the Security Council' (2005) 2(2) *International Organizations Law Review* 337.
85 UNGA Res 2625 (XXV) (24 October 1970) UN Doc A/RES/25/2625.
86 Definition of Aggression, UNGA Res 3314 (14 December 1974).
87 UN Charter (1945) art 2(1).
88 ibid art 2(7).
89 ibid.
90 ibid art 25.
91 US, UNSC Verbatim Record (15 October 1999) UN Doc S/PV.4051 at 3.
92 Few instances of Council discussion on terrorism prior to 1999 could be found eg UNSC Res 286 (9 September 1970) UN Doc S/RES/286 appealed for an end to hijacking of commercial aircraft and release of passengers held; UNSC Res 457 (4 December 1979) UN Doc S/RES/457 condemned Iranian taking of US hostages in Tehran; UNSC Res 579 (18 December 1985) UN Doc S/RES/579 condemned acts of hostage-taking and abduction; UNSC Presidential Statement 3 (1995) UN Doc S/PRST/1995/3 condemned a terrorist attack in Israel.
93 See Weiss and others (n 83) 130.
94 UNSC Res 1377 (12 November 2001) UN Doc S/RES/1377 Annex.
95 UNSC Res 1368 (12 September 2001) UN Doc S/RES/1368 para 4.
96 eg UNSC Res 1390 (16 January 2002) UN Doc S/RES/1390 para 2(a). See also eg UNSC Res 1333 (19 December 2000) UN Doc S/RES/1333 para 8(c); UNSC Res 1267 (15 October 1999) UN Doc S/RES/1267 para 4(b).
97 UNSC Res 1373 (28 September 2001) UN Doc S/RES/1373.
98 See eg Simon Chesterman, Thomas M Franck and David M Malone, *Law and Practice of the United Nations* (Oxford University Press 2008) 110; Stefan A Talmon, 'The Security Council as world legislature' (2005) 99 *American Journal of International Law* 175.
99 UNSC Res 1373 (28 September 2001) UN Doc S/RES/1373 preamble.
100 The resolution is phrased extremely vaguely and in the passive.
101 eg the International Convention for the Suppression of Terrorist Bombings (1997); the International Convention for the Suppression of the Financing of Terrorism (1999); the International Convention for the Suppression of Acts of Nuclear Terrorism (2005); High Level Panel on Threats, Challenges and Change (2004).
102 UNGA Res 51/210 (16 January 1997) UN Doc A/RES/51/210 para 2.
103 See eg Syria, UNSC Verbatim Record (15 April 2002) UN Doc S/PV.4512 at 10; Malaysia, ibid (Resumption) 10; Pakistan, UNSC Verbatim Record (18 January 2002) UN Doc S/PV.4453 at 30.

104 UNSC Res 1566 (8 October 2004) UN Doc S/RES/1566 para 3.
105 1963 Convention on Offences and Certain Other Acts Committed on Board Aircraft (Tokyo Convention); 1970 Convention for the Suppression of Unlawful Seizure of Aircraft (Hague Convention); 1971 Convention for the Suppression of Unlawful Acts against the Safety of Civil Aviation (Montreal Convention); 1973 Convention on the Prevention and Punishment of Crimes Against Internationally Protected Persons; 1979 International Convention against the Taking of Hostages (Hostages Convention); 1980 Convention on the Physical Protection of Nuclear Material (Nuclear Materials Convention); 1988 Protocol for the Suppression of Unlawful Acts of Violence at Airports Serving International Civil Aviation; 1988 Convention for the Suppression of Unlawful Acts against the Safety of Maritime Navigation; 1988 Protocol for the Suppression of Unlawful Acts Against the Safety of Fixed Platforms Located on the Continental Shelf; 1991 Convention on the Marking of Plastic Explosives for the Purpose of Detection; 1997 International Convention for the Suppression of Terrorist Bombings; 1999 International Convention for the Suppression of the Financing of Terrorism.
106 The ICJ has not defined terrorism. See eg Rosalyn Higgins, 'The general international law of terrorism' in Rosalyn Higgins and Maurice Flory (eds), *Terrorism and International Law* (Routledge 1997) 28.
107 UK, UNGA Verbatim Record (1 October 2001) UN Doc A/56/PV.12 at 18–19.
108 ibid 18.
109 ibid 2 ff.
110 ibid para 6.
111 President, UNSC Verbatim Record (12 November 2001) UN Doc S/PV.4413 at 19: 'There were 15 votes in favour'.
112 UK, UNSC Verbatim Record (30 November 2001) UN Doc S/PV.4432 at 5.
113 France, UNSC Verbatim Record (18 January 2002) UN Doc S/PV.4453 at 7. See also eg UK, UNSC Verbatim Record (12 November 2001) UN Doc S/PV.4413 at 15; Singapore, UNSC Verbatim Record (15 October 2001) UN Doc A/56/PV.25 at 10; Turkey, UNSC Verbatim Record (12 November 2001) UN Doc A/56/PV.48 at 9; UNGA 'Letter dated 20 December 2001 from the Representatives of Belgium and India to the United Nations addressed to the Secretary-General' (26 December 2001) UN Doc A/56/757 at 4 and UNSC Verbatim Record (18 January 2002) UN Doc S/PV.4453 at 21; Kazakhstan, UNSC Verbatim Record (19 November 2001) UN Doc A/56/PV.59 at 34; Guatemala, UNSC Verbatim Record (31 October 2001) UN Doc A/56/PV.34 at 13.
114 Angola, UNSC Verbatim Record (22 April 2004) UN Doc S/PV.4950 at 9–10.
115 US, UNSC Verbatim Record (18 January 2002) UN Doc S/PV.4453 at 6.
116 UK, ibid 5.
117 UK, UNGA Verbatim Record (1 October 2001) UN Doc A/56/PV.12 at 18.
118 UK, UNSC Verbatim Record (18 January 2002) UN Doc S/PV.4453 at 4.
119 UK, UNGA Verbatim Record (1 October 2001) UN Doc A/56/PV.12 at 18.
120 See eg Syria, UNSC Verbatim Record (18 January 2002) UN Doc S/PV.4453 at 9.
121 Pakistan (n 103) 31.
122 UNSC Res 1566 (8 October 2004) UN Doc S/RES/1566 para 3.
123 ibid para 2.
124 UNSC Res 2178 (24 September 2014) UN Doc S/RES/2178.
125 ibid para 6.
126 ibid preamble (emphasis added).

127 ibid para 1.
128 Chile, UNSC Verbatim Record (22 April 2004) UN Doc S/PV.4950 at 10. Resolution 1373 is referred to numerous times in the discussions on UNSC Res 1540 (2004). See eg France, ibid 9; Russia, ibid 16 (2004); Germany, ibid 19; India, ibid 23.
129 Spain, ibid 7. See also Angola (n 114) 10, where UNSC Res 1540 (2004) was 'in accord with the objectives stated in resolution 1373 (2001)'.
130 Pakistan, UNSC Verbatim Record (22 April 2004) UN Doc S/PV.4950 at 15.
131 ibid.
132 South Africa, ibid 22.
133 See Joyner, 'The Security Council as a legal hegemon' (n 39) 227.
134 Daniel Joyner, *International Law and the Proliferation of Weapons of Mass Destruction* (Oxford University Press 2009) 189.
135 Daniel Joyner, 'The Security Council as a Legal Hegemon' (2012) 43 *Geo J Int'l L* 225, 231.
136 ibid 237.
137 Mexico, UNSC Verbatim Record (22 April 2004) UN Doc S/PV.4950 (Resumption 1) 4. See also Chile, UNSC Verbatim Record (28 April 2004) UN Doc S/PV.4956 at 6; Pakistan, ibid 3.
138 India, UNSC Verbatim Record (22 April 2004) UN Doc S/PV.4950 at 23.
139 ibid.
140 Pakistan, ibid 15.
141 South Africa, ibid 22.
142 Mexico, ibid (Resumption 1) 5 (emphasis added).
143 Pakistan, UNSC Verbatim Record (28 April 2004) UN Doc S/PV.4956 at 2.
144 See Brazil, ibid 8: 'We sought to safeguard the integrity of the existing international treaties and conventions – including the Non-Proliferation Treaty – and the balance of rights and duties contained therein'.
145 Spain, ibid 8.
146 Under art 39 of the Charter, Chapter VII must include the determination of a threat to the peace. The US attempted this in the discussions on resolution 1540: ibid 5. Nonetheless, the general nature of the threat undermines the authority of the resolution and is precisely what Pakistan alluded to as 'fudging' definition of terrorism for hegemonic political interests. Moreover, the Council does not clearly state what gaps exist in existing international treaties and conventions that spurred it into action for the purposes of a threat to the international peace.
147 US, ibid 5.
148 Spain, ibid 8.
149 Chile, UNSC Verbatim Record (22 April 2004) UN Doc S/PV.4950 at 11.
150 ibid.
151 UN Charter (1945) art 2(7).
152 New Zealand, UNSC Verbatim Record (10 July 2002) UN Doc S/PV.4568 at 5.
153 Uruguay, UNSC Verbatim Record (12 June 2003) UN Doc S/PV.4772 at 11.
154 See eg Canada, UNSC Verbatim Record (10 July 2002) UN Doc S/PV.4568 at 3; Samoa, ibid (Resumption 1) 7; Germany, UNSC Verbatim Record (10 July 2002) UN Doc S/PV.4568 at 9; Canada, UNSC Verbatim Record (12 June 2003) UN Doc S/PV.4772 at 5–6; Lichtenstein, ibid 7–8; Trinidad and Tobago, ibid 15, Elberling (n 84) 337; see de Wet (n 2).
155 UN Charter (1945) art 25.
156 ibid art 103.
157 For further discussion of this argument see generally Daniel Joyner, *Interpreting the Nuclear Non-proliferation Treaty* (Oxford University Press 2011).

158 Iran, UNSC Verbatim Record (12 June 2003) UN Doc S/PV.4772.

159 See eg *Tadic case* (Decision by Appeals Chamber) IT-94-1-AR72 (2 October 2000) para 43, where 'there exists no corporate organ formally empowered to enact laws directly binding on international legal subjects'. See also Michael C Wood, 'The interpretations of Security Council resolutions' (1998) 2 *Max Planck Yearbook of United Nations Law* 73; Derek W Bowett, 'Judicial and political functions of the Security Council and the International Court of Justice' in Hazel Fox (ed), *The Changing Constitution of the United Nations* (BIICL 1997) 79–80.

160 Vienna Convention on the Law of Treaties (adopted 22 May 1969, entered into force 27 January 1980) 1155 UNTS 331 art 31(3.b).

161 Egypt, UNSC Verbatim Record (27 August 2008) UN Doc S/PV.5968 (Resumption 1) 3.

162 UNSC Res 1737 (27 December 2006) UN Doc S/RES/1737.

163 UNSC Res 1929 (9 June 2010) UN Doc S/RES/1929.

164 UNSC Res 1718 (14 October 2006) UN Doc S/RES/1718 para 3.

165 Vienna Convention on the Law of Treaties (adopted 22 May 1969, entered into force 27 January 1980) 1155 UNTS 331 art 34, 'A treaty does not create either obligations or rights for a third State without its consent'. At the core of the Convention, in its preamble, is 'free consent' and the Convention also provides for the 'withdrawal of a party . . . in conformity with the provisions of the treaty', as the DPRK did. Moreover, the use of coercion or threat of force in resolution 1718 may have invalidated any subsequent accession by the DPRK under art 52 of the Vienna Convention.

166 See Bedjaoui (n 9) 28.

10 The equitable participation in decision-making processes

> The Council remains a closed club. Informal consultations apart, the Council's real work and decision-making transpires often in smaller and more secretive conclaves, which in some cases exclude even some members of the Council.[1]

Introduction

Equitable participation in the decision-making process of the Council is one of the central reasons for the validity of imposing a rule of law framework upon the Council; the Council's composition of 15 member stats, as well as the existence of permanent seats on the Council, underline the need for an equitable and fair decision-making process. However, perhaps the most common criticism of the Council in relation to equitable participation in decision-making processes is that the Council operates within a framework wherein five permanent member states are capable of overruling the decisions of the entire Council on non-procedural matters by use of the *veto* power.[2] There are, however, other examples within the Charter where the equitable participation of member states should take place. As a primarily political organ, the composition of the Council should arguably effectively reflect the modern political landscape as opposed to that of post-Second World War at the time of its creation; moreover, elements of the UN Charter relating to how the Council exercises its function to 'act on [UN Member States'] behalf'[3] should be carried out to the letter.

Aside from the existence and use of the veto, three central themes exhibit the extent to which the Council allows for the equitable participation of member states in the decision-making process. As the UN organ vested with the responsibility to act on behalf of UN member states[4] and power to command member states to comply with its resolutions,[5] it is not necessary for all member states to contribute to the decision-making process in the same manner as that of the General Assembly; with one vote to each Council member state as opposed to one vote to each UN member state, 'prompt and effective action by the United Nations'[6] is more likely to take place albeit – as we have seen – not guaranteed. However, it is nonetheless inherent in the voting structure of the Council – which requires an affirmative vote of nine members[7] – that matters are discussed openly, fully and extensively on the Council itself and not purely between a sub-section of the 15 member states. This matter has already been discussed and, as concluded, the Council has yet to reform itself adequately to include all member states insofar as the openness of its meetings is concerned.

Equitability of participation extends further than simply the transparency of meetings and the inclusion of all relevant parties to a discussion; the composition of the Council should also reflect an effort to establish equitable participation. The 10 non-permanent state members of the Council should be representative of the wider UN community, as evidenced by the necessity for 'equitable geographical distribution' in article 23(1) of the Charter; this must be balanced with their contribution 'to the maintenance of international peace and security and to the other purposes of the Organization'[8] but the composition and number of Council members should reflect the wider community of the UN that the Council was designed to represent. Moreover, state Members affected by matters[9] or party to a dispute[10] under consideration by the Council should be included in any relevant discussions, not only in the interests of equality but also those of transparency; similarly, there is the implicit expectation that such inclusion in discussions would not simply be formality but rather that the Council would accommodate any issues, concerns or comments raised during the course of debate.

Arguing the expansion of the Council

The only official reform of the Security Council since its creation has been the expansion of the number of Members from eleven to fifteen, under UNGA Resolution 1991 (1963),[11] later ratified by the Council in 1965. The same document assigned to the now 10 non-permanent seats five members from African and Asian states, one from Eastern European states, two from Latin American states and two from Western European and other states.[12] This decision was taken as a result of the increase in the membership of the United Nations, which swelled from the original 51 nations in 1945 to 113 in 1963.[13] With over half the UN membership consisting of recently decolonised African and Asian countries, the Council was amended to reflect not only numbers but also issues and priorities represented within the UN system.

Both the reasoning behind the decision to expand the Council and the subsequent action itself are worth examining within the context of today's geo-political landscape. One way to look at the ballooning of UN membership in the first two decades of its existence would be that numbers more than doubled; another would be that membership increased by 62 states. Since 1965 – when the Council ratified the GA resolution – membership of the UN has expanded by a further 80 nations, most recently with South Sudan in 2011. In fact, in the decade of 1990–2000 alone, 30 states declared independence or sought to be recognised by the UN, many of which was attributable to the end of the Cold War; the independence of so many former USSR territories and declared independence of smaller island states are analogous to the decolonisation of nations in the mid-20th century.

However, almost two decades into the 21st century, reform of the Council through expanding its number of seats has not materialised; the current assignment of non-permanent seats on the Council has remained the same for almost half a century while the geographical groups have expanded in number – in comparison to 1965, there are now five seats to be divided between an African group of 54 states and Asia–Pacific group of 55, totalling 109 states. This figure equates to over 56 per cent of the total UN membership;[14] including the permanent seat of China, this equates to six seats out of 15, a total of 40 per cent of Council seats[15] or one seat for every 18 states. The Latin American and Caribbean Group (GRULAC) has no permanent seats assigned to it and 32 states – or 17 per cent of UN member states – to be represented by only two non-permanent seats; this is one seat for every 15 states, of which neither has the power to block Council resolutions in the interests of the region, as most other groups do.[16]

Conversely, the Western European and Other Group (WEOG) consists of 29 states and is assigned three permanent seats[17] in addition to two non-permanent seats – a total of five seats or one-third of all Council seats – for a mere 15 per cent of UN membership: one seat for every six states. In between these two poles lies the smallest of the groups – the Eastern European Group – with one seat for every 12 states: Russia's permanent seat in addition to another non-permanent rotating seat to represent 12 UN members, or 12 per cent of the UN membership. There is clearly an extreme disparity in the composition of the Council that does not reflect equitable participation by or representation of UN member states and calls for reform to expand it appear entirely warranted.[18]

This position is further amplified by two elements: first, the difficulty with which states Member of a large groups, such as Africa or the Asia–Pacific, will actually have to achieve the goal of sitting on the Council owing to the wider pool and therefore smaller chance of succeeding; and, secondly, the discriminate nature of the selection of states to fill these limited non-permanent seats, which at times appear to be given to the same candidates on repeat occasions – 69 states – over a third of UN members – have never served on the UN Security Council in its history, whereas other nations have served up to 10 times.[19] Although many of these virgin states are newly-declared independent and perhaps understandably have not had the opportunity to sit on the Council, other states like the Dominican Republic and Haiti joined in the UN in 1945 – the same time as Argentina[20] and Colombia[21] – but neither has represented the GRULAC at the Council; even the comparable nations of Panama[22] and Cuba[23] have fared better.

In Asia, while Pakistan has sat in the Asia–Pacific seat seven times, Afghanistan has been overlooked entirely, despite having joined a year before; in Africa, South Africa – a front runner for a permanent seat within the African Group plan – has sat only twice, both within the last decade, despite joining in 1945, whereas Egypt was one of the first to represent the African Group and has done so five times. This disparity affects not only the perspectives of the issues discussed at the Council level, but also the nature of issues brought to light to the Council.

A stark example of this is climate change, which affects more than any other group that of the Alliance of Small Island States (AOSIS) – a coalition of 44 states that is at greatest risk of rising sea levels; as the Prime Minister of Tuvalu noted during his address to the General Assembly in 2008, climate change is 'without doubt, the most serious threat to the global security and survival of mankind . . . [and] an issue of enormous concern to a highly vulnerable small island state like Tuvalu'.[24] Yet of the 44 members of the AOSIS, only eight states[25] have had the opportunity to sit on the Council where they might highlight such issues.

The stagnation of reform flies in the face not only of all states' resolution in the UN Millennium Declaration to intensify efforts 'to achieve a comprehensive reform of the Security Council *in all its aspects*'[26] but also of many states' support for an enlarged Council, including the P5 members themselves,[27] who recognise the need for 'a Security Council that better represents twenty-first-century realities and is maximally capable of carrying out its mandate and effectively meeting the global challenges of this century'.[28]

Wider support for Council enlargement

Heavy support for Council reform through enlargement has also been pushed by the wider community; at least three major initiatives external to the P5 members have been put forward. The common denominator in all proposals was, ironically, the lack of coherency from member states in finding a suitable compromise. In 2005, former Secretary-General Annan proposed his *In Larger Freedom* report[29] with an aim to 'make it more broadly representative of the international community as a whole, as well as of the geopolitical realities of today, and thereby more legitimate in the eyes of the world';[30] in this he advocated[31] an enlarged council of 24 members under one of two plans,[32] either of which he believed would allow the Council to become more 'broadly representative of the realities of power in today's world'.[33] The Secretary-General urged a vote prior to the summit in September 2005[34] – none took place.

Also in 2005, the G4 – comprising Brazil, Germany, India and Japan – proposed[35] 10 new members to the Council, of which six seats would be permanent and held by them in addition to two African states. Perhaps unsurprisingly, there is opposition from numerous angles to each of these bids,[36] most notably the larger *Uniting for Consensus* group – containing Argentina, Italy, Canada, Colombia and Pakistan – which opposed this proposal and countered with a plan to bolster the existing 15 seats with an additional 10 *non-permanent* seats and granting all members the right to re-election.[37] Finally, African states have not stayed silent; they also submitted a draft plan expanding the Council.[38] Nonetheless, in 2008, efforts were redoubled by the UN and multiple rounds[39] of negotiations on a suitable text were conducted during which caucuses such as the African Group[40] and L69[41] emerged and the Uniting for Consensus group gained momentum;[42] however, even at the 10th round of Intergovernmental Negotiations on Security Council reform (IGN) talks in March 2014, '[t]he positions of the various groups remained unchanged, pointing to the manifest deadlock in terms of what should be the specific way ahead'.[43]

At what was hailed a landmark decision in September 2015 the Assembly reaffirmed its central role in the questions of equitable representation on and increase in the membership of the Council in a resolution adopted without vote.[44] Though the decision was the first of its kind to be adopted through an official formal Assembly document, many states[45] saw it as a technical roll-over rather than a substantive reform effort. Despite nine meetings on the issue in this 70th session, actual reform remains a pipe dream.

Notwithstanding the efforts and official stances of states to expand the Council as part of wider reform, it is key also to examine the real impact of enlargement and whether it will achieve the purported goals of ensuring a more equitable participation experience for those included. While there appears to be a general consensus over the notion that the Council should expand to reflect more accurately the landscape of the modern political world, there are two major flaws to the implementation. Primary, since the Council is a political organ, is the issue of whether expansion would actually reflect not only the number of countries in the world and how statistically well represented they are but also the distribution of power. It can be argued that France certainly, and potentially the UK along with it, are no longer the powerhouses that they were in 1945 with a sprawling colonial empire at their discretion; others would point at the economic rise of countries such as Brazil, India, South Africa, and Nigeria. Secondly, the logistics of expansion should be measured against the potential impact on the efficiency and potency of the Council; it would be counterproductive if an expansion were to have a negative impact on the work of the Council.

The logistics of expansion

On the first point, it is unclear that any Group's reform proposals attempt to address the de facto imbalance between seats granted on the Council and the military, economic and political potency outside of it; it is perhaps unsurprising that all P5 members are among the top eight countries in terms of GDP,[46] the top six countries in terms of both military firepower[47] and expenditure[48] and all possess nuclear weaponry. To extend these trends, however, is difficult; India, Brazil, Japan and Germany are nations that are often touted as likely potential candidates for permanent seats on the Council, but it is up for debate whether any bring a rounded package in the same form as the existing P5 members.

With respect to the logistics of Council expansion, as has been shown, there is general consensus that the Council should be expanded. However, while much of the focus has been directed towards suitable candidates for permanent or non-permanent seats,[49] precisely how many seats the Council should be expanded by[50] or what rights any new seats would confer on Council Members that occupied them – especially the veto – little prudent debate has been had over the wisdom of actually expanding the Council and what impact this will have on the decision-making process. Secretary-General Annan emphasised that reforms of the Council 'should not impair the effectiveness of the Security Council';[51] to ignore this advice simply to achieve adherence to standards of the rule of law might be considered short-sighted since, if by expanding the number of Council members one also undermines the work of the principal organ entrusted with maintenance of the international peace, a great blow would be struck to the UN as a whole and the wider community that relies on the actions of the Council. A logical balance must be struck.

An expanded Council of 24 states might more easily contribute towards the highlighting of a wider range of issues that are prioritised by the newer members; however, it may also serve to dilute the efficacy and potency of the Council. The resources at the disposal of the Council would need to be spread wider; consequently, larger states may well be more reluctant to contribute towards causes that are not high on their agenda and therefore at least one of the purposes of enlarging the Council – widening the horizons of Council action – would have failed. Moreover, in expanding the Council, the voting system would need to be changed, requiring a greater majority of votes in order to pass a resolution; accounting for divergent views based on regional affiliation, the discussions at the Council would not only be more time-consuming but may also inevitably result in an increase in stalemates or failures of resolution to be adopted. Finally, it would still be debateable whether an increased Council would represent the Council as a whole; while at first glance the Council would move towards the democratic representation of the General Assembly, the fact remains that enlarging the group excessively – even if the number of seats proportionally reflected the number of states in each group – would hinder serious negotiations while still leaving the veto in the hands of at least five member states. Moreover, issues of which states would fill the seats and the selection process would open an entirely new avenue of debate – many view themselves as ideal candidates.

A question emerges, then, whether expanding the Council to include these states would weaken the image of the Council, which is primarily tasked with maintaining peace and security worldwide. The P5 members have *global* reach not only in terms of sheer numbers on paper – such as military expenditure, armed forces strength or GDP – or their geographical location, distributed around the world almost evenly, but also in terms of political influence. The lengthier answer to this question beyond the core scope of this book but expanding the Council does risk crippling its work and such moves towards equality under the rule of law may be self-defeating for the rule of law, which operates best within a robust and efficient system.[52]

As such, strictly from a legal perspective, the lack of Council expansion contravenes the principle of the equitable participation; in reality, however, this may be a necessary departure from the letter of the law in an effort to maintain the power of the Council to act quickly, efficiently and decisively in the event of a threat to the international peace. As contrasting as it may appear to advocate practicality over equality and fairness, it may be that the Council – as a political organ that must be necessarily rapid in its responses – requires such a compromise.

Consultation of relevant parties to a situation or matter of discussion

In accordance with its Rules of Procedure,[53] the Council should generally meet in public; however, as already established, it has become common practice for the Council to meet in private where a great deal of the discussion and decisions themselves take place, away from the eye not only of the general public and wider UN community, but also from other Council Members. Any opacity of decision-making on the Council is even more acutely felt when the discussions are around a topic to which an affected or involved party is not privy; where article 31 of the Charter grants the Council discretion over inviting a UN Member to the discussion, article 32 imposes an obligation on the Council to include relevant Parties in the discussion.[54]

However, in practice, the liberty granted to the Council in article 31 is relied upon more heavily than that of article 32; the Council may be more inclined to deem a situation to 'specially affect' a member state thereby triggering article 31 than it may be to consider that state a party to a dispute covered by article 32 in order to avoid the necessity of including that state in discussions. This appears to have been the case with South Africa during discussions over the question in Namibia; in this case the ICJ found that South Africa was not entitled to demand inclusion in discussions owing to the classification of the Namibia question as a situation rather than a dispute.[55] Moreover, there is little room for states to object to such classification.[56]

Council practice shows that states that should logically be party to a discussion are often side-lined in a variety of ways. First, there is the possibility that articles 31 and 32 will be overlooked altogether and states that are clearly relevant and even central to the discussion are left out of the Council when it broaches topics. In 1998, when both Pakistan[57] and India[58] conducted nuclear tests in their respective territories, the Council met to discuss their action in the absence of both parties. Presidential statements condemning the actions of both nations[59] – emerging from meetings[60] that neither India nor Pakistan were invited to attend – were followed by UNSC Resolution 1172,[61] to which in addition to the 15 Council members of the time, 12 nations[62] were invited to participate in the discussion.[63]

India, however, was not invited to participate, nor did any state remark on its absence in the discussions of UNSC Resolution 1172, despite a letter circulated by the Permanent Representative of India to the Council two days prior to the Council meeting on the resolution[64] regretting 'that the Council has disregarded this Charter provision [of article 31] by not giving India an opportunity to participate in the discussions on this draft'.[65] India raises a valid and awkward point for the Council, hinting at a bias that the Council would find difficult to respond to, given that the other party to the dispute – Pakistan – was granted the opportunity to respond publicly to both Council members and non-Council members alike during discussion in a lengthy and defensive speech.[66] A decade later, the matter was still the subject of criticism at the Council,[67] suggesting that little had changed.

Secondly, even when states are invited to take part in proceedings, there are no safeguards in place to ensure that their contributions take place prior to the decision being taken;[68] for example, in the discussion on UNSC Resolution 1172, Canada took the opportunity to 'express [its] regret that the views of Member States not members of the Security Council are being heard only after consideration and after adoption of such a resolution, dealing as it does with matters of such vital concern to all Member States';[69] a view reiterated almost a decade later by Iran.[70] The denial of representation prior to a vote undermines the concept of transparency and openness on the Council; just as private meetings may be construed as eliciting a 'clique' mentality between certain members of the Council – most notably the P5 members – so too giving the floor to representatives to speak only *after* a vote has taken place gives the impression that their contributions are neither valued nor have impact on the Council members. To relegate speeches in such a way devalues the input of these states, suggests that their arguments are mere afterthoughts to a process that includes neither their perspective nor political stances. The components of transparency, fairness and equitable participation are all challenged when the Council adopts 'a presidential statement and a resolution without even allowing the views of the concerned party to be heard'.[71]

The infringement on sovereign rights

There is also the possibility that states may be overruled in the discussions by more powerful members, even when matters primarily affect their own sovereignty, with no clear explanation for the decision. This was the case with Rwanda, which initially approached the Council for assistance after the Rwandan genocide in 1994 and requested the Council to set up 'as soon as possible an international tribunal to try the criminals'[72] for four principal reasons.[73] However, less than two months later, they voted against UNSC Resolution 955[74] establishing the ICTR; Rwanda was the only state to have voted against the tribunal, with China abstaining. Put simply, Rwanda was excluded from input into redressing 'genocide and other systematic, widespread and flagrant violations of international humanitarian law'[75] that had taken place on its own territory, not only – as flippantly claimed by New Zealand[76] – owing to the avoidance of the death penalty, but as a result of seven serious concerns[77] that Rwanda found unacceptable.

Rwanda is a prime example of a nation that has suffered grave, catastrophic conflict that has stemmed from and caused even further ethnic division amongst its peoples, which it attempted to highlight in the first of its objections to the Council on *ratione temporis*.[78] Even after the vote, the Rwandan representative believed that '[t]he changes proposed by the Rwandese Government, with all good will, could very well have been accommodated by international law and do not run counter to the idea of international jurisdiction . . . [and] that an international tribunal for Rwanda, taking into account Rwandese realities, [was] possible and feasible';[79] nonetheless, all seven of its objections – including the inclusion of candidates and judges for the ICTR from states with nationals alleged to have perpetrated the very crimes they intended to try – were ignored by the

Council, which is unsurprising given that Rwanda was permitted to give its speech only after the vote had been taken in a manner that suited more an explanation of its vote than a coherent attempt by the Council to expand its base of information upon which to take a balanced decision.

This appears to be a trend that has continued to affect international peacekeeping as well. In July 2016, despite acknowledgement that 'United Nations peacekeeping operations and special political missions should be deployed on the basis of full consultation with the country concerned and follow the principle of the consent of the host country'[80] – noted as being particularly pertinent owing to the fact that 'the resolution has been adopted outside of Chapter VII of the Charter of the United Nations, and is consistent with the principles of peacekeeping operations calling for the participation and agreement of host countries'[81] – the consent of Burundi was neither sought nor received in the creation of a 'United Nations police officers component in Burundi for an initial period of one year'[82] under UNSCR 2303; in fact, Burundi was not even present at the Council meeting discussing the French-proposed resolution. Despite allegations that the text of the resolution would 'violate the country's sovereignty, international law and the Charter of United Nations, and it sets a negative precedent for the international community', it passed with four abstentions and 11 affirmative votes. The forceful imposition of a policing contingent has followed the track of Chapter VII resolutions; consent of a host nation is no longer seen as a prerequisite. Ironic insult is added to injury through the specific French reference to the Rwandan genocide,[83] which the Council failed to prevent and – as seen above – subsequently led to the forcing through of the ICTR against the will of the Rwandan government.

On the situation in South Sudan, the Council at least heard the protestations of the government that the 'adoption of the resolution goes against a basic principle of United Nations peacekeeping operations, which is the consent of the main parties to the conflict, and against the Charter of the United Nations, which urges Members to respect the sovereignty, territorial integrity and political independence of other States';[84] however, this took place *after* the vote and – in the same vein as the rationale behind the policing agenda above – had no impact on its decision under UNSCR 2304 to 'increase the force levels of UNMISS up to a ceiling of 17,000 troops, including 4,000 for the Regional Protection Force'.[85] Despite similar objections and abstention by three of the same Council members as those abstaining on UNSCR 2303 – China, Egypt and Venezuela – for the same reasons that it 'is inconceivable that this Government should not be party to a detailed agreement on the deployment of a force that is to operate on its territory',[86] the vote passed, again, with 11 affirmative votes and four abstentions.

These omissions and acts are coupled with miscellaneous errors in the procedure and implementation of Council rules that also have the result of undermining equitable participation in the decision-making process for states – invitations to participate are sometimes late[87] and the draft resolutions and statements that are circulated to Council members

> often trimmed and edited before reaching informal consultations . . . mak[ing] it hard for non-members to be readily informed of the work of the Council . . . [and] difficult for non-members to provide meaningful input into the process, even in rare opportunities such as open debates.[88]

The Council risks having undermined the equitable participation of states in the decision-making process, not only by failing to expand appropriately or redress the geo-political imbalance of its composition, but also through various methods of exclusion of states from debates, discussions and decisions. Insofar as Council practice in the field of equitable representation, it has not shown a willingness for meaningful reform, nor has it displayed any pattern or comprehensive future plan of action for ameliorating the shortfalls in which its behaviour hitherto has resulted.

The veto

The most contentious issue on the Council when any discussion on reform or equitable participation in the decision-making process is broached is undoubtedly the existence, and resort to the veto by the P5 members. The mechanism of the veto, however, is enshrined[89] in the foundations of the Charter,

> meticulously inserted into every nook and cranny of the Charter. No important decision could be taken by the Organization without their approval. Any Great Power, if it chose, could block the admission of new members. It could prevent the expulsion of a member or the suspension of membership rights. It could hold up the appointment of the Secretary-General. It could block the admission of a state to the International Court of Justice. More important still, it could prevent the adoption of an amendment to the Charter. Thus the veto power was imbedded with what seemed to be eternal finality in the fundamental law of the United Nations.[90]

To suggest that any debate on the value of the existence, or indeed abolition, of the veto is anything but strictly academic would be asinine; amendment of the UN Charter requires the consent of the same P5 members[91] that refuse even consideration of relinquishing the control it grants them. Accordingly, any examination of the Council's behaviour must take place within the existing framework of the UN Charter, which clearly allows for the use of the veto in its article 27(3) and with the explicit realisation of the inherent inequality of the mechanism. The pattern of usage, however, and reasoning behind its invocation can be subjects to standards of equitability.

The intended purpose of the veto

> [E]ach of the five permanent members of the Council possesses the right to prevent any [substantive] decision of the Council being reached. And that is

> why the right implied in this formula has been called the 'veto'. *Some objection was taken to using the name 'veto', but the name is quite an accurate description of the right itself.*[92]

The veto was 'the most controversial, perhaps, of all the problems with which the Conference [was] faced'[93] at San Francisco in 1945; strong opposition to the notion of permanent seats on the Council coupled with the power unilaterally to block the adoption of non-procedural resolutions was rife amongst delegates.[94] Indeed, so irregular was the notion of the veto that confusion as to its method of applicability led to the first veto, exercised by Russia, being discounted in 1946.[95] The veto was nonetheless a non-negotiable element of the Council for the major powers of the time – the UK, Russia, the US and China.[96] Nonetheless, the veto was initially due to be afforded to every Council Member under the principle of unanimity, but was removed from all but the P5 – a decision that, to the UK delegate, 'may be considered to be unequal treatment . . . [and] undesirable, but . . . not entirely unreasonable'.[97]

From the perspective of the member states, the veto represented the utmost confidence and trust instilled in the Great Powers to use the veto not only selflessly, but invariably sparingly, and only as a result of the debt owed to them in the aftermath of the Second World War:

> We believe that it is necessary that on every occasion when the veto power be applied by any one of the great powers *it should be recalled that the great majority of this Conference has granted them such a tremendous amount of confidence in the certainty that the veto shall not be applied except in exceptional cases* and then only when the exercise of that faculty may contribute to consolidate the peace and to maintain security in the world – in other words that the Conference *being as it is opposed to the proposed system* has given its approval to it only because it believes that the great powers which have carried this war to a victorious culmination deserve such *an exorbitant proof of confidence from the other countries associated in the United Nations Organization.*[98]

Following a great deal of compromise, the right of a veto for the Great Powers was semantically altered to reflect a 'categoric imperative of unanimity'[99] – a shift took place from the *right* of the P5 members to a permanent seat and veto power, to the *necessity* for unanimity on the Council. In short, the veto was designed to ensure that the P5 Members acted in perpetual unison with respect to any non-procedural action taken under the aegis of the Council. As a result, the veto was seen 'not as a question of privileges, but of using the present distribution of military and industrial power in the world for the maintenance of peace'[100] without which 'the [United Nations] would break down in the event that enforcement action were undertaken against a Permanent Member'.[101] One might note the use of the term 'present distribution' as an indication that it was seen as imperative that the P5 Members with their sheer strength of military and populations, moved in a coordinated effort at every step; moreover, although this does not remain the case, the P5 at the time represented 'probably more than half the population of the world, and account has to be taken of that fact'.[102] Ultimately, the acceptance of the existence of the veto was not smooth, but pragmatically accepted;[103] the reality of the situation was that 'if the veto . . . was removed the Powers responsible for Dumbarton Oaks Proposals would say they couldn't accept the decision and the inevitable alternative would be to drop the Proposals altogether',[104] meaning that the United Nations would never have come into existence. In the words of one commentator, '[t]he veto was the price we had to pay for the Charter. It was the price we had to pay for the cooperation of the Great Powers'.[105]

The veto was unabashedly part of a flawed system[106] and remains so to this day. However, it is clear that the reason for the creation of the veto for the Council was not to ensure that the Great Powers were exalted or placed atop an institutional hierarchy but rather to reflect the political, military and demographic realities of the world at the time of the establishment of the UN. While the geo-political landscape has changed drastically in the decades that have passed, the reasoning and purpose behind the veto remains the same: to ensure that the P5 Members moved in unison towards the goal of maintaining international peace and security. Certainly, the veto was never intended to be 'used capriciously and . . . the Soviet Delegate had told the press that the five great powers would rarely exercise the veto'.[107]

The veto record of the Council

History, however, recounts a different story and since the creation of the United Nations, over 190 draft Council resolutions have been subject to veto;[108] of these, the vast preponderance overall has been cast by the USSR/Russian Federation,[109] the very same P5 member that granted the above assurances. With the exception of two vetoes used by France and the UK in 1956,[110] no other state used its veto until 1970[111] – a Soviet monopoly lasting a quarter of a century. In fact, throughout the Cold War, the veto was frequently resorted to, almost exclusively by the USSR and the US in 'a story of the pursuit of national interests – even in the face of contrary world opinion and reasoned judicial decisions'.[112] In the years 1945–1989, a total of 646 resolutions were adopted while the veto was exercised a total of 162 times – therefore, almost one in five resolutions debated at the Council failed. This surely falls short of the standard expected by the delegates at San Francisco, who believed that

> the great powers can perform a great service to the world if they demonstrate in practice that the special power of veto given to each and every one of them individually under this Charter will be used with restraint and in the interest of the United Nations as a whole. It might be put in a phrase with which most of us are familiar, 'It is excellent to have a giant's strength but it is tyrannous to use it as a giant.'[113]

Deeper inspection of the use of veto relates unequivocally to interests unaffiliated with international peace and security, and in many cases central to the national interests of states : both the USA[114] and USSR[115] alike exercised their veto in the admission of numerous states to the UN 'for no better reason than that . . . [a P5 Member] sees them as pawns in the cold war';[116] the USSR used its veto to avoid action over its invasion of Afghanistan[117] and Czechoslovakia;[118] the US blocked resolutions against its own actions in Grenada[119] and Nicaragua;[120] and the UK blocked numerous resolutions criticising or threatening sanctions on South Africa.[121] Although the UN 'was not meant to be a club in which [veto-holders] competed to admit [their] friends and to blackball candidates supported by [their] opponents',[122] political and strategic alliances became central to the decisions of the Council when to use their veto. Violating the authority and entrusted guardianship upon which the veto was established, the Council's veto record between the years 1945 and 1990 is a damning tale of the superiority of domestic foreign policy above the interests of international peace and security, and indeed looks to have continued beyond the collapse of the Berlin Wall.

While the end of the Cold War heralded a new era in cooperation at the Council and a distinct decline in the number of vetoes used can be noted throughout the 1990s,[123] the number of vetoes being exercised have crept up since the turn of the century.[124] France and the UK last used their vetoes in 1989, prior to the post-Cold War period under examination in this book, and France has even been active in its pursuit of less frequent recourse to the veto, advocating a return to the original principles underlying the purpose of the veto and calling for 'the five permanent members of the Security Council voluntarily and collectively suspending their right to exercise the veto when mass atrocities are under consideration'.[125] As such, the sole users of the veto since 1990 have been the US, the Russian Federation and China; moreover, when the subjects of their veto usage is examined, it is highly evident that national interests lie at the heart of their objections.

The United States

By far the subject of the most vetoes at the Council is the Palestinian Question, on which the US has exercised its veto rights no less than 30 times; almost half of these have taken place since 1990. Despite the recognition that the Palestinian Question poses a threat to the international peace by fellow P5 Members[126] the US most recently took the stance that a draft resolution condemning settlements that they themselves recognise to be illegal under international law[127] 'risks hardening the positions of both sides . . . could encourage the parties to stay out of negotiations and, if and when they did resume, to return to the Security Council whenever they reached an impasse';[128] yet when discussing the situation in Syria, the US adamantly imposed the prerogative that: '[i]t is the Council's responsibility to stop atrocities if we can and, at a minimum, to ensure that the perpetrators of atrocities are held accountable'.[129]

Indeed, one P5 Member has gone on record to state that '[a]s the principal organ responsible for the maintenance of international peace and security, the Security Council can and should continue to play an important role in resolving the question of Palestine, in promoting the Middle East peace process and in safeguarding the peace and security of that region'.[130] Moreover, it seemed hypocritical to cite as a reason for the use of its veto to block the adoption of S/2006/878 a 'characterization of Israeli military actions as excessive and disproportionate [which] constitutes a legal judgement [sic] that the Security Council would be ill-advised to make'[131] in light of the legislative role and norm-setting that the Council engaged in recently before in resolutions 1373, 1422 and 1540. The Council's failure to adopt resolutions condemning the disproportionate violence perpetrated by Israeli forces 'conveyed to Israel that it can continue to behave as though it were above international law . . . [and] conveyed to the Palestinian people that, with regard to their issue, the Security Council is not dealing with justice in the proper way'.

The intense and mutually beneficial relationship between Israel and the US is difficult to deny: for decades, the US leadership has highlighted the importance of Israel to the nation.[132] Israel also provides key strategic importance that, while historically providing a bastion against the USSR during the Cold War,[133] remains integral to strategic cooperation and mutual security to this day. In fact, so close are the US and Israel, that the concept of damaging Israel or siding against it has been likened at the highest echelons of US government as tantamount to political suicide.[134] As a result, despite the fact that the Israeli–Palestinian conflict repeatedly features on the agenda of the Council – which in itself underscores the importance, acuteness and urgency of the situation – only 13 resolutions have been passed on the subject of the Israeli/Palestinian conflict since 1990;[135] the US has vetoed more resolutions on the Palestine Question since 1990 than it has allowed to pass. At the root of the vetoes are claims that the resolutions are 'lopsided and unbalanced'[136] despite assertions from fellow Council Members to the contrary[137] and the US's own biased analysis of the situation in 2014.[138] This is an unprecedented situation on the Council – never has a single situation been the subject of so many vetoes by one state.

The US – and the wider Council too – was eerily silent throughout the Israeli bombings in Gaza Strip in 2014, despite the 'appalling'[139] toll, including the bombing of UNRWA schools 'on six occasions', where 'almost 2,000 Palestinians have been killed, of whom 459 are children and 239 are women'.[140] The Council met no less than 13 times in 2014 to discuss or remain seized of the situation in the Gaza Strip; nonetheless, only one Presidential Statement emerged. As the UN High Commissioner for Human Rights has noted, '[s]hort-term geo-political considerations and national interests, narrowly defined, have repeatedly taken precedence over intolerable human suffering and grave breaches of and long-term threats to international peace and security'.[141]

This was certainly true of the veto used by the US that led to the adoption of UNSC Resolution 1422.[142] In its original incarnation of S/2002/712, the resolution extending the mandate of the UN Mission was blocked by the US owing to 'concerns on the question of the International Criminal Court (ICC), in particular the need to ensure [their] national jurisdiction over [their] personnel and officials involved in United Nations peacekeeping and in coalition-of-the-willing operations'.[143] Despite lamentation that '[t]he fact that any permanent member can unilaterally decide to exercise its veto privilege to defeat the efforts of the other 14 members to extend the mandate of an agreed United Nations peacekeeping mission holds disturbing implications for the other 174 members of the United Nations and for the entire world in general',[144] UNSC Resolution 1422, accommodating the US demands for postponement of any investigation of peacekeeper personnel from a non-signatory state to the Rome Statute before the ICC was adopted unilaterally. Gone, also, were charades that the use of the veto was for anything other than national interests, contrary to the intended purpose of the veto:

> it is clear that our veto of the draft resolution on the United Nations Mission in Bosnia and Herzegovina (UNMIBH) did not reflect rejection of peacekeeping in Bosnia. But it did reflect *our frustration* at *our inability* to convince our colleagues on the Security Council to take seriously *our concerns* about the legal exposure of *our peacekeepers* under the Rome Statute.[145]

The reason, then, for the US veto – far from the wholesome purposes of the principle of unanimity in the advancement or maintenance of peace and security – was, by its own admission, entirely one of self-preservation and non-subordination to the ICC. Simply put, as non-signatories to the Rome Statute, they did not wish to have their 'decisions second-guessed by a court whose jurisdiction [they] do not recognize'.[146] While in domestic foreign policy national interest can be argued as paramount, the Council P5 are entrusted with responsibilities that extend beyond their domestic spheres and immediate situations of focus. States recognised that the veto exercised against renewal of the mission in Bosnia and Herzegovina had potentially far reaching consequences and 'not only [for] the existence of the United Nations Mission in Bosnia and Herzegovina . . . [but also] the other 14 operations [at the time] deployed'.[147] Nonetheless, in the face of criticism and pressure from other P5[148] and non-permanent[149] Members, the US maintained its stance until the remainder of the Council acquiesced.

Since the end of the Cold War, the US has not once exercised its veto in a manner consistent with the principles and spirit of the veto power granted by the Charter drafters at San Francisco. In fact, the use of the veto by the US has been exclusively in the pursuit of either its own national interests or the interests of arguably its closest ally, from which it 'has never flinched from its commitment [towards] – a commitment which remains unshakeable'.[150] Regrettably, the US appears to exemplify the criticism of veto by other states Member: 'its use and the threat of its use operate as a procedural device when permanent members pursue their national interests, a process that affects both the working methods and the effectiveness of the Council in achieving its objective of enforcing international peace and security'.[151]

The Russian Federation and China

Following the flurry of vetoes during the Cold War when the overwhelming number of vetoes exercised came from the USSR, the Russian Federation has exercised the veto eleven times since 1990.[152] While their first veto of financing for the mission in Cyprus had 'no political basis of any kind . . . [and was] dictated solely by practical considerations of the Government of the Russian Federation concerning the way to develop further the expanding United Nations peace-keeping operations and concerning, approaches to financing the expenditures for such operations',[153] later uses of the veto were attributable to situations that were deemed 'politically inadmissible'.[154] In fact, both of these stances are incompatible with the intended purpose of the veto; a Russian negative vote over funding of a peacekeeping mission can be argued to embody the same national interests as the protection of peacekeepers, albeit without the international legal ramifications and potential abuse of an international treaty. Even more brazenly, as a party to the conflict in Georgia, the Russian Federation did not hesitate to use its veto to block the adoption of S/2009/310 on the subject, owing to 'its continued insistence on removing all references to Georgia's territorial integrity in the draft resolution'.[155] As a result, UNMIG, established in 1993, ceased to exist in 2009 – a prime example of the derogatory effect of national interests on the maintenance of international peace and security.

Of the three P5 members to have used the veto power since 1990, China has been the most sparing, having exercised its right to the veto a total of eight times since 1990.[156] More telling, perhaps, is the Sino–Russian regional cooperation on the Council that becomes evident upon examination of voting records. China has used its veto alongside Russia in six of these eight draft resolutions,[157] has abstained in one of Russia's other vetoed draft resolutions[158] and has been supported by Russian abstention in another of its own,[159] suggesting that – in contrast to Western P5 Members of the Council – China and Russia appear far more closely aligned and willing openly to provide mutual support on the Council.[160]

This is not, however, to say that national interest has not underscored some Chinese decisions at the Council: the Chinese veto of a 1999 draft resolution[161] that would have authorised 'the attachment to MINUGUA of a group of 155 military observers'[162] was the direct result of Guatemalan recognition of Taiwanese independence and support for their readmission to the General Assembly,[163] a stance that China interpreted as 'actions to infringe upon China's sovereignty and territorial integrity'.[164] The observer attachment was later endorsed by the Council,[165] but not before Guatemala severely toned down its support for and interaction with Taiwan,[166] 'thereby removing the obstacles to China's support for the draft resolution'.[167] Similar situations have also befallen Macedonia[168] and Haiti[169] over their links with the island.

What is most interesting, however – particularly in contrast with the use of the veto by the US, which overwhelmingly seeks to protect Israeli interests in its use of the veto – is the self-declaration of Russia and China as protectors of state sovereignty and territorial integrity. Whereas the US is highly partisan in its use of the veto towards a state, Sino–Russian voting records on the Council suggest that they use the veto in pursuit of the *principle* of non-intervention. It is no coincidence that both P5 Members vote in unison against resolutions involving intervention in what they consider to be the domestic affairs of states, since both have proclaimed themselves quasi-guardians not only of the sovereignty of non-Council states Member of the UN but also of the purity of the meaning of the Charter. Certainly this appears to be the central theme that runs through the vast majority of the resolutions blocked by Russia and China in recent years on Myanmar,[170] Zimbabwe[171] and Syria.[172]

Both Russia and China have made clear their opposition to the abuse of power and derogation from the strict verse of the Charter. During discussions on draft resolution S/2008/447 (2008), Russia was unequivocal in its condemnation of what it saw to be the expanding scope of Council action:

> In the positions of a number of Council members, we have of late seen an increasingly obvious attempt to take the Council beyond its Charter prerogatives and beyond the maintenance of international peace and security. We believe such practices to be illegitimate and dangerous and apt to lead to a realignment of the entire United Nations system. The Russian Federation intends to continue to counter such trends, so that all States without exception will firmly comply with the Charter of the Organization.[173]

The Chinese veto of a draft resolution on the situation in Myanmar[174] exemplifies this attitude; the government mandated military attacks on civilians in ethnic minority regions was deemed to be 'mainly the internal affair of a sovereign State . . . [and did] not constitute a threat to international or regional peace and security'[175] and, accordingly, any Council involvement in the situation would 'not only exceed the mandates of the Council, but also hinder discussions by other relevant agencies'.[176] Russia concurred, stating that it 'believe[d] that the situation in that country does not pose any threat to international or regional peace. . . . [and] deem[ed] unacceptable any attempt to use the Security Council to discuss issues outside its purview'.[177]

The situation in Syria, however, has been the crux of Sino–Russian veto cooperation in recent times, with a total of four draft resolutions 'double-vetoed' in as many years.[178] In the aftermath of Council authority for military action in Libya[179] – from which Russia and China abstained – both disapproved of the manner and results of Council-mandated NATO action,[180] rendering them hesitant to support any similar authorisation of action in Syria.[181] Yet the situation in Syria continues to pose great suffering and danger to the people of Syria, lending credibility to charges made by other Council Members that 'they have chosen to block efforts to achieve justice for the Syrian people'.[182] These allegations are difficult to negate when Syrian orders for weaponry from Russia are said to amount to $3.5 billion[183] and Russia maintains a naval station in the Syrian port of Tartus; as such, Russian vetoes on Syria may not be as entirely morally based or defensive of international legal principles as they may first appear.

Moreover, territorial integrity has not barred Russia from annexing Crimea in 2014, in a series of events that culminated at the Council in a 2014 Russian veto of draft resolution S/2014/189, which declared illegal the contested shotgun referendum of March 16, 2014 and led to several rounds of sanctions imposed by Japan, Canada, the EU and the US.[184] At the core of the vetoed draft resolution was the 'commitment to the sovereignty, independence, unity and territorial integrity of Ukraine within its internationally recognized borders'.[185] Numerous representatives pointed to the inviolable and non-derogable elements of the principles at its core, notably 'the illegality of the acquisition of territory through the threat or use of force and the obligation to settle disputes by peaceful means'.[186]

Nevertheless, despite meeting no less than 14 times[187] since the beginning of 2014 to discuss the situation in the Ukraine, the Council has successfully passed one resolution condemning the downing of flight MH370 in Ukrainian territory,[188] while the other has been vetoed by Russia. Meanwhile, a pro-Russian Prime Minister has been installed, a Treaty signed on 18 March to initiate Crimea's accession to the Russian Federation and Ukrainian Armed Forces have been evicted from their bases. The recognition of the Republic of Crimea and Sevastopol as federal subjects of Russia by Syria[189] only serves to fuel allegations of the interconnectivity of national interests at the root of the use of the veto in the Syrian conflict. While this reflects poorly on Russia at the international level, it has not impacted as greatly on its work at the Council as the US stance towards Israel; though an ideal role model for a Council Member, Russia's disparity between its stance on the Council and its political impact outside of the UN is perhaps an example of the dual roles that P5 members are required to play and highlights the importance of a disconnect between the role of a P5 Member when dealing with Council business and when dealing as a sovereign state in its domestic and foreign policy.

China and Russia maintain that their interest in using the veto strictly complies with the letter of the Charter provisions; their insistence on the territorial integrity of states and the prohibition of extending the scope of the Council to include elements within the definition of peace and security is an admirable principle to maintain, which supports other components of the rule of law, such as the separation of powers and transparency. However, their actions do not always comply with the standards that they set out to maintain; accusations of political bias have been exchanged from both pro-interventionist[190] and pro-sovereignty[191] camps, but Russia and China remain – on paper and at the Council, at least – firm in their resolve to ensure territorial integrity and sovereignty in the majority of their uses of the veto.

Efforts to reform the use of the veto

> The veto power, which guarantees the dominance of the five permanent members, has to be re-examined. It is our view that the veto power has now become untenable and anachronistic. If we need to accept some kind of weighting in terms of asymmetries within the Council, we cannot accept a

> situation in which one, two or three in the Council are more powerful than the rest of the membership of the United Nations.[192]

Efforts to regulate the use of the veto have traditionally fallen within the framework of the general reform of the Council.[193] Throughout discussions 'the veto continued to come under criticism, with many delegations emphasizing the need to either abolish it or limit its use'.[194] In the aftermath of the Cold War, the veto was not exercised for several years, leading to its designation as a 'power . . . instituted in response to realities and situations that no longer obtain'.[195] Proposals by UN member states for veto reform included subjects of debate where the veto could be prohibited, such as the voluntary abolition of the veto when dealing with the election of the Secretary-General of the UN[196] and matters of reform.[197] There were numerous ideas, also, with respect to amendments to the practice of veto-usage, in essence to avoid the maintenance of international peace and security from being held 'hostage to the dictates of one State that has the power to veto its resolutions whenever it has to';[198] proposals included the requirement of two P5 members for the exercise of the veto[199] – which would not resolve alliances such as the Sino–Russian stance on Syria – or the 'granting to the General Assembly or to the enlarged Security Council, specially expanded for such cases, of the right to overrule the veto by qualified majority if the veto is invoked by only one permanent member of the Security Council'.[200] States generally took the view that, although 'each Member State has to protect its national objectives and interests, this approach needs to include an appreciation for the broader interests of the United Nations and of the general membership'[201] and that equitable participation was central to reform of the veto.[202]

Conclusions

The situation today remains the same as over two decades ago: 'reform of the veto power is not viable'.[203] There has been recognition on the part of states as early as 1993 during General Assembly debates that '[t]he cases in which recourse was made to the veto have demonstrated that it has been used, in most cases, not in the service of principles, but in the service of special interests'.[204] This is as true today as it was in 1993, as shown in the analysis of the veto usage by Russia, China and the US. The establishment of an Open-ended Working Group on Equitable participation[205] has done little in the way of improving the situation; despite annual reports for a decade, the Working Group's functions and efforts have trailed off with the last report in 2008[206] despite the group being revived in 2015. The question of equitable representation on and increase in the membership of the Council has been included on every Assembly agenda since well before the establishment of the Working Group,[207] yet any change on the Council composition has yet to be achieved. Despite forming a key element of UN reform, the Council has been a disappointingly stationary subject of discussion with no action having been taken. This should come as no surprise, however, against the backdrop of the inclusion of the veto itself in 1945, when the entire organisation of the

United Nations risked being derailed as a result of the loggerheads reached over the inclusion of the veto,[208] with the P5 adamant on its inclusion and a number of states opposing it, as discussed previously.

There is, therefore, a clear pattern of inequitable participation in the decision-making process on the Council, from the apparent ostracism of states that hold entitlement to participate in discussions and debates to the use of the veto in denying the passing of resolutions for national interests of the P5 members; the lack of Council reform owes much to a combination of confusion as to the correct path towards reform, failure to follow verbal acknowledgements and pledges with action, and the inevitable impact of domestic interests of the P5 members on the reform process. As a result, this component of the rule of law is one of the poorest complied with by the Council and, moreover, there seems to be little appetite for or signs of improvement on the horizon. In direct opposition to the intended purpose of the veto, domestic interests continue to reign supreme for the US, Russia and China, which have exercised their right of veto six times since 2010 alone.[209] France's proposal that the veto be voluntarily suspended by P5 members when the Council is debating humanitarian matters has not been adopted and despite grave situations in Syria and the Occupied Arab Territories, there have been numerous vetoes cast by China and the Russian Federation, and the US respectively. The efforts on the part of the UK and France to move away or limit the use of vetoes have been undermined by the continued abuse of the power by the US, Russia and China.

Expansion of the Council has also stagnated. Despite several rounds of reform talks and numerous plans put forward by groups of states and individual states, none has come to fruition. Although the P5, which ultimately must decide to endorse the expansion of the Council through a Charter amendment in accordance with article 108, appears to support the expansion of the Council in word but not in deed; stumbling blocks of the extent of power to be granted as well as the number of new seats to be created have meant that the Council has remained as unchanged on paper as 1965, when the number of non-permanent seats were last expanded,[210] and in practice since 1991, when the USSR notified the UN that the Russian Federation was its designated successor.[211] As the world has changed around the Council, the constituent permanent members have remained the same, undermining the legitimacy and relevance of the Council in the modern world.

Security Council reform is once again on the agenda of the 70th General Assembly Session of 2016–17[212] since the 'need to reform the Security Council is urgent, as reflected in the 2005 World Summit Outcome'.[213] One might also cynically predict that it will remain on future agendas for many years to come. As noted by the President of the General Assembly, urgent reform of the Council was highlighted almost a decade ago[214] and the Open-ended Working Group considering Council reform has been in operation since 1993;[215] yet little, if anything, has been done. In over 20 years, despite reports by the Open-ended working group,[216] an Austrian Initiative,[217] the 2005 World Summit[218] and numerous member state groups in support of expansion or reform of the veto and other elements of equitable participation,[219] there has been no reform of the

Council on this front. Rather, in contrast to the environment under which reform of the Council was initially tabled in 1993, where the veto had not been used for three years, for several years the veto has been regularly made use of in relation, as shown, to overtly national interest matters.

The criticisms made by member states in 1993 are as relevant today with respect to the make-up of the Council. 'It is . . . essential that the Security Council, which acts on behalf of all the Members of the Organization, pursuant to Article 24 of the Charter, should have a membership that reflects adequately the increase in the membership of the Organization, and also its regional, political, cultural and religious diversity'.[220] The current Council reflected none of these in 1993 and presents an even more skewed representation of the geo-political situation today. The Council – and more importantly, the P5 Members – have acknowledged that reform of the composition of the Council is necessary; the General Assembly has also identified that the situation should be resolved urgently. Nonetheless, these oral intentions have not translated into action by either party and the Council remains, even omitting the existence of the veto as an inherent element of the UN Charter, an imbalanced and inequitable decision-making forum that has a great way to go before reaching any adequate standard of the rule of law.

Notes

1 Pakistan, UNSC Verbatim Record (27 August 2008) UN Doc S/PV.5968 (Resumption 1) 24.
2 UN Charter (1945) art 27(3).
3 ibid art 24(1).
4 ibid.
5 ibid art 25.
6 ibid art 24(1).
7 ibid art 27(2).
8 ibid art 23(1).
9 ibid art 31.
10 ibid art 32.
11 UNGA Res 1991A (1963) UN Doc A/RES/17/1991A para 1(a)–(d).
12 ibid.
13 'Growth in United Nations membership, 1945–present'.
14 109 states from 193 is 56.5%.
15 6 out of 15 seats on the Council.
16 The WEOG has France, the UK and the US; the Eastern European Group has Russia; and the Asia–Pacific group (and arguably the African Group) has China.
17 France, UK, US.
18 Iran, UNSC Verbatim Record (27 August 2008) UN Doc S/PV.5968 (Resumption 1) 11.
19 Brazil represented the GRULAC on a non-permanent seat in 1946/7, 1951/2, 1954/5, 1963/4, 1967/8, 1988/9, 1993/4, 1998/9, 2004/5 and 2010/11; Japan represented Asia–Pacific in a non-permanent seat in 1958/9, 1966/7, 1971/2, 1975/6, 1981/2, 1987/88, 1992/3, 1997/8, 2005/6 and 2009/10.
20 Which finished its ninth rotation on the Council in December 2014.
21 Which has sat eight times on the Council.
22 Which has sat five times.
23 Which has sat three times.

24 'Statement delivered by Honourable Apisai Ielemia, Prime Minister and Minister of Foreign Affairs of Tuvalu, at the 63rd Session of the United Nations General Assembly Open Debate' (26 September 2008).
25 Cape Verde, Cuba, Guinea Bissau, Guyana, Jamaica, Mauritius, Singapore and Trinidad and Tobago. In total, they have sat 13 times.
26 UNGA Res 55/2 (18 September 2000) UN Doc A/RES/55/2 para 30 (emphasis added).
27 There is broad support from the P5 for Council reform on the question of enlargement: France calls for the inclusion of the so-called 'G4' of 'Germany, Brazil, India and Japan as permanent members of the Security Council and an increased presence of African countries', France, UNGA Verbatim Record (7 November 2013) UN Doc A/68/PV.46 at 28; the UK (ibid 20) and China (ibid 26) support this proposal; Russia is 'in favour of keeping the Council as it is, namely, compact. Its optimal number should not exceed 20 members' (ibid 18); and the US 'is open to modest expansion of the Council in both the permanent and non-permanent categories' (ibid 22).
28 US, UNGA Verbatim Record (7 November 2013) UN Doc A/68/PV.46.
29 UNGA 'Report of the Secretary-General: In larger Freedom: Towards Development, Security and Human Rights for All' (21 March 2005) UN Doc A/59/2005.
30 ibid 60.
31 ibid para 170.
32 ibid 43 (Box 5).
33 ibid para 169.
34 ibid para 170.
35 UNGA Draft Res (6 July 2005) UN Doc A/59/L.64.
36 eg Argentina, Colombia and Mexico oppose Brazil's bid; China and South Korea oppose the appointment of Japan; Pakistan opposes giving a seat to India.
37 UNGA Draft Res (21 July 2005) UN Doc A/59/L.68.
38 UNGA Draft Res (14 December 2005) UN Doc A/60/L.41.
39 March/April 2009; May 2009; September 2009; November 2009; June – November 2010; December 2010; March 2011; January – May 2012.
40 54 Member States from Africa, coordinated by the C10 – Algeria, DRC, Equatorial Guinea, Kenya, Libya, Namibia, Senegal, Sierra Leone, Uganda, and Zambia.
41 A group of developing countries active from 2007 onwards, including Brazil, India and approximately another 40 states.
42 Italy is the focal point of the group and its other core members are Argentina, Canada, Colombia, Costa Rica, Malta, Mexico, Pakistan, Republic of Korea, San Marino, Spain, and Turkey. Support for the group likely totals around 40 UN Members, including permanent member China.
43 UNGA 'Remarks at the Informal General Assembly Meeting of the Intergovernmental Negotiations on Security Council Reform' (New York, 27 June 2013).
44 UNGA Res 69/L.92 (11 September 2015) UN Doc A/69/L.92.
45 e.g. UNGA Verbatim Records (14 September 2015) UN Doc A/69/PV.104: China at 5, Pakistan at 11, Spain at 11, Turkey at 14, Argentina at 17, Italy at 2.
46 'GDP and its breakdown at current prices in US Dollars', UN Statistics Division (2013).
47 'Countries Ranked by Military Strength' (3 April 2014) *Global Firepower*.
48 Sam Perlo-Freeman and Carina Solmirano, 'Trends in world military expenditure, 2013' (April 2013) *Stockholm International Peace Research Institute*, Table 1; International Institute of Strategic Studies, *The Military Balance: 2014* (Routledge 2014) 3.

49 In addition to Japan, Germany, India and Brazil vying for permanent seats, Egypt, Nigeria and South Africa all feel they have strong reasons to sit on an 'African seat'.
50 The smallest expansion remains that of the Secretary-General, advocating an expansion to 24 seats in both plans.
51 UNGA 'Report of the Secretary-General: In larger Freedom: Towards Development, Security and Human Rights for All' (21 March 2005) UN Doc A/59/2005 para 169(c).
52 Austria, UNSC Verbatim Record (16 December 2014) UN Doc S/PV.3483 at 19.
53 UNSC Provisional Rules of Procedure (1946) UN Doc S/96/Rev.7, r 48.
54 UN Charter (1945) arts 31–32.
55 *Legal Consequences for States of the Continued Presence of South Africa in Namibia (South West Africa) notwithstanding Security Council Resolution 276 (1970)* (Advisory Opinion) [1971] ICJ Rep 16 para 22.
56 Under article 25 of the Charter, States are bound to comply with the decisions of the Council. There is no mechanism for review of Council decision; in the case of *Namibia* ibid, South Africa was found to have been required to object to the classification of the question at the beginning and the matter could not be reclassified on the fly.
57 28 May 1998.
58 11 and 13 May 1998.
59 UNSC Presidential Statement 12 (1998) UN Doc S/PRST/1998/12 condemned India; UNSC Presidential Statement 17 (1998) UN Doc S/PRST/1998/17 condemned Pakistan.
60 UNSC Verbatim Record (14 May 1998) UN Doc S/PV.3881 and UNSC Verbatim Record (29 May 1998) UN Doc S/PV.3888 note no additional attendees beyond the 15 Council members.
61 UNSC Res 1172 (6 June 1998) UN Doc S/RES/1172.
62 Argentina, Australia, Canada, Egypt, Iran, Mexico, New Zealand, Norway, Pakistan, the Republic of Korea, Ukraine and the United Arab Emirates.
63 UNSC Verbatim Record (6 June 1998) UN Doc S/PV/3890 at 2.
64 UNSC 'Letter dated 4 June 1998 from the Permanent Representative of India to the United Nations addressed to the President of the Security Council' (4 June 1998) UN Doc S/1998/464 was sent two days prior to the Council's 3890th meeting on 6 June 1998, discussing the recent nuclear tests by India and Pakistan.
65 ibid para 2.
66 UNSC Verbatim Record (6 June 1998) UN Doc S/PV/3890 at 28–32.
67 Philippines, UNSC Verbatim Record (27 August 2008) UN Doc S/PV.5968 (Resumption 1) 9.
68 Belarus, UNSC Verbatim Record (27 August 2008) UN Doc S/PV.5968 (Resumption 1) 5.
69 UNSC Verbatim Record (6 June 1998) UN Doc S/PV/3890 at 18.
70 Iran, UNSC Verbatim Record (27 August 2008) UN Doc S/PV.5968 (Resumption 1) 12.
71 Iran, UNSC Verbatim Record (31 July 2006) UN Doc S/PV.5500 at 7.
72 'Letter dated 28 September 1994 from the Permanent Representative of Rwanda to the United Nations addressed to the President of the Security Council' (29 September 1994) UN Doc S/1994/1115.
73 UNSC Verbatim Record (8 November 1994) UN Doc S/PV. 3453 at 14.
74 UNSC Res 955 (8 November 1994) UN Doc S/RES/955.
75 ibid preamble.

76 UNSC Verbatim Record (8 November 1994) UN Doc S/PV.3453 at 5.
77 ibid 14 ff.
78 ibid 14.
79 ibid 16.
80 China, UNSC Verbatim Records (29 July 2016) UN Doc S/PV.7752 at 9. See also Angola at 4.
81 Egypt, ibid at 3.
82 UNSC Res 2303 (29 July 2016) UN Doc S/RES/2303 para 13.
83 France, UNSC Verbatim Records (29 July 2016) UN Doc S/PV.7752 at 3.
84 UNSC Verbatim Records (12 August 2016) UN Doc S/PV.7754 at 12.
85 UNSC Res 2304 (12 August 2016) UN Doc S/RES/2304 para 14.
86 Egypt, UNSC Verbatim Records (12 August 2016) UN Doc S/PV.7754 at 10.
87 Libya, UNSC Verbatim Record (16 September 2013) UN Doc S/PV.7031 at 6.
88 Tonga, UNSC Verbatim Record (27 August 2008) UN Doc S/PV.5968 (Resumption 1) 21.
89 UN Charter (1945) art 27(3).
90 Francis O Wilcox, 'The rule of unanimity in the Security Council' (1946) 40 *Proceedings of the American Society of International Law* 51, 54.
91 UN Charter (1945) art 109(2).
92 Australia, United Nations Conference on International Organization (UNCIO) Vol 11 (1945) 19–20 (emphasis added).
93 Egypt, ibid 5.
94 See eg ibid 20; Norway, United Nations Conference on International Organization (UNCIO) Vol 12 (1945) 2.
95 UNSC Verbatim Record (16 February 1946) UN Doc S/PV.23 at 367.
96 UK, United Nations Conference on International Organization (UNCIO) Vol 11 (1945) 5.
97 UK, ibid 1.
98 Colombia, United Nations Conference on International Organization (UNCIO) Vol 12 (1945) 3 (emphasis added).
99 Peru, ibid 5.
100 US Secretary of State, quoted in Kanhaya R Gupta, *Reform of the United Nations: Vol 1* (Atlantic Publishers 2007) 26.
101 P5 statement, ibid.
102 UK, United Nations Conference on International Organization (UNCIO) Vol 11 (1945) 4.
103 New Zealand, ibid 2.
104 New Zealand, ibid 1.
105 See Wilcox (n 90) 55.
106 UK, ibid 6.
107 United Nations Conference on International Organization (UNCIO) Vol 11 (1945) 5.
108 'Security Council Veto list, prepared and maintained by the Dag Hammarskjold library'.
109 90 vetoes cast as USSR, 11 as Russian Federation.
110 UNSC 'Letter dated 29 October 1956 from the Representative of the United States of America, addressed to the President of the Security Council, concerning: "The Palestine Question: Steps for the Immediate Cessation of the Military Action of Israel in Egypt" (30 October 1956) UN Doc S/3710; letter dated 29 October 1956 from the Representative of the United States of America, addressed to the President of the Security Council, concerning: 'The Palestine Question: Steps for the Immediate Cessation of the Military Action of Israel in Egypt' (30 October 1956) UN Doc S/3713/Rev.1.

111 UNSC Draft Res (11 March 1970) UN Doc S/9696.
112 Emma McClean, 'Hard evidence: who uses veto in the UN Security Council most often – and for what?' *The Conversation* (31 July 2014).
113 Australia, United Nations Conference on International Organization (UNCIO) Vol 11 (1945) 19–20.
114 Vietnam (1975 and 1976), Angola (1976).
115 Italy (1952 and 1955), Libya (1952), Japan (1952 and 1955), Vietnam (1952, 1957 and 1958), Laos (1952), Cambodia (1952), Portugal (1955), Ireland (1955), Jordan (1955), Guatemala (1954) and Korea (1957 and 1958) amongst others.
116 UK, UNSC Verbatim Record (30 November 1961) UN Doc S/PV.985 para 52.
117 UNSC Draft Res (6 January 1980) UN Doc S/13729.
118 UNSC Draft Res (22 August 1968) UN Doc S/8761.
119 UNSC Draft Res (27 October 1983) UN Doc S/16077/Rev.1.
120 UNSC Draft Res (28 October 1986) UN Doc S/18428; UNSC Draft Res (31 July 1986) UN Doc S/18250.
121 UNSC Draft Res (7 March 1988) UN Doc S/19585; UNSC Verbatim Record (8 March 1988) UN Doc S/PV.2797; UNSC Draft Res (19 February 1987) UN Doc S/18705; UNSC Draft Res (17 June 1986) UN Doc S/18163; UNSC Draft Res (23 May 1986) UN Doc S/18087/Rev.1; UNSC Draft Res (26 July 1985) UN Doc S/17354/Rev.1; UNSC Draft Res (31 August 1981) UN Doc 5558S/14664/Rev.2; UNSC Draft Res (26 October 1977) UN Doc S/12312/Rev.1; UNSC Draft Res (26 October 1977) UN Doc S/12311/Rev.1; UNSC Draft Res (26 October 1977) UN Doc S/12310/Rev.1; UNSC Draft Res (24 October 1974) UN Doc S/11543.
122 UK, UNSC Verbatim Record (30 November 1961) UN Doc S/PV.985 para 52.
123 Fewer vetoes were exercised in the entire decade 1990–99 as in the two years 1989–89 alone: nine vetoes versus 12, one for every year versus six for every year.
124 In the 14 years since 2000 there have been 20 vetoes, an average of 1.5 for every year.
125 France, UNGA Verbatim Record (7 November 2013) UN Doc A/68/PV.46 at 28.
126 UK, UNSC Verbatim Record (18 February 2011) UN Doc S/PV.6484 at 5.
127 US, ibid 4.
128 ibid 4–5.
129 US, UNSC Verbatim Record (22 May 2014) UN Doc S/PV.7180 at 4.
130 China, UNSC Verbatim Record (27 March 2001) UN Doc S/PV.4305 at 4–5.
131 US, UNSC Verbatim Record (11 November 2006) UN Doc S/PV.5565 at 2.
132 See eg Gerald Ford, 'Remarks welcoming PM Rabin to USA' (10 September 1974); Jimmy Carter, 'The President's News Conference' (12 May 1977); George Bush Sr, Address to the 46th Session of the United Nations General Assembly (23 September 1991); Barack Obama, 'Remarks at the 2011 AIPAC Policy Conference' (22 May 2011).
133 Stephen Wenne, 'It has one of world's best armies, but US may expect too much help in case of Soviet attack' *Christian Science Monitor* (31 July 1981).
134 Jimmy Carter, 'Los Angeles, California remarks at a Democratic National Committee Fundraising Dinner' (22 October 1977).
135 UNSC Res 904 (23 September 1994) UN Doc S/RES/904; UNSC Res 1322 (7 October 2000) UN Doc S/RES/1322; UNSC Res 1397 (12 March 2002) UN Doc S/RES/1397; UNSC Res 1402 (29–30 March 2002) UN Doc S/RES/1402; UNSC Res 1403 (4 April 2002) UN Doc S/RES/1403; UNSC Res 1405 (19 April 2002) UN Doc S/RES/1405; UNSC Res 1435 (24 September

2002) UN Doc S/RES/1435; UNSC Res 1450 (13 December 2002) UN Doc S/RES/1450; UNSC Res 1515 (19 November 2003) UN Doc S/RES/1515; UNSC Res 1544 (19 May 2004) UN Doc S/RES/1544; UNSC Res 1624 (14 September 2005) UN Doc S/RES/1624; UNSC Res 1850 (16 December 2008) UN Doc S/RES/1850; UNSC Res 1860 (8 January 2009) UN Doc S/RES/1860.

136 US, UNSC Verbatim Record (5 October 2004) UN Doc S/PV.5051 at 2. See also eg US, UNSC Verbatim Record (11 November 2006) UN Doc S/PV.5565 at 2; US, UNSC Verbatim Record (25 March 2004) UN Doc S/PV.4934 at 2; US, UNSC Verbatim Record (27 March 2001) UN Doc S/PV.4305 at 5.

137 See eg France, UNSC Verbatim Record (5 October 2004) UN Doc S/PV.5051 at 4; Algeria, UNSC Verbatim Record (25 March 2004) UN Doc S/PV.4934 at 4.

138 A seemingly one-sided condemnation of Gazan aggression was issued in January 2014. See US, UNSC Verbatim Record (20 January 2014) UN Doc S/PV.7096 at 17.

139 Special Coordinator for the Middle East Peace Process and Personal Representative of the Secretary-General, UNSC Verbatim Record (18 August 2014) UN Doc S/PV.7243 at 2.

140 ibid.

141 Navi Pillay, UNSC Verbatim Record (21 August 2014) UN Doc S/PV.7247 at 4.

142 UNSC Res 1422 (12 July 2002) UN Doc S/RES/1422.

143 US, UNSC Verbatim Record (30 June 2002) UN Doc S/PV.4563 at 2.

144 New Zealand, UNSC Verbatim Record (10 July 2002) UN Doc S/PV.4568 at 7.

145 US, ibid 9 (emphasis added).

146 US, UNSC Verbatim Record (30 June 2002) UN Doc S/PV.4563 at 2.

147 Cuba, UNSC Verbatim Record (10 July 2002) UN Doc S/PV.4568 (Resumption 1) 15.

148 France, UNSC Verbatim Record (10 July 2002) UN Doc S/PV.4568 at 11.

149 Iran, UNSC Verbatim Record (10 July 2002) UN Doc S/PV.4568 at 15; Canada, ibid 3–4; New Zealand, ibid 7; Cuba, ibid (Resumption 1) 15.

150 See Wenne (n 133).

151 Argentina, UNSC Verbatim Record (27 August 2008) UN Doc S/PV.5968 (Resumption 1) 16.

152 UNSC Draft Res (22 May 2014) UN Doc S/2014/348; UNSC Draft Res (15 March 2014) UN Doc S/2014/189; UNSC Draft Res (19 July 2012) UN Doc S/2012/538; UNSC Draft Res (4 February 2012) UN Doc S/2012/77; UNSC Draft Res (4 October 2011) UN Doc S/2011/612; UNSC Draft Res (14 June 2009) UN Doc S/2009/310; UNSC Draft Res (11 July 2008) UN Doc S/2008/447; UNSC Draft Res (12 January 2007) UN Doc S/2007/14; UNSC Draft Res (21 April 2004) UN Doc S/2004/313; UNSC Draft Res (2 December 1994) UN Doc S/1994/1358; UNSC Draft Res (29 April 1993) UN Doc S/25693.

153 Russia, UNSC Verbatim Record (11 May 1993) UN Doc S/PV.3211 at 4–5. This is supported by the passing of UNSC Res 831 (1993), which resolved the funding issue that Russia objected to earlier.

154 Russia, UNSC Verbatim Record (2 December 1994) UN Doc S/PV.3475 at 10.

155 UK, UNSC Verbatim Record (15 June 2009) UN Doc S/PV.6143 at 6.

156 UNSC Draft Res (22 May 2014) UN Doc S/2014/348; UNSC Draft Res (19 July 2012) UN Doc S/2012/538; UNSC Draft Res (4 February 2012) UN Doc S/2012/77; UNSC Draft Res (4 October 2011) UN Doc S/2011/612;

UNSC Draft Res (11 July 2008) UN Doc S/2008/447; UNSC Draft Res (12 January 2007) UN Doc S/2007/14; UNSC Draft Res (25 February 1999) UN Doc S/1999/201; UNSC Draft Res (9 January 1997) UN Doc S/1997/18.

157 UNSC Draft Res (22 May 2014) UN Doc S/2014/348; UNSC Draft Res (19 July 2012) UN Doc S/2012/538; UNSC Draft Res (4 February 2012) UN Doc S/2012/77; UNSC Draft Res (4 October 2011) UN Doc S/2011/612; UNSC Draft Res (11 July 2008) UN Doc S/2008/447; UNSC Draft Res (12 January 2007) UN Doc S/2007/14.

158 UNSC Draft Res (2 December 1994) UN Doc S/1994/1358.

159 UNSC Draft Res (25 February 1999) UN Doc S/1999/201.

160 The UK has abstained on several resolutions concerning the Palestinian Question, objecting to the language or lean of the text, but has never used its veto to block their adoption. See eg UNSC Draft Res (5 October 2004) UN Doc S/2004/783; UNSC Draft Res (11 November 2006) UN Doc S/2006/878; UNSC Draft Res (27–28 March 2001) UN Doc S/2001/270.

161 UNSC Draft Res (7 March 1997) UN Doc S/1997/199.

162 ibid para 1.

163 On 29 December 1996, a Taiwanese envoy attended the signing of peace accords in Guatemala City. Guatemala also voted consistently for the adoption of Taiwan as an item on the agenda of the General Assembly. See eg UNGA 'Provisional Agenda of the Fifty-first regular session of the General Assembly' (19 July 1996) UN Doc A/51/150 para 159.

164 China, UNSC Verbatim Record (10 January 1997) UN Doc S/PV.3730 at 20.

165 UNSC Res 1094 (20 January 1997) UN Doc S/RES/1094.

166 Guatemala, UNSC Verbatim Record (20 January 1997) UN Doc S/PV.3732 at 4.

167 China, ibid 3.

168 Although not explicitly stated in the records as forming the reason for the use of the veto by China, Macedonia's agreement with Taiwan for direct economic aid and investments were alluded to in the Canadian representative's speech. See UNSC Verbatim Record (25 February 1999) UN Doc S/PV.3982 at 7 and denied by China as 'totally groundless', ibid 9.

169 In both 1996 and 2007, resolutions relating to Haiti were jeopardised by links to Taiwan. Following an invitation to Taiwanese Vice-President li Yuan-zu to attend the inauguration of former President René Préval on 7 February 1996, the Chinese only voted in favour of UNSC Res 1048 (1996) '[i]n view of the fact that the draft resolution before us has basically incorporated the amendments by the Chinese delegation', China, UNSC Verbatim Record (29 February 1996) UN Doc S/PV.3638 at 12. In response to Haitian diplomatic ties with Taiwan, in adopting UNSC Res 1743 (15 February 2007) UN Doc S/RES/1743, China agreed only to 'an extension for a reasonable period, as an ad hoc arrangement, beyond the original six months', UNSC Verbatim Record (15 February 2007) UN Doc S/PV.5631 at 3.

170 UNSC Draft Res (12 January 2007) UN Doc S/2007/14.

171 UNSC Draft Res (11 July 2008) UN Doc S/2008/447.

172 UNSC Draft Res (18 February 2011) UN Doc S/2011/24; UNSC Draft Res (4 October 2011) UN Doc S/2011/612; UNSC Draft Res (4 February 2012) UN Doc S/2012/77; UNSC Draft Res (19 July 2012) UN Doc S/2012/538; UNSC Draft Res (22 May 2014) UN Doc S/2014/348.

173 Russia, UNSC Verbatim Record (11 July 2008) UN Doc S/PV.5933. See also China, ibid 13.

174 UNSC Draft Res S/2007/14 (12 January 2007) UN Doc S/2007/14.

175 China, UNSC Verbatim Record (12 January 2007) UN Doc S/PV.5619 at 3.

176 ibid.

177 Russia, ibid 6.
178 UNSC Draft Res (22 May 2014) UN Doc S/2014/348; UNSC Draft Res (19 July 2012) UN Doc S/2012/538; UNSC Draft Res (4 February 2012) UN Doc S/2012/77; UNSC Draft Res (4 October 2011) UN Doc S/2011/612.
179 UNSC Res 1970 (26 February 2011) UN Doc S/RES/1970.
180 See eg Russia, UNSC Verbatim Record (4 October 2011) UN Doc S/PV.6627 at 4.
181 Russia, UNSC Verbatim Record (19 July 2012) UN Doc S/PV.6810 at 8.
182 UK, UNSC Verbatim Record (22 May 2014) UN Doc S/PV.7180 at 7. See also Luxembourg, ibid 8; France, ibid 15; US, ibid 4.
183 'Why Russia is standing by Syria's Assad' *BBC News* (London, 15 June 2012).
184 Both the EU and the US have blacklisted individuals, businesses, and the State's finance, energy and arms sectors. France recently cancelled an arms deal with Russia. See eg 'How far do EU–US sanctions go?' *BBC News* (5 September 2014); Dan Lamothe, 'France backs off sending Minstral warship to Russia in $1.7 billion deal' *Washington Post* (Washington DC, 3 September 2014).
185 UNSC Draft Res (15 March 2014) UN Doc S/2014/189.
186 Australia, UNSC Verbatim Record (15 March 2014) UN Doc S/PV.7138 at 9. See also Nigeria, ibid.
187 UNSC Verbatim Record (28 August 2014) UN Doc S/PV.7253; UNSC Verbatim Record (8 August 2014) UN Doc S/PV.7239; UNSC Verbatim Record (21 July 2014) UN Doc S/PV.7221; UNSC Verbatim Record (18 July 2014) UN Doc S/PV.7219; UNSC Verbatim Record (24 June 2014) UN Doc S/PV.7205; UNSC Verbatim Record (28 May 2014) UN Doc S/PV.7185; UNSC Verbatim Record (29 April 2014) UN Doc S/PV.7165; UNSC Verbatim Record (16 April 2014) UN Doc S/PV.7157; UNSC Verbatim Record (19 March 2014) UN Doc S/PV.7144; UNSC Verbatim Record (15 March 2014) UN Doc S/PV.7138; UNSC Verbatim Record (13 March 2014) UN Doc S/PV.7134; UNSC Verbatim Record (10 March 2014) UN Doc S/PV.7131; UNSC Verbatim Record (3 March 2014) UN Doc S/PV.7125; UNSC Verbatim Record (1 March 2014) UN Doc S/PV.7124; UNSC Verbatim Record (28 February 2014) UN Doc S/PV.7123.
188 UNSC Res 2166 (21 July 2014) UN Doc S/RES/2166.
189 Matthew Rosenburg, 'Breaking with the West, Afghan leader supports Russia's annexation of Crimea' *New York Times* (New York, 23 March 2014).
190 France, UNSC Verbatim Record (19 July 2012) UN Doc S/PV.6810 at 3; UK, ibid 3.
191 Russia, ibid 8.
192 Malaysia, UNGA Verbatim Record (23 November 1993) UN Doc A/48/PV.61 at 10.
193 See eg UNGA 'Report of the Open-ended Working Group on the Question of Equitable Representation on and Increase in the Membership of the Security Council and Other Matters related to the Security Council' (1 January 2004) UN Doc A/58/47 para 14.
194 ibid para 12. See eg Canada, UNSC Verbatim Record (27 August 2008) UN Doc S/PV.5968 (Resumption 1) 11; Vietnam, UNSC Verbatim Record (27 August 2008) UN Doc S/PV.5968 at 11; Cuba, ibid 33; Egypt, ibid (Resumption 1) 3; Syria, UNGA Verbatim Record (23 November 1993) UN Doc A/48/PV.61 at 2.
195 Syria, UNGA Verbatim Record (23 November 1993) UN Doc A/48/PV.61 at 2. See also Iran, UNGA Verbatim Record (24 November 1993) UN Doc A/48/PV.64 at 2.
196 Chile, ibid 4.

197 New Zealand, UNGA Verbatim Record (24 November 1993) UN Doc A/48/PV.64 at 9.
198 Libya, UNGA Verbatim Record (23 November 1993) UN Doc A/48/PV.62 at 10.
199 Belize, UNGA Verbatim Record (24 November 1993) UN Doc A/48/PV.64 at 12.
200 Ukraine, ibid 16.
201 Singapore, UNGA Verbatim Record (23 November 1993) UN Doc A/48/PV.61 at 6.
202 See eg Vietnam, UNGA Verbatim Record (23 November 1993) UN Doc A/48/PV.62 at 2; Indonesia, ibid 4; Argentina, ibid 15; Portugal, UNGA Verbatim Record (24 November 1993) UN Doc A/48/PV.64 at 19; Nigeria, ibid 19; Spain, ibid 27.
203 Chile, UNGA Verbatim Record (23 November 1993) UN Doc A/48/PV.61 at 3.
204 Libya, UNGA Verbatim Record (23 November 1993) UN Doc A/48/PV.62 at 10.
205 UNGA Res 48/26 (3 December 1993) UN Doc A/RES/48/26 para 1 established the Open-ended Working Group on the Question of Equitable Representation on and Increase in the Membership of the Security Council and Other Matters related to the Security Council.
206 UNGA 'Report of the Open-ended Working Group on the Question of Equitable Representation on and Increase in the Membership of the Security Council and Other Matters related to the Security Council' (9 October 2008) UN Doc A/62/47.
207 See eg UNGA 'Agenda of the forty-seventh session of the General Assembly' (18 September 1992) UN Doc A/47/251 para 40; UNGA 'Agenda of the forty-sixth session of the General Assembly' (20 September 1991) UN Doc A/46/251 para 38; UNGA 'Agenda of the forty-fifth session of the General Assembly' (21 September 1990) UN Doc A/45/251 para 41.
208 Tom Connally, *My Name is Tom Connally* (Thomas Y Crowell 1954) 282–83; Townsend Hoopes and Douglas Brinkley, *FDR and the Creation of the UN* (Yale University Press 1997) 126.
209 UNSC Draft Res (22 May 2014) UN Doc S/2014/348; UNSC Draft Res (15 March 2014) UN Doc S/2014/189; UNSC Draft Res (19 July 2012) UN Doc S/2012/538; UNSC Draft Res (4 February 2012) UN Doc S/2012/77; UNSC Draft Res (4 October 2011) UN Doc S/2011/612; UNSC Draft Res (18 February 2011) UN Doc S/2011/24.
210 UNGA Res 1991A (XVIII) (1963) UN Doc A/RES/17/1991A.
211 President of the Russian Federation, letter to the Secretary-General from the President of the Russian Federation (24 December 1991) UN Doc 1991/RUSSIA at 1.
212 UNGA 'Provisional agenda of the sixty-ninth regular session of the General Assembly' (18 July 2014) UN Doc A/69/150 para 122. UN reform is an agenda item that has been carried over from previous years to little avail.
213 UNGA 'Opening address by the President at the opening of the 69th session' (16 September 2014).
214 UNGA Res 60/1 (24 October 2005) UN Doc A/RES/60/1 para 153.
215 UNGA Res 48/26 (3 December 1993) UN Doc A/RES/48/26 para 1.
216 UNGA 'Report of the Open-ended Working Group on the Question of Equitable Representation on and Increase in the Membership of the Security Council and Other Matters related to the Security Council' (1 January 2004) UN Doc A/58/47; UNGA 'Report of the Open-ended Working Group on the Question of Equitable Representation on and Increase in the Membership of the Security

Council and Other Matters related to the Security Council' (September 2007) UN Doc A/61/47; UNGA 'Report of the Open-ended Working Group on the Question of Equitable Representation on and Increase in the Membership of the Security Council and Other Matters related to the Security Council' (9 October 2008) UN Doc A/62/47.

217 Simon Chesterman, 'The UN Security Council and the rule of law: the role of the Security Council in strengthening a rules-based international system: final report and recommendations from the Austrian Initiative, 2004–2008' (Institute for International law and Justice 2008).

218 UNGA Res 60/1 (24 October 2005) UN Doc A/RES/60/1.

219 South Africa, UNSC Verbatim Record (26 November 2012) UN Doc S/PV.6870 at 16.

220 Chile, UNGA Verbatim Record (23 November 1993) UN Doc A/48/PV.61 at 3.

11 Accountability

Introduction

Accountability was identified by the Secretary-General as one of the integral components of the rule of law[1] and provides mechanisms for safeguarding all standards of the rule of law. It requires detailed reporting and explanation[2] as well as a mechanism to which the Council is answerable. Where Council decisions are poorly explained, arbitrarily taken, obscured behind closed-door meetings or otherwise taken in contravention of the rule of law, there can be no accountability; similarly, where the Council appears to be acting *legibus solutus*, there is an even greater need for an oversight body for the Council to bring it in line with its obligations to abide by the rule of law. Accountability for the Council would, therefore, involve the existence of a structure or entity to combat impunity and deliver consequences for transgressions and violations of the Charter and its meaning.

As the overarching document that governs the behaviour of the Council and sibling organs, the Charter is the appropriate starting point when searching for measures of accountability for the Council; however, the Charter is vague in its stipulations for this. Sparse reference to examples of accountability include Article 24(3) of the UN Charter, which specifies that the Council is to 'submit annual and, when necessary, special reports to the General Assembly for its consideration';[3] these reports 'shall include an account of the measures that the Security Council has decided upon or taken to maintain international peace and security'.[4] While the Assembly is obliged to 'receive and consider'[5] these reports, the Charter is unclear on the precise reasoning behind this practice and gives no indication of any Assembly capacity or obligation to monitor the Council's behaviour. In fact, the Charter makes explicit reference to the capacity of the Council to 'adopt its own rules of procedure',[6] including the method and content of the reports to the Assembly. In the absence of Charter guidance on accountability, it is necessary to examine the powers of other internal organs to review the Council decision-making process, including the Council itself.

Self-regulation

While the Council has shown an increased willingness to promote accountability in its work promoting the rule of law at the domestic level,[7] there has been much less discussion on turning the focus inwards and the Council itself abiding by any mechanisms for accountability for its actions. Discussions have taken place sporadically[8] but despite the recognition that 'it is high time to enhance the Security Council's accountability to the wider membership'[9] no progress has been made in recent years. Of the seven meetings in 2013 on Presidential Note S/2010/507 providing guidance in 'efforts to enhance the efficiency and transparency of the Council's work'[10] six have been closed meetings[11] to which the wider UN audience and global population were not privy; similarly, in 2014, there have been almost as many closed meetings as open – four of ten.[12] Incongruously, one of the matters contained in the document discussed behind closed doors was the Council's 'commitment to increase recourse to open meetings',[13] a matter that four years later the organ has trouble implementing even as the President confirms the need for 'more effective use . . . of public meetings, informal interactive dialogues and Arria-formula meetings'.[14] As discussed earlier, transparency 'constitute[s] a "prerequisite" of accountability'.[15]

Efforts to reform the Council from an accountability perspective have hitherto failed in gaining notable traction. Despite recognition that '[t]ransparency, accountability and coherence are key elements that the Security Council should observe in all its activities, approaches and procedures'[16] and that 'decisions on behalf of the membership of the United Nations are more effective when they are taken in a transparent, inclusive and accountable manner',[17] any active movement in this direction has been almost static. For example, the initiative pioneered by Brazil of 'interaction with the broader membership through briefings, not only at the beginning of each presidency, but also at the conclusion . . . [was] see[n] as a voluntary exercise in accountability . . . which has, unfortunately, not been replicated by other members of the Council'.[18]

The most notable recent attempt for internal Council accountability reform came in the shape of a draft General Assembly resolution[19] proposed by the Small Five Group[20] that laid 'out a clear road map . . . for improving the Council's transparency, accountability, distribution of tasks and fulfilment of responsibilities through a stronger use of [UN] legal and political instruments';[21] however, 'opposition to the proposal was fierce, particularly on the part of the five permanent members . . . [and] procedural legalism, which was unjustified but institutionally legitimate . . . forced [the withdrawal of] the draft resolution'.[22] This simple five page document contained recommendations for improved relationship with the Assembly,[23] increased input from member states[24] and most importantly, pivotal accountability elements such as

> [e]xplaining the reasons for resorting to a veto or declaring its intention to do so, *in particular with regard to its consistency with the purposes and principles of the Charter of the United Nations and applicable international law*. A copy

of the explanation should be circulated as a separate Security Council document to all members of the Organization.[25]

The rejection, however, signalled the start of another initiative, calling for increased accountability and addressing both the Council's internal functioning, as well as its relations to the broader UN membership.

The Accountability, Coherence and Transparency (ACT) group

Founded in May 2013, ACT 'is a cross-regional group of 27 small and medium-sized countries aiming at enhancing the effectiveness of the Security Council through the improvement of its working methods'.[26] The group does not fall within the traditional school of Council reform – it assumes the Council's continuation in its present composition – but attempts to find pragmatic methods of increasing elements related to Council accountability and 'to strengthen the responsibility, coherence and transparency of the Security Council'.[27] Its focus for activities have to date revolved around increased transparency in the selection of the Secretary-General, advocacy for the voluntary suspension of the veto in cases of atrocity crimes, and calls for the Council to improve the substantive and analytical quality of its annual reports. However, as a relatively new initiative, it is difficult to measure its efficacy and until now it has limited itself to supporting initiatives taken by existing mechanisms rather than making concrete recommendations itself.[28]

It can be argued that ACT has had limited impact on increasing transparency at the Council; various Presidential Notes have committed the organ to make 'more effective use . . . of public meetings, informal interactive dialogue and Arria-formula meetings',[29] 'enhancing interaction and consultation with troop- and police-contributing countries',[30] and that 'any member of the Security Council may be a penholder'.[31] In reality, however, penholder positions remain overwhelmingly granted to P5 members[32] and despite the support of P5 member France's support for a limitation of the use of veto, ACT's 2015 'Code of Conduct regarding Security Council action against genocide, crimes against humanity or war crimes'[33] – which calls upon members of the Council to refrain from voting against credible draft resolutions intended to prevent or halt mass atrocities – there has not been wide support or adoption of the initiative.

The Office of the Ombudsperson

Externally-facing, too, the Council has made hesitant efforts to ensure accountability to individuals affected by its decisions. The Ombudsperson Office[34] appears to be the sole attempt by the Council itself to self-regulate on any notable level; yet, this is limited in its scope – focusing only on the list of Al-Qaeda targeted sanctions list.[35] There have been no efforts to instigate similar processes for other sanctions regimes, which led to criticism by the Ombudsperson herself in a recent discussion on Council reform that 'it remains a procedure applicable only in the context of one targeted sanctions regime'.[36] Aside from the lack of judicial review[37] in the appointment of the Ombudsperson[38] and transparency in disclosure of the reasoning behind a decision,[39] the Office of the Ombudsperson has no powers of recommendation to maintain or remove individuals from the sanctions list and the Council is in no way answerable to it.

Rather, the Ombudsperson's mandate is curtailed to preparing a 'Comprehensive Report that will exclusively . . . [b]ased on an analysis of all the information available . . . lay out for the [Al-Qaeda Sanctions] Committee the principal arguments concerning the delisting request'.[40] Indeed, the decision is taken by the committee – which itself monitors the implementation of the sanctions rather than measuring Council compliance with the rule of law[41] – and later informs the Ombudsperson of this decision.[42] However, even with respect to full access to documents in order to create such reports, former Ombudsperson Kimberly Prost has repeatedly made the same comments regarding increased transparency in each report that she filed since 2013[43] and in July 2014 raised concerns that the Council may choose to ignore its reasoning.[44]

In fact, accountability in this respect appears to be taking steps backwards; whereas in 2011, where a delisting request has been rejected, description to the petitioner of reasoning 'to the extent possible and drawing upon the Ombudsperson's Comprehensive Report'[45] was a requirement, in 2014 the 'Comprehensive Report, and any information contained therein, should be treated as strictly confidential and not shared with the petitioner or any other Member State'.[46]

Sibling UN organs

Of the four[47] remaining organs of the UN, there are only two that are potentially eligible or suitable for review of the Council – the ICJ and the General Assembly. As the 'principal judicial organ of the United Nations'[48] the ICJ is the sole candidate for judicial review of the Council. Despite the political nature of the Council in its decision-making process, this is not mutually exclusive to assessment of the legality of its actions. As the Council is bound by the parameters of its powers under the Charter and is obliged to observe the limitations of both international norms and the rule of law, judicial review – at least of the procedure followed and its adherence to the components of the rule of law – should be a task for the ICJ. The decision-making process of the Council impact myriad other elements of international law, particularly the Council's bold ventures into legislating and the impact this has on establishing international norms and precedent. However, other elements also touch on the international legal plane, such as the intersection between international human rights law and Council-mandated sanctions or military action. As a result, the ICJ's power to review the Council must be examined.

The Assembly, too, has powers of review that can be invoked to review decisions of the Council. As the democratic counterweight to the exclusive Council, the Assembly potentially provides a forum for discussion and action that is more representative of the international community. Under the Charter, it is authorised to 'discuss *any questions or any matters within the scope of the present Charter or relating to the powers and functions of any organs provided for in the present Charter*'.[49] This has overwhelming potential and in essence translates into a competency to not only review the Council's powers itself in the Assembly but to discuss the ICJ's powers to review the Council should such powers not exist. Moreover, the Assembly is tasked with considering 'general principles of co-operation in the maintenance of international peace and security'[50] and was designed for extensive interaction with both the Council in an advisory role[51] and as an organ 'encouraging the progressive development of international law and its codification'.[52] In light of recent Council practice of legislating, this latter responsibility should be addressed under the powers granted to the Assembly in Article 10.

The International Court of Justice

While there is no explicit provision for it in the Charter, it has long been identified by the ICJ and others[53] that the United Nations as an organisation has a legal personality.[54] Judicial review of the Council's resolutions has been also touched upon at the ICJ in previous years, most notably in 1992 when the Court declined to grant Provisional Measures to Libya in its *Lockerbie* case;[55] from the perspective of ICJ judicial review of the Security Council, this was a disappointing decision. During the course deliberations, it was identified that:

> . . . the Court is the guardian of legality for the international community as a whole, *both within and without the United Nations*. One may therefore legitimately suppose that the intention of the founders was not to encourage a blinkered parallelism of functions but a fruitful interaction.[56]

This acceptance of concurrent jurisdiction and the Court's previous rulings in support of this principle in its *Hostages*[57] and *Nicaragua*[58] cases belies the reality that the Court appears to have folded before the fact that the resolution of Council[59] on the matter had been issued. The Council's Chapter VII resolution demanding the extradition of suspects in the Lockerbie bombings would have been in direct opposition to any Provisional Measures issued by the Court and Judge Bedjaoui highlights the crux of the matter when he alludes to 'the grave question of . . . the possible inconsistency between the decisions of the two organs and of how to deal with so delicate a situation'.[60]

Despite the fact that UNSC Resolution 748 was adopted *after* the Libyan Applications to the ICJ and lengthy discussions at the Court and even in light of the recognition that 'the Court . . . was not obliged to take into account a resolution passed after the closure of the proceedings and to apply it, retroactively as it were, to the case which had been submitted to it',[61] the Court considered the resolution. In short, aware of the case pending before the ICJ, the Council nonetheless adopted a resolution in an apparent effort to either circumvent or eclipse any decision of the Court; reciprocally, even though the resolution was adopted *ex post facto* to the Court's initial consideration of the case, the Court recognised its admissibility and chose to dismiss the request for Provisional Measures.

In this case, the Council was well aware of its powers under Charter Article 96(1) to request an advisory opinion from the Court; indeed, it had already done such in the 1971 *Namibia* case[62] subsequent to UNSC Resolution 276.[63] The absence of a referral to the Court 'may be regrettable, but there is, alas, no provision in the Charter making it mandatory to consult the Court'.[64] Joyner has recommended a revisitation of the 'arguments of long provenance regarding the Court's jurisdiction *rationae personae*, and amendment of Article 36 of its Statute to make its compulsory jurisdiction truly universal'[65] but it is questionable how this can be realistically implemented. For the time being, at least, the jurisdiction of the ICJ over the Council remains exclusively advisory and instigated by the Council itself on an ad hoc basis. Key to this, certainly, is the recognition by certain judges that the Court is not empowered to

> . . . exercise judicial review of the decisions of the Security Council. . . [and is] particularly without power to overrule or undercut decisions of the Security Council made by it in pursuance of its authority under Articles 39, 41 and 42 of the Charter to determine the existence of any threat to the peace, breach of the peace, or act of aggression and to decide upon responsive measures to be taken to maintain or restore international peace and security.[66]

Although the ICJ has previously held that it is 'not the function of a court merely to provide a basis for political action if no question of actual legal rights is involved',[67] this cannot be interpreted to be the case in situations where the Council's action has legislative or legally binding effects.[68] Moreover, for the Council to adopt a resolution on the same subject that the Court has begun addressing that later emerged to be contradictory suggests a lack of inter-organ cooperation; a similar complementarity must be forthcoming from the Council, notwithstanding the capacity of both to be seized of the same matter simultaneously. That is to say, for a resolution contrary to the content of a case seised by the Court to emerge *after* the Court has begun consideration of the matter is likely – particularly in light of the political considerations of the Council – to be an effort to prejudice the course of justice at the Court. Indeed, such action by the Council is a step away from accountability rather than a move towards; rather than using the powers granted to the Council to refer a question to the Court for an advisory opinion on its legality, the Council mobilised to undermine the activity of the Court. This fact was recognised in the dissenting opinion of Judge El-Kosheri on the *Lockerbie* case.[69]

Naturally, there is an argument to be made for the dismissal of the case and for judicial review to be limited from a pragmatic perspective. To empower the Court to decide a case in opposition to an existing Chapter VII resolution risks 'appearing to offer to recalcitrant States a means to parry and frustrate decisions of the

Security Council by way of appeal to the Court'.[70] However, the Court has previously differentiated between advisory opinions a sterner judicial review of the Council.[71] Martenczuk acknowledges that there 'might be disagreement over the effect of a judgment finding a Council resolution to be invalid'[72] but finds that 'justiciability could not act to prevent the judicial review of Security Council resolutions by the Court'.[73]

The political nature of a dispute is therefore no bar to the intervention of the Court. Indeed, an examination of the ICJ Statute shows that the 'Court shall have the power to indicate, if it considers that circumstances so require, any provisional measures which ought to be taken to preserve the respective rights of either party'[74] and that '[p]ending the final decision, notice of the measures suggested shall forthwith be given to the parties and to the Security Council',[75] indicating that the Court is well within its jurisdiction to ensure that provisional measures are adopted where necessary. Moreover, the decision to dismiss the *Lockerbie* case – irrespective of its consideration after a further six years of sanctions[76] on Libya – underscores Judge Shahabuddeen's questions at the time, which remain valid to this very day:

> Are there any limits to the Council's powers of appreciation? . . . [I]s there any conceivable point beyond which a legal issue may properly arise as the competence of the Security Council to produce such overriding results? *If there are any limits, what are those limits, and what body, other than the Security Council, is competent to say what those limits are?*[77]

Potential coordination with the ICJ

The Court can, however, assess the legality of enforcement action both within the Charter and against international norms and law. One might argue that 'it does not appear . . . that it was the intention of the Charter to preclude the examination of the validity of decisions of the UN political organs, for instance when this validity is relevant to the decision of a dispute between two UN Member States'.[78] Sanctions regimes, for example, can be measured against international human rights norms; the scope of military intervention can be analysed against international humanitarian law; and the very extent of the powers that the Council has assumed can be assessed on an *ad hoc*, even retrospective, basis. In the event that an advisory opinion is sought by the Council from the Court on the legality of a decision that it has taken – such as the imposition of general and open-ended legislation upon states through Chapter VII resolutions – the jurisdiction *rationae materiae* of the Court is clear and the motion itself would augment the faith of the wider UN and international community in the volition of the Council to increase its transparency and accountability efforts.[79]

Even if – owing to the inevitable delay that a referral to the ICJ would take and which would be incompatible with the urgency that is frequently encompassed by a threat to the peace and the need for a response – an advisory opinion is sought *after* the adoption of a Chapter VII resolution, the advisory opinion would serve multiple functions. Primarily, referral to the Court may partially eliminate the necessity for reform of the Council's composition, as many of the sentiments of injustice and exploitation by P5 Members of their positions on the Council would be undermined by the validity of judicial review.[80] Moreover, as a focused, reasoned and legal opinion, the Council can make use of the Court's advisory judgment as precedent in its future decision-making process on both the same threat and specifically analogous threats and, in the same way that it refers to previous resolutions and UN documents in its preamble, can refer to the advisory opinion in both its discussions[81] and in subsequent resolutions. For the Council to seek an advisory opinion from the ICJ for a situation and later referred to by the Council's within the framework of its desire to 'remain seized of the situation'[82] would be a marked step towards accountability for the Council. This would allow for so-called 'course-correction' in the response to – but not the identification of – a threat to the peace.

More fundamentally, the reasoning behind the outcome of the advisory opinion can be used to better shape the response of the Council in its general decision-making process. Frequent recourse to the ICJ would result in recommendations for general best practice, legitimacy of the scope of powers of the Council[83] and increased authority to the Council. From such advisory opinions, the Council could confirm or seek to modify its behaviour and enforcement action: agreement by the Court of a Council response would free the Council from the burden of justification of its actions and allegations of ulterior motives; similarly, a statement by the Court that the Council has exceeded its mandate of powers would set the threshold beyond which the Council would be trespassing. This is particularly important in cases where the Council takes new action, such as its foray into generic legislation; were the Council to have submitted UNSC Resolution 1373 for analysis, for example, subsequent disagreement with the legality of the contents of the resolution would have been moot, as the ICJ would have pronounced its legal opinion. Subsequent resolutions such as 1540 and 2178 which build upon the model of UNSC Resolution 1373 would have unequivocally been either valid or *ultra vires* in their foundation. Such decisions on *ultra vires* action can also be included in the ICJ advisory opinions; in this way, the ICJ could pronounce on the scope of the Council's powers to respond to an international threat, while avoiding entering into any discussions on the determination of the threat itself.

Nonetheless, this has not been the case and the Council has made no efforts to refer to the Court any significant questions of either Charter interpretation or substantive matters for judicial review despite intensive calls in 2009 by members of the Non-Aligned Movement.[84] While in recent years, the Council has 'emphasized the key role of the [ICJ] . . . in adjudicating disputes among States and the value of its work and call[ed] upon States that have not yet done so to consider accepting the jurisdiction of the Court in accordance with its Statute',[85] the Council has not made any attempts to make use of its powers to seek advisory opinions. This, despite the fact that advisory opinions were recognised as a means to enhance international peace and security that have been successfully resorted to in the past and to promote the rule of law by the Council.[86]

It would appear, therefore, that the Council has no intention to refer any element of the legality of its decision-making process – even *ex post facto* – to the ICJ for any form of judicial review. As a result, although the Council is not *legibus solutus*, at least from the perspective of the ICJ there is neither a willingness from the Court to rule on the legality of the political decisions of the Council, nor is there any volition from the Council as an organ to request legal clarification on the extent of its Charter powers, the legality of the ramifications of its political decisions or any other aspect of the decision-making process.

The General Assembly

If the Court is either unwilling or unable to rule on the legality of the Council's decision-making process, then one may also turn to the Assembly for a form of review albeit non-judicial. Charter Article 10 grants the most expansive powers to the Assembly in its review of the 'powers and functions'[87] of the Council, allowing it to discuss both and make 'recommendations to . . . the Security Council . . . on any such question or matters',[88] notwithstanding Charter Article 12. In essence, the Assembly may discuss the scope, content and function of the Council's Charter powers, provided this does not interfere with a dispute or situation that the Council is addressing; it may also recommend for them to alter or curb its behaviour based on Assembly discussions. The Assembly has made use of or hinted at this privilege in over 40 resolutions since 1990 and has discussed the scope of reform of Council working methods,[89] reflecting the assertion that:

> [i]t is impossible to read Article 30 in such a way as to make it immune from the General Assembly's explicit authority to discuss and make recommendations on any matters within the scope of the Charter relating to the functions of any organ of the United Nations – including the Council – and to make recommendations to the Council on these matters . . . The Council may have the responsibility of formally adopting its rules of procedure, but the General Assembly is clearly empowered not only to discuss the Council's working methods but to make recommendations to the Council, whether or not those recommendations touch on and concern the rules of procedure.[90]

However, the Assembly has not requested action from the Council in recent years on peace and security issues, nor has it requested action from the Council in accordance with Article 11 of the Charter, although it has 'encourage[d] the Security Council to consider appropriate measures to ensure accountability in the Syrian Arab Republic'[91] and felt it necessary to remind the Council of its 'primary responsibility for the maintenance of international peace and security'.[92] Despite numerous previous references to Article 11 of the Charter and the repeated reaffirmation of 'the role and authority of the General Assembly, including on questions relating to international peace and security',[93] the Assembly has failed to make an impact on the working methods of the Council. Several efforts of states to support the powers of the Assembly under Article 10 have not borne fruit;[94] the Council is still stagnant in its reform and remains inwards-looking for review and implementable guidance.

While Article 10 permits the Assembly to make recommendations on the scope of the Council's powers – which is has not done – as well as matters of reform – which appear to have been ignored – it does not, however, issue the Assembly with the power to monitor or review the actual decisions of the Council. That is to say, the Assembly does not have a mandate that, even in the most liberal of interpretations, would permit it the power of review of Council actions or decisions. The Assembly can choose to make use of UNGA Resolution 377A (1950)[95] – also known as the *Uniting for Peace* resolution – to intervene in situations where 'the Security Council, because of lack of unanimity of the permanent members, fails to exercise its primary responsibility for the maintenance of international peace and security'[96] but this lacks the potential to excel beyond a mere auxiliary measure to the Council. *Uniting for Peace* does not authorise the Assembly to review the Council itself, but rather to attempt to fill in where the Council has reached an impasse.

The working methods, legality of Council action, scope of Council powers and other integral elements of Charter interpretation have been eliminated from discussion at the Assembly despite their potential for inclusion under Article 10. The Assembly is incapable of grasping fully the matters under examination at the Council owing to a lack of cooperation between the two organs. The Council's reports to the Assembly have been labelled as 'a bland summary and listing of meetings and outcome documents'[97] and it has been identified that 'there is a need to ensure more informative annual Security Council reporting to the General Assembly'.[98] Although it is known to the Council that 'there is a need to increase transparency and coordination between the Security Council and the General Assembly',[99] little reform has materialised; 'despite the current positive trends in the working methods of the Security Council, [it has] yet to live up to the expectations of the 2005 World Summit, mainly with respect to representativity and legitimacy, to efficiency and effectiveness, to transparency and accountability, and to the implementation of Council decisions'.[100]

Conclusions

The ICJ presents the best option among existing mechanisms for accountability of Council action and compliance with the rule of law. Despite an explicit mechanism for review of the Council by the ICJ under Article 96, however, this has not been made use of by either organ for the purposes of subjecting Council behaviour to a standard of review. Under Article 96, in combination with its mandate under Article 10 of the Charter, it is also discouraging to note that the Assembly has not made use of its prerogative to request advisory opinions from the ICJ in order to review Council behaviour. De Wet's summation over a decade ago that the ICJ be used by means of an authorisation of 'the Secretary-General to request advisory opinions that can guide the United Nations political organs in relation to the legality of their own actions . . .'[101] was by her own admission unlikely, and has been proven correct; the Assembly, despite having numerous tools at its discretion to review the Council or refer the process of decision-making to the ICJ, has failed to utilise them in the promotion of the rule of law.

In both cases, the Council has made no efforts to ensure that it subjects its decision-making process to the minimum legal standards expected from a rule of law. Such advisory opinions, although technically not legally binding, would be significantly influential in the evolution of Charter interpretation and defining the parameters of Council powers; moreover, given the primacy of the ICJ as the 'principal judicial organ of the United Nations', a legal opinion on matters of Council practice based on its history would be integral to any genuine efforts of reform – indeed, it is difficult to imagine how the Council might achieve this without such judicial input.

Notes

1 Report of the Secretary-General, 'The rule of law and transitional justice in conflict and post-conflict societies' (2004) UN Doc S/2004/616 para 6.
2 See eg Argentina, UNSC Verbatim Record (27 August 2008) UN Doc S/PV.5968 (Resumption 1) at 16.
3 UN Charter (1945) art 24(3).
4 ibid art 15(1).
5 ibid.
6 ibid art 30.
7 See eg UNSC 'Letter dated 7 June 2006 from the Permanent Representative of Denmark to the United Nations addressed to the Secretary-General' (7 June 2006) UN Doc S/2006/367; UNSC Presidential Statement 28 (2006) UN Doc S/PRST/2006/28; UNSC Presidential Statement 11 (2010) UN Doc S/PRST/2010/11; USA, UNSC Verbatim Record (19 January 2012) UN Doc S/PV.6705 at 9.
8 eg UNSC 'Note by the President of the Security Council' (26 July 2010) UN Doc S/2010/507; UNSC Verbatim Record (26 November 2012) UN Doc S/PV.6870; UNSC 'Note by the President of the Security Council' (5 June 2012) UN Doc S/2012/402.
9 Netherlands, UNSC Verbatim Record (26 November 2012) UN Doc S/PV.6870 (Resumption 1) 5.
10 UNSC 'Note by the President of the Security Council' (26 July 2010) UN Doc S/2010/507 para 1.
11 UNSC Official Communiqué (31 January 2013) UN Doc S/PV.6914; UNSC Official Communiqué (28 February 2013) UN Doc S/PV.6927; UNSC Official Communiqué (30 April 2013) UN Doc S/PV.6958; UNSC Official Communiqué (30 May 2013) UN Doc S/PV.6972; UNSC Official Communiqué (27 June 2013) UN Doc S/PV.6992; UNSC Official Communiqué (29 August 2013) UN Doc S/PV.7027.
12 UNSC Official Communiqué (27 February 2014) UN Doc S/PV.7122; UNSC Official Communiqué (31 March 2014) UN Doc S/PV.7151; UNSC Official Communiqué (30 April 2014) UN Doc S/PV.7166; UNSC Official Communiqué (29 May 2014) UN Doc S/PV.7189.
13 UNSC 'Note by the President of the Security Council' (26 July 2010) UN Doc S/2010/507 para 28.
14 UNSC 'Note by the President of the Security Council' (28 August 2013) UN Doc S/2013/515 para 2(a).

15 Antonios Tzanakopoulos, 'Transparency in the Security Council' in Andrea Bianchi and Anne Peters (eds), *Transparency in International Law* (Cambridge University Press 2012) 392.
16 Guatemala, UNSC Verbatim Record (29 October 2013) UN Doc S/PV.7052 at 7. See also eg South Africa, UNSC Verbatim Record (30 November 2011) UN Doc S/PV.6672 at 11; Brazil, ibid 16; Senegal, UNSC Verbatim Record (26 November 2012) UN Doc S/PV.6870 (Resumption 1) 10.
17 Switzerland, UNSC Verbatim Record (30 November 2011) UN Doc S/PV.6672 at 18.
18 Brazil, ibid.
19 UNGA Draft Res (15 May 2012) UN Doc A/66/L.42/Rev.2.
20 Costa Rica, Jordan, Liechtenstein, Singapore and Switzerland.
21 Costa Rica, UNSC Verbatim Record (26 November 2012) UN Doc S/PV.6870 (Resumption 1) 4.
22 ibid.
23 UNGA Draft Res (15 May 2012) UN Doc A/66/L.42/Rev.2 paras 1 ff.
24 ibid para 8.
25 ibid para 19 (emphasis added).
26 UNSC 'Letter dated 19 September 2013 from the Permanent Representative of Switzerland to the United Nations addressed to the President of the Security Council' (23 September 2013) UN Doc S/2013/568 at 1.
27 Luxembourg, UNSC Verbatim Record (29 October 2013) UN Doc S/PV.7052 at 4.
28 See eg UNSC 'Letter dated 19 September 2013 from the Permanent Representative of Switzerland to the United Nations addressed to the President of the Security Council' (23 September 2013) UN Doc S/2013/568 at 1.
29 UNSC 'Note by the President of the Security Council' (28 August 2013) UN Doc S/2013/515.
30 UNSC 'Note by the President of the Security Council' (28 October 2013) UN Doc S/2013/630.
31 UNSC 'Note by the President of the Security Council' (14 April 2014) UN Doc S/2014/268.
32 In 2016, seven non-P5 members held pens over situations on the Council's agenda; P5 members held 29; Bosnia and Herzegovina has a rotating penholder position and Peace and Security in Africa has no penholder.
33 'Letter dated 14 December 2015 from the Permanent Representative of Liechtenstein to the United Nations addressed to the Secretary-General', Annex I (14 December 2015) UN Doc A/70/621–S/2015/978.
34 Established under UNSC Res 1904 (17 December 2009) UN Doc S/RES/1904.
35 UNSC Res 1267 (15 October 1999) UN Doc S/RES/1267.
36 Ms Prost, UNSC Verbatim Record (23 October 2014) UN Doc S/PV.7285 at 2.
37 Both in terms of the process of appointing an Ombudsperson and the function of the Office of the Ombudsperson.
38 UNSC Res 1904 (17 December 2009) UN Doc S/RES/1904 para 20.
39 UNSC 'Report of the Office of the Ombudsperson pursuant to Security Council resolution 2161 (2014)' (31 July 2014) UN Doc S/2014/553 para 46.
40 ibid Annex II para 7.
41 UNSC Res 1267 (15 October 1999) UN Doc S/RES/1267 para 6 (1999).
42 UNSC Res 1904 (17 December 2009) UN Doc S/RES/1904, Annex II para 11.
43 UNSC 'Report of the Office of the Ombudsperson pursuant to Security Council resolution 2083 (2012)' (31 January 2014) UN Doc S/2014/73 para 71. See also UNSC 'Report of the Office of the Ombudsperson pursuant to Security Council

resolution 2083 (2012)' (31 July 2013) UN Doc S/2013/452 para 58; 'Report of the Office of the Ombudsperson pursuant to Security Council resolution 2083 (2012)' (31 January 2013) UN Doc S/2013/71 para 60; 'Report of the Office of the Ombudsperson pursuant to Security Council resolution 1989 (2011)' (30 July 2012) UN Doc S/2012/590 para 58.

44 UNSC 'Report of the Office of the Ombudsperson pursuant to Security Council resolution 2161 (2014)' (31 July 2014) UN Doc S/2014/553 para 51.

45 UNSC Res 1989 (17 June 2011) UN Doc S/RES/1989 para 14(a).

46 UNSC Res 2161 (17 June 2014) UN Doc S/RES/2161 para 13(c).

47 The Trusteeship Council has been disbanded.

48 ibid art 92.

49 ibid art 10 (emphasis added).

50 ibid art 11(1).

51 ibid arts 11–12.

52 ibid art 13.

53 *Reparation for Injuries Suffered in the Service of the United Nations* (Advisory Opinion) [1942] ICJ Rep 174, 179. See also eg Nigel D White, *The United Nations System: Towards International Justice* (Lynne Rienner 2002) 28 ff.

54 *Reparations case*, ibid 179.

55 *Questions of Interpretation and Application of the 1971 Montreal Convention arising from the Aerial Incident at Lockerbie (Libyan Arab Jamahiriya v United States of America)* (Provisional Measures: Order) [1992] ICJ Rep 114, 127.

56 ibid Separate Opinion of Judge Lachs at 138 (emphasis added).

57 *United States Diplomatic and Consular Staff in Tehran* (Judgment) [1980] ICJ Rep 3 para 37.

58 *Military and Paramilitary Activities in and against Nicaragua (Nicaragua v United States)* (Merits, Judgment) [1986] ICJ Rep 14 para 106.

59 UNSC Res 748 (31 March 1992) UN Doc S/RES/748.

60 *Questions of Interpretation and Application of the 1971 Montreal Convention arising from the Aerial Incident at Lockerbie (Libyan Arab Jamahiriya v United States of America)* (Provisional Measures: Order) [1992] ICJ Rep 114, Dissenting Opinion of Judge Bedjaoui at 143.

61 ibid 151.

62 *Legal Consequences for States of the Continued Presence of South Africa in Namibia (South West Africa) notwithstanding Security Council Resolution 276 (1970)* (Advisory Opinion) [1971] ICJ Rep 16, 17.

63 UNSC Res 276 (30 January 1970) UN Doc S/RES/276.

64 *Questions of Interpretation and Application of the 1971 Montreal Convention arising from the Aerial Incident at Lockerbie (Libyan Arab Jamahiriya v United States of America)* (Provisional Measures: Order) [1992] ICJ Rep 114, Dissenting Opinion of Judge Bedjaoui at 152.

65 Daniel Joyner, *International Law and the Proliferation of Weapons of Mass Destruction* (Oxford University Press 2009) 189.

66 *Questions of Interpretation and Application of the 1971 Montreal Convention arising from the Aerial Incident at Lockerbie (Libyan Arab Jamahiriya v United States of America)* (Preliminary Objections) [1992] ICJ Rep 115, 127, Dissenting opinion of President Schwebel at 53–54.

67 *Case concerning the Northern Cameroons (Cameroon v United Kingdom)* (Preliminary Objections) [1963] ICJ Rep 15, 37.

68 *Accordance with International Law of the Unilateral Declaration of Independence in Respect of Kosovo* (Advisory Opinion) [2010] ICJ Rep 403 para 46.

69 *Questions of Interpretation and Application of the 1971 Montreal Convention arising from the Aerial Incident at Lockerbie (Libyan Arab Jamahiriya v United*

States of America) (Provisional Measures: Order) [1992] ICJ Rep 114, Dissenting opinion of Judge El-Kosheri at 210.

70 *Questions of Interpretation and Application of the 1971 Montreal Convention arising from the Aerial Incident at Lockerbie (Libyan Arab Jamahiriya v United States of America)* (Preliminary Objections) [1992] ICJ Rep 115, Dissenting opinion of President Schwebel at 53.

71 *Accordance with International Law of the Unilateral Declaration of Independence in Respect of Kosovo* (Advisory Opinion) [2010] ICJ Rep 403 para 33.

72 Bernd Martenczuk, 'The Security Council, the International Court and judicial review: what lessons from Lockerbie?' (1999) 10(3) *European Journal of International Law* 517, 528.

73 ibid 529.

74 Statute of the International Court of Justice (1945) art 41(1).

75 ibid art 41(2).

76 UNSC Res 1192 (1998) suspended the sanctions following the arrival of the two accused Pan Am flight bombers.

77 *Questions of Interpretation and Application of the 1971 Montreal Convention arising from the Aerial Incident at Lockerbie (Libyan Arab Jamahiriya v United States of America)* (Provisional Measures: Order) [1992] ICJ Rep 114, Judge Shahabuddeen's Separate Opinion at 142 (emphasis added).

78 See Martenczuk (n 72) 526–27.

79 The Court may base its decisions on an interpretation of the Charter as well as general principles and customary international law.

80 This may, of course, be hindered by the fact that the P5 States always have judges on the Court, but would at the very least demonstrate a willingness on the part of the Council to request legal advice from a valid, legitimate source.

81 Verbatim records would be the ideal place to search for reference to the Court in deliberations and negotiations on the Council.

82 This phrase concludes the vast majority of resolutions dealing with ongoing situations and paves the way for future resolutions or decisions on a matter. To incorporate the ICJ advisory opinion as a source of input into the decision-making process going forward would allow the Council a wider yet more thorough perspective on a situation.

83 If the Court were to agree with the legality of Council action after having studied them in depth, despite protestations of Member States, this would add legitimacy to the actions of the Council.

84 UNGA 'Letter dated 24 July 2009 from the Permanent Representative of Egypt to the United Nations addressed to the Secretary-General' (14 September 2009) UN Doc A/63/965-S/2009/514, Annex para 18.9.

85 UNSC Presidential Statement 11 (2010) UN Doc S/PRST/2010/11 para 2.

86 South Africa, UNSC Verbatim Record (29 June 2010) UN Doc S/PV.6347 (Resumption 1) 16.

87 UN Charter (1945) art 10.

88 ibid.

89 See eg Saint Vincent and the Grenadines, UNSC Verbatim Record (22 April 2010) UN Doc S/PV.6300 at 27; Qatar, ibid (Resumption 1) 26; Egypt, UNSC Verbatim Record (30 November 2011) UN Doc S/PV.6672 at 25.

90 Saint Vincent and the Grenadines, ibid.

91 UNGA Res 68/182 (30 January 2014) UN Doc A/RES/68/182 para 10.

92 ibid para 12.

93 See eg UNGA Res 68/307 (18 September 2014) UN Doc A/RES/68/307 para 6; UNGA Res 68/297 (18 September 2013) UN Doc A/RES/67/297 para 4; UNGA Res 66/294 (8 October 2012) UN Doc A/RES/66/294 para 4; UNGA Res 65/315 (11 October 2011) UN Doc A/RES/65/315.

94 eg Switzerland, UNSC Verbatim Record (22 April 2010) UN Doc S/PV.6300 at 27, representing the Group of five small nations (S5) and stressing the outcome of the 2005 World Summit in line with Article 10; Jordan, UNSC Verbatim Record (30 November 2011) UN Doc S/PV.6672 at 23, presenting a new draft Assembly resolution containing measures to enhance the implementation of UNSC Presidential Note S/2010/507 (2010).
95 UNGA Res 377(V) (3 November 1950) UN Doc A/RES/377(V).
96 ibid para 1.
97 India, UNSC Verbatim Record (22 April 2010) UN Doc S/PV.6300 at 19.
98 India, UNSC Verbatim Record (29 October 2013) UN Doc S/PV.7052 at 23.
99 Jordan, UNSC Verbatim Record (23 October 2014) UN Doc S/PV.7285 at 18.
100 Rwanda, ibid 14.
101 Erika de Wet, *The Chapter VII Powers of the United Nations Security Council* (Hart Publishing 2004) 373.

Final conclusions

The Security Council is entrusted with primary responsibility for the maintenance of peace and security; the chapters of this book have argued that in fulfilling this responsibility, it should comply with standards of the rule of law that have been derived from domestic, international and supranational principles. It has therefore identified the eight core components of the rule of law relevant to the Security Council and evidenced using primary material such as resolutions and verbatim records both the intentions and resulting decisions that have emerged from the Council, examining the extent to which it has complied with these rule of law components in its decision-making process. It seems clear that – while Council practice since 1990 appears to have evolved in some cases – on many fronts it has stagnated or deteriorated and there has been little serious volition for transition in the quarter of a decade that have passed since the fall of Communism that signalled the seismic shift in its political composition and renewed vigour of passing resolutions. In fact, certain elements of the rule of law were stronger in 1946 than they are today.

The Council has undoubtedly improved in its human rights considerations, moving from a sanctions regime that crippled entire nations in the early 1990s to more targeted sanctions and measures that, as a result of being more focused, produce less collateral effects on the populations of target states. It has also made efforts to establish committees to monitor its sanctions regimes and has created and established an ombudsperson to monitor the enforcement of anti-terrorism measures taken under Chapter VII. However, more action is needed to incorporate human rights and humanitarian considerations into its resolutions. While advances have been made on the front of compliance with human rights standards, the Council remains an exclusive club primarily governed by the national interests of the P5 members. It would appear that seizure of a matter by the Council remains arbitrary and that even once seized, effective Council action is taken only where a decision or resolution does not run contrary to the national interests of one of the P5 Members: responses to the continuing situations in Israel and Syria are muted despite their key strategic value to international peace and importance to redressing the balance of international peace in the Middle East region; meanwhile, during the same time period, sanctions and the use of 'all necessary means' are authorised against states that pose threats to international peace and are not close political or economic allies of the P5, such as South Sudan,[1] the Congo[2] and Libya.[3]

At times, these interests are in direct conflict: the situation in Syria is permissive, if not supportive, of the spread of international terrorist groups such as Daesh and, despite resolutions condemning and even authorising the military intervention against international terrorist groups such as the Taliban and Al-Qaeda[4] as well as general resolutions condemning international terrorism,[5] little action under Chapter VII has been taken thus far against state or non-State actors in Syria.[6] At other times, the standards imposed by the Council appear malleable to the country in question: while India was engaged with the European Union in talks to sign a civil nuclear pact in 2014[7] and Pakistan continue to test nuclear warheads capable of mid-range payload delivery, Iran and the DPRK have been subject to numerous rounds of sanctions by the Council for civilian and military nuclear aspirations.

The Council's record on transparency appears also in critical need of reform, with use being made of the private meetings in contravention of the working methods it has adopted itself. Moreover, the transparency afforded by public promulgation of information is superficial, since minutes or verbatim records of private meetings are not publicly disseminated. The decision-making process itself remains obscure, with the Council relying increasingly on closed-door meetings after a failed period of attempted transparency; where invitations to meetings are distributed, at times these are delayed, thereby eliminating the opportunity for non-Council Member states to attend and participate. Allegations of cliques or 'mini-Councils' are also concerning from the perspective of transparency, where some member states have expressed their discontent at the *fait accompli* attitude taken on the Council. Whereas during the Cold War years, the P5 would explain their vote and the reasoning behind any use of the veto in the interests of transparency and mutual understanding, recent verbatim records display an increased recourse to opacity in statements of P5 member state representatives. Despite non-P5 member state calls for more openness and their warnings of the derogatory effect such Council behaviour has on the legitimacy of the organ the use of closed meetings is on the rise.

This trend is continued in the Council's attitude towards legal certainty, which remains lacking in its decisions. There is a renewed effort by the Council to use the gateway Article 39 determination in its Chapter VII resolutions, even at times referring explicitly to the Article of Chapter VII under which action is taken;[8] yet, while at times there does appear a pattern of determinations under Article 39 of the Charter, the Council is not consistent in this practice, which in turn undermines the nature of its work, calls into question its integrity and raises questions of arbitrary behaviour. Moreover, resolutions are not always clear in establishing the precise nature of the threat, nor indeed how the measures taken seek to impart international peace to the situation the Council is tackling in a resolution; while the Council clearly makes efforts to establish the grounds for the use of Chapter VII resolutions under Chapter 39, it has increasingly grown lax in specifying the legal basis for its action or the precise threat to which it is responding. This type of action, more than simply leading to accusations that the Council is misusing its prerogative to invoke Chapter VII powers, is in fact more serious: Chapter VII may only be invoked once a determination of a threat to the peace is made. As such, the use of Article 41 and 42 of the Charter by the Council without such determination is an ultra vires action on the part of the Charter – a clear contravention of the rule of law.

This is even more serious given the lack of equality before the law, as highlighted by the juxtaposition of the Iranian and Japanese nuclear situations. Indeed, coupled with the lack of legal certainty, the absence of equality before the law in situations that the Council deals with is even more damning for its decision-making process. The selective nature with which it addresses situations and its varied responses to analogous threats to the international peace cannot be overcome by simply citing the need for ad hoc responses to different situations. The Council should ensure that the same standard is applied not only to similar situations and threats, but also that it holds itself accountable to the same standard. Without ensuring that all member states are treated equally under international law and by the Council itself, the organ risks creating a hierarchy where some states are above the law, which is a grave violation of this component of the rule of law as well as contravening standards of predictability.

The Council has also shown that it has encroached upon the jurisdiction and powers of sibling UN organs, as well as over-reaching in its own jurisdiction by imposing legislative obligations upon UN member states. The frequently self-serving use of the veto by some P5 members, coupled with the decision to abuse the powers of Chapter VII and to foray into the judicial or norm-setting roles of the ICJ or Assembly are overt displays of a disregard for the separation of powers and indifference to the *ultra vires* nature of certain actions that other member states have warned against. Rather than working in unison with other organs as the Council was accustomed to doing in the early years of the UN, the Council has, over the past 20 years, grown bolder in the exploitation of its ***kompetenz kompetenz***, aware of the absence of a steering committee or overarching governing body to reign in its actions. Indeed, the ICTY, the ICJ and the ECJ have all rejected the opportunity to give legal opinions on the actions of the Council, preferring to address the specific issue they are tasked with rather than offer any general rules or guidance.

Finally, the most damaging component of the rule of law for the integrity and legitimacy of the Council is that of equitable participation, which for decades has been paid lip service without a single shred of reform. Notwithstanding the de facto reform of the Russian Federation filling the seat of the former USSR, which was a move of necessity, the Council is a snapshot of an antiquated political landscape that pre-dates not only the fall of the second superpower, but also the rise of numerous other significant nations on the international plane. The current composition of the Council all but ignores the post-colonialist rise of BRICS nations, the global South and the African continent, which at 54 recognised nations forms over a quarter of the entire UN membership. Nations and regions that rightfully should be represented on the Council as permanent members – with or without the veto – have been shunned in favour of more talks that result in the perpetual inclusion of reform on the agenda of the Assembly and no action taken. In what appears to be a manner idiosyncratic to the Council, protection of national interests has become paramount even with respect to any equitable, democratic element of its composition.

While state actions and regional mechanisms in the aftermath of a resolution can in certain cases counter-balance any violations or omissions of the Council with respect to the rights of the individual, there is little that can be done at the subordinate level.[9] I have focused on how to ensure that the Council complies with the rule of law in its decision-making process, rather than how the Council's decisions themselves comply with the international rule of law, and accordingly, any change needs to be effected internally, at the deliberative stages of a resolution and prior to this in the composition of the Council itself. The Council has not succeeded at effectively monitoring and curbing its own powers, processes and accessibility and therefore resort must be made to an independent mechanism to monitor and advise it. In light of the construction of the Charter, the exclusive jurisdictions granted to the Council and the requirement for at least the acquiescence of the P5 Council Members to any changes, initiatives to reform the Council have thus far failed. By removing the review mechanism from the Council itself and granting powers of recommendation and review to a the ICJ as the sole UN judicial organ, mandated to deal with the decisions and decision-making process of the Council as part of an advisory process, a large part of the political considerations that have typically plagued the Council's efficiency, barred the organ from taking action, hindered its maintenance of the international peace and stalled any efforts towards equitable participation may be removed.

If the Charter were to be rewritten today, it would not be difficult to imagine a drastically different Council with largely dissimilar permanent members to the current P5. In order to remain relevant to the world today and in the absence of an entire overhaul of the Charter and the United Nations system, the Council's voluntary adherence to a rule of law framework is the most effective and feasible option for it to comply with the principles of international law, the components of the rule of law, and the principles upon which the UN has been founded.

Notes

1 UNSC Res 1996 (8 July 2011) UN Doc S/RES/1996.
2 UNSC Res 1925 (28 May 2010) UN Doc S/RES/1925; UNSC Res 1991 (28 June 2011) UN Doc S/RES/1991.
3 UNSC Res 1973 (17 March 2011) UN Doc S/RES/1973.
4 UNSC Res 1386 (20 December 2001) UN Doc S/RES/1386 led to the expansion of ISAF's mandate under UNSC Res 1510 (13 October 2003) UN S/RES/1510. This enabled NATO to expand outside of Kabul to the remainder of Afghanistan once they had assumed control of the mission in August 2003.
5 See eg UNSC Res 2178 (24 September 2014) UN Doc S/RES/2178; UNSC Res 2170 (15 August 2014) UN Doc S/RES/2170; UNSC Res 1624 (14 September 2005) UN Doc S/RES/1624.
6 UNSC Res 2268 (26 February 2016) UN Doc S/RES/2268; UNSC Res 2254 (18 December 2015) UN Doc S/RES/2254.

7 See eg 'India, EU to sign civil nuclear pact by 2015' *CNN-IBN* (16 November 2014).

8 See eg UNSC Res 2141 (5 March 2014) UN Doc S/RES/2141, which explicitly states that the Council is '[a]*cting under Article 41 of Chapter VII of the Charter of the United Nations*' (emphasis in original).

9 While the international plane is horizontal, I use the term 'subordinate' here to refer to the subjects of binding resolutions – states – and those subsequently lower in the vertical domestic hierarchy – individuals.

Index

For Product Safety Concerns and Information please contact our EU representative GPSR@taylorandfrancis.com
Taylor & Francis Verlag GmbH, Kaufingerstraße 24, 80331 München, Germany

www.ingramcontent.com/pod-product-compliance
Ingram Content Group UK Ltd.
Pitfield, Milton Keynes, MK11 3LW, UK
UKHW011009180926
475701UK00004B/638
9780367193409